THE ERNST & YOUNG RESOURCE GUIDE
TO GLOBAL MARKETS 1991

The Wiley/Ernst & Young Business Guide Series

THE ERNST & YOUNG RESOURCE GUIDE TO GLOBAL MARKETS 1991

CHARLES F. VALENTINE
GINGER LEW
ROGER M. POOR
Ernst & Young International Trade Advisory Services
Washington, D.C.

JOHN WILEY & SONS
New York • Chichester • Brisbane • Toronto • Singapore

Copyright © 1991 by Ernst & Young.
Published by John Wiley & Sons, Inc.

Library of Congress Cataloging-in-Publication Data:

Valentine, Charles F.
  The Ernst & Young resource guide to global markets, 1991 / Charles F. Valentine, Ginger Lew, Roger M. Poor.
    p.   cm. — (The Wiley/Ernst & Young business guide series)
  Includes bibliographical references.
  ISBN 0-471-52829-3. — ISBN 0-471-53006-9 (pbk.)
  1. International trade—Handbooks, manuals, etc.   2. International business enterprises—Management—Handbooks, manuals, etc. I. Lew, Ginger. II. Poor, Roger M. III. Ernst & Young (Firm) IV. Title. V. Title: Ernst and Young resource guide to global markets, 1991 VI. Series.
HF1379.V36 1991
658.1'8—dc20
                                     90-41068
                                      CIP

Printed in the United States of America

91 92 10 9 8 7 6 5 4 3 2 1

CONTENTS

ACKNOWLEDGMENTS

This first edition of The Ernst & Young Resource Guide to Global Markets 1991 owes its existence to the fine efforts of the international business specialists at Ernst & Young. We wish to thank the various partners and employees of Ernst & Young who have provided specific advice and have supported the efforts of this work who are acknowledged in the companion volume to this work, *The Ernst & Young Guide to Expanding in the Global Market*. Specifically, we would like to thank Steven Graubart, Marianna Bertucci, and Joanna Pineda for their contributions to the research and writing of this volume.

INTRODUCTION

This book is intended to serve as a companion volume to *The Ernst & Young Guide to Expanding in the Global Market*. While that book presents key issues and approaches for companies expanding internationally, this work focuses on contemporary issues and provides key market, economic, demographic and trade data. *The Ernst & Young Resource Guide to Global Markets* will be updated on a yearly basis. As such, it will serve as a handy source for information on a range of regions, countries and trends. We believe this information will meet the practical purpose of supporting key company decisions regarding international expansion, but will also serve as a useful reference on a need-to-know basis.

This book is organized as follows:

Section 1, Current Key Issues in International Business, covers a variety of key topics affecting international businesses. First, an overview of the Triad is presented. These are the three key world geographic regions and represent the most important markets for U.S. companies. Following this, we present an overview of The European Community's "Project 1992" and a discussion of the markets in Southeast Asia. After an analysis of the U.S.-Canada Free Trade Agreement there are two sections on the international trading system: The General Agreement on Tariffs and Trade and Intellectual Property Protection.

Section 2, Regional Overviews and Country Profiles, presents a comparative analysis of countries on a regional basis. These regional overviews are followed by a fact sheet on each country, containing key economic and trade indicators. We have tried to highlight that information which would be most useful to companies across a range of industries. Key contacts are provided for each of the countries.

Section 3 provides a glossary of common international business terms. In **Sections 4 through 7,** we provide the names of key contacts for further information on international trade matters. Finally, **Section 8** provides a reading list that contains the names of key publications on international trade.

While no one work can serve as the all encompassing guide and reference source to international business, we believe that this work will serve as one of the most compact and comprehensive works of its kind. We have tried to make the book accessible and concise; hence its limited size. Too many reference works on international business go unused on library shelves or the top of office filing cabinets because they are too cumbersome and too poorly organized for an executive to bring with him or her and use on an international trip.

We recognize that much of the data in this book is available from public sources and that with a sufficient degree of effort it could be obtained from the Department of Commerce, local embassies, etc. The busy international executives of the 1990s cannot wait, however, for their staffs to locate, collate, chart and digest all of this information. For these reasons we trust that this work will be useful to many in the corporate world, from the Chairman level down to the new research assistant just graduated from college.

NOTE: We have made every effort to obtain the most current information available. The data contained in this book is current as of July 20, 1990.

SECTION 1

CURRENT KEY ISSUES IN INTERNATIONAL BUSINESS

Here we discuss a number of topics which will be of importance to international business in the coming years. Initially we will present an overview of The Triad, the three regions which are of greatest strategic importance to U.S. businesses. Following the Triad overview is a more detailed discussion of selected regions and issues of which businesses must be aware as they plan their international market entry programs for the 1990s.

THE TRIAD

The three most important areas of the world for U.S. businesses are North America, the Pacific Rim, and the European Community. Together, they comprise what is termed "The Triad." These regions are comprised of the countries listed in Figure 1.

The countries of the Triad combined account for 80 percent of world Gross Domestic Product (GDP) and 75 percent of world imports and exports. U.S. exports to the Triad account for over 77 percent of total U.S. exports. As these regions are the fastest growing economic regions in the world, it is likely that they will continue to account for an increasing portion of U.S. exports.

Figure 2 compares GDP, exports, and imports of the Triad. As illustrated by the chart in Figure 2, GDP is the greatest in North America, totaling $5.0 trillion in 1988. The importance of trade to the overall economy is greatest in the European Community (EC). While overall trade figures for North America and the Pacific Rim are close to equal,it is interesting to note the imbalance of exports and imports in those two regions. In North America, imports exceed exports, reflecting the large U.S. trade deficit. In the Pacific Rim, exports exceed imports, reflecting the strong efforts these countries have made in developing export markets.

Figure 1. The "Triad"—Definition

North America	Pacific Rim	EC
United States	Japan	Belgium
Canada	S. Korea*	Denmark
Mexico	Taiwan*	France
	Hong Kong*	W. Germany
	Malaysia†	Greece
	Singapore*†	Ireland
	Thailand†	Italy
	Indonesia†	Luxembourg
	Brunei†	Netherlands
	Philippines†	Portugal
	Australia	Spain
	New Zealand	UK

* Newly Industrialized Countries (NICs)
† Association of South East Asian Nations (ASEAN)

FIGURE 2. The Triad—Exports, Imports, GDP, 1988
(Source: The World Bank)

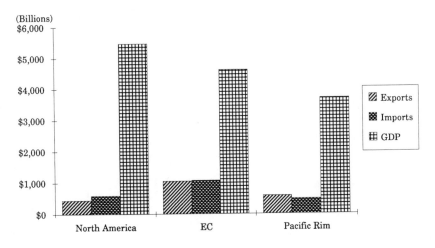

Within each of the legs of the Triad there has been a trend toward the development of regional trading blocs. For example, EC 1992 integrates the economies of the European leg and will lead to increased inter-regional trade. Likewise, the United States–Canada Free Trade Agreement will increase trade between the United States and Canada and the integration of these two markets. Each of these issues is discussed in a separate section later in this chapter.

This development of trading blocs presents both obstacles and opportunities for companies from outside the region. On the downside, companies within the region will have advantages over outsiders for obtaining new business. On the other hand, once a company establishes itself within the region it will have opportunities to exploit the rest of the region. For example, to capitalize on integration of regional markets, a U.S. company could establish operations in Singapore and use this as a base for operations in the other Pacific Rim countries.

Several of the largest and most important Japanese companies have recognized the new reality of the Triad global economy. Yamaha, Sony, Honda, Omron, and Matsushita, among others, have decentralized responsibility for strategy and operations to a regional headquarters located in each of the Triad areas. From regional headquarters in Triad member countries, these companies manage regional markets far more effectively than from a distance. The company headquarters in Japan is responsible only for corporate services and resource allocation.

Case Study

One U.S.-based multinational corporation tried for years to control its Far Eastern operations from the headquarters of its international division in the United States. The manager of operations in Japan ended up commuting to the United States twenty times a year—first for approval of his annual plans, then for debates on altering the plans to reflect changes in his markets.

Even when the company began to lose market share in the Far East, headquarters adhered to plans put in place earlier rather than adapting to the changing market conditions.

The company finally, at great expense, moved its international headquarters and key personnel to Tokyo. The head of Far East activities is now given the freedom to make local decisions locally (and is also free of constant travel back and forth to the United States). The division's performance and profits are booming, reflecting the wisdom of making decisions closest to the customers those decisions will affect. (Kenichi Ohmae, *Harvard Business Review*, July/August 1989.)

Case Study

Fujitsu, one of the largest Japanese electronics manufacturers, held groundbreaking ceremonies in October 1989 for its North American Telecommunications Centre. The $80 million complex will be involved in research and development, and manufacturing. It is expected to employ about 1,200 people by the end of 1992.

> ## Case Study (Continued)
>
> According to a company spokesperson, "The Texas facilities represent a blueprint for the way Fujitsu intends to address the global telecommunications market." Fujitsu is planning to establish a similar operation in Europe. (*Financial Times*, October 25, 1989, page 8.)

The trend toward integration within and across the Triad areas is evidenced by increased international merger, acquisition, and direct investment activities. U.S. companies are acquiring European companies; European companies are investing in the United States, and the Japanese are shopping and buying on both sides of the Atlantic. Figure 3 illustrates Japan's growing presence in Europe. Figure 4

FIGURE 3. The Japanese in Europe
(Source: European Affairs, 3/89 Autumn, page 98)

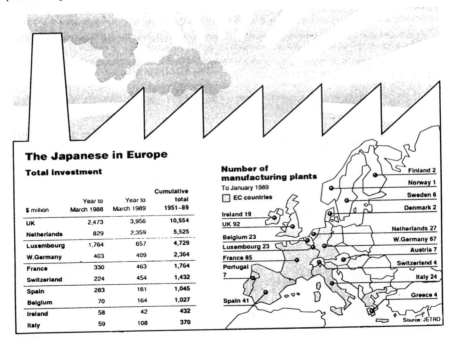

The Japanese in Europe

Total Investment

$ million	Year to March 1988	Year to March 1989	Cumulative total 1951–89
UK	2,473	3,956	10,554
Netherlands	829	2,359	5,525
Luxembourg	1,764	657	4,729
W.Germany	403	409	2,364
France	330	463	1,764
Switzerland	224	454	1,432
Spain	283	161	1,045
Belgium	70	164	1,027
Ireland	58	42	432
Italy	59	108	370

Number of manufacturing plants
To January 1989
☐ EC countries

Ireland 19
UK 92
Belgium 23
Luxembourg 23
France 85
Portugal 7
Spain 41

Finland 2
Norway 1
Sweden 6
Denmark 2
Netherlands 27
W.Germany 67
Austria 7
Switzerland 4
Italy 24
Greece 4

Source: JETRO

FIN TIMES

FIGURE 4.   European Merger and Acquistion Activity, 1988
(Source: European Affairs, 3/89 Autumn, page 82)

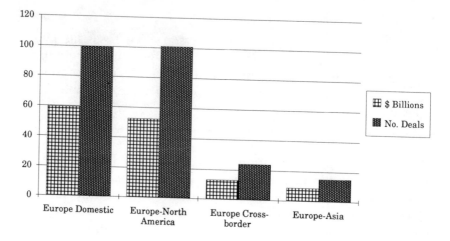

shows data on European merger and acquisition activity for 1988.
Note the high level of trans-Atlantic merger and acquisition activity,
reflecting U.S. firms positioning themselves for 1992.

European Community

Individual markets within each of the regions vary greatly as to
their export potential. As can be seen in the Table 1 on page 7,
within the European Community markets range from the large
economies of West Germany and France to the smaller economies
of Ireland and Portugal. The "Big Four" economies in the EC, West
Germany, France, Italy and the UK, account for over 80 percent of
GDP and 70 percent of trade. However, some of the smaller countries, for example Spain, have witnessed strong growth in recent
years. A detailed analysis of the European Community's 1992 initiative follows this overview of the Triad.

Table 1. EC Key Economical Data, 1988 (US$billions)

Country	GDP	Exports	Imports
West Germany	1,201.8	322.6	249.0
France	949.4	161.7	176.7
Italy	828.9	128.5	135.5
UK	702.4	145.1	189.4
Spain	340.3	40.5	60.4
Netherlands	228.3	103.2	99.7
Belgium†	153.8	89.0	91.1
Denmark	90.5	27.8	26.5
Portugal	41.7	10.2	16.0
Greece	40.9	5.4	12.0
Ireland	27.8	18.7	15.6
EC Total	**4,605.8**	**1,052.7**	**1,072.2**

† Includes Luxembourg.
Source: The World Bank

The United Kingdom is the leading EC market for U.S.exports, followed by West Germany and France. Figure 5 shows U.S. exports to the EC for 1989.

Figure 6 shows the key products exported to the EC from the United States. Office equipment and computers are by far the largest U.S. commodity exported to the EC, a trend that is expected to continue into the 1990s. Other promising export opportunities for U.S. companies include telecommunications equipment, electronic and electrical components, and pollution control technologies.

U.S. investments in the EC are also growing, reflecting the number of firms positioning themselves in Europe for the projected completion of the EC's single internal market in 1992. The EC 1992 project is discussed later in this chapter.

Pacific Rim

Within the Pacific Rim, the economies range in size from Japan to Brunei. Japan, as is well known, has become one of the world's lead-

Figure 5. U.S. Exports to the EC, 1989
(Source: U.S. Department of Commerce)

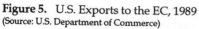
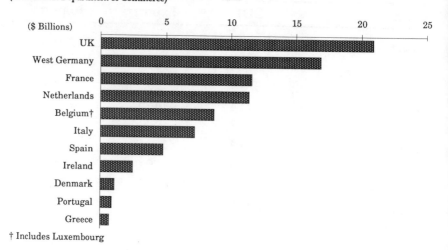

† Includes Luxembourg

Figure 6. Key U.S. Exports to the EC, 1989, Total: $86.6 Billion
(Source: U.S. Department of Commerce)

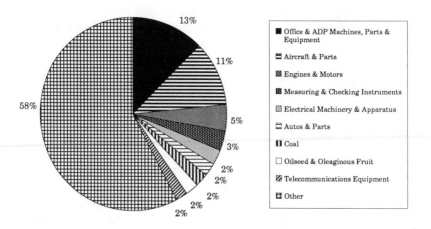

ing economic powers and is significantly larger than the other countries in the region. Table 2 shows GDP, exports, and imports for the countries in the Pacific Rim.

Table 2. Pacific Rim Key Economic Data, 1988 (US$ billions)

Country	GDP	Exports	Imports
Japan	2,843.7	264.8	183.3
Australia	246.0	25.3	29.3
South Korea	171.3	60.7	51.8
Taiwan	118.9	60.4	44.6
Indonesia	83.2	19.7	15.7
Thailand	58.0	15.8	17.9
Hong Kong	44.8	63.2	63.9
New Zealand	39.8	8.8	7.3
Philippines	39.2	7.1	8.2
Malaysia	34.7	20.8	16.6
Singapore	23.9	39.2	43.8
Brunei†	3.1	2.1	0.8
Pacific Rim Total	**3,706.5**	**587.8**	**483.1**

† 1987 data.
Source: The World Bank

As illustrated in Figure 7, Japan, Taiwan, and Korea are the three largest markets for U.S. exports. Japan imports more from the United States than Korea and Taiwan combined. Each of these countries has begun programs to assist U.S. companies export to their markets. For example, in the fall of 1989 the Government of Japan announced the establishment of two programs to assist U.S. firms seeking to export to Japan: (i) export promotion offices for U.S. manufactured goods and (ii) hot line information offices on exporting to Japan. Export promotion offices have been established at the U.S. subsidiaries of Japanese trading

Figure 7. U.S. Exports to the Pacific Rim, 1989
(Source: U.S. Department of Commerce)

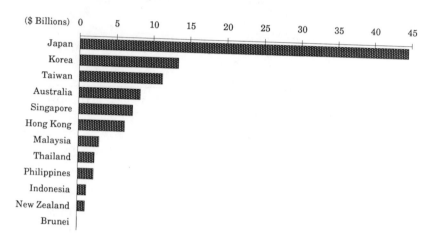

companies in nineteen U.S. cities. Hot line offices have been established in The Japanese External Trade Organization's (JETRO) seven U.S. offices. The hot line is intended to handle complaints raised by American businesses regarding exports to Japan. The Korean Government Trade Promotion Agency (KOTRA) and the Taiwanese Trade Promotion Agency (CETRA) have also set up programs to assist firms export to their respective countries. This assistance can include market information and advice on entering the markets.

U.S. exports to Japan account for over 20 percent of Japan's total imports. Less than two-thirds of U.S. exports are manufactured goods. Agricultural goods and primary commodities make up the rest. Many U.S. companies are hesitant to attack the Japanese market, having heard "horror stories" from their predecessors. However, the Japanese appear to be making sincere efforts to increase access to their home market as well as to decrease informal impediments to imports. Although the Japanese market can be daunting, many U.S. companies are thriving there, through patience and due diligence.

Case Study—Amway Corporation

Amway (Japan) Ltd., subsidiary of Amway Corporation of Ada, Michigan, is among the top ten most profitable foreign companies in Japan, just behind Shell Petroleum and ahead of NCR Corporation. Amway's cult-like corporate culture and direct-selling tactics are credited with their success. In 1988, Amway Japan sales totaled $524 million, making it Amway Corporation's top overseas affiliate.

Amway sells in homes through its 500,000 distributors (as Amway calls salespeople), enabling the company to get around one of the toughest obstacles in Japan: the local retailers and wholesalers who often demand huge markups or refuse to carry products. The distributors work on commission.

Amway has set up three automated distribution centers with on-site customs inspection that allow them to fill orders within two days. Amway's "near-religious zeal" appeals to the Japanese who prefer to identify strongly with their employers.

Although rivals such as Avon Corporation and Shaklee Corporation are way behind Amway in Japan, Amway may soon face challenges in the Japanese market. More and more Japanese competitors are starting to imitate the company. The trend toward Japanese women entering the workplace may also make traditional sales techniques (i.e. Tupperware parties) more difficult. (*Business Week*, September 4, 1989.)

Case Study—Mentor Graphics

Mento Graphics, based in Beaverton, Oregon, makes graphics design software and has sales of $300 million. Twenty percent of its sales are to Japan, where Mentor has a more than 50 percent share of the market. (According to a Mentor spokesperson, no American company, not even Coca Cola, has as large a market share in Japan.)

Case Study (Continued)

The high quality of Mentor's products partly accounts for the company's success. Another major factor is "doing as the Romans do."

In 1983, Mentor was approached by an arm of one of the largest Japanese trading companies wanting to try to sell Mentor products in Japan. Mentor had an ultimate goal of establishing a direct sales presence in Japan but since "you can't just go into Japan," Mentor saw the offer as a means of acquiring know-how in selling in Japan and providing customer service to the Japanese. Mentor entered into a sales agreement with the company, while making it clear that Mentor's goal was to have its own Japanese subsidiary.

The sales effort went so well it was converted into a joint venture in 1985 and became a wholly owned subsidiary in 1986. In the process of conversion to a wholly owned subsidiary, an event occurred that Mentor considers to be the key to their success in Japan. The 40 employees of the trading company who had been handling Mentor's sales left en masse to join Mentor.

The Japanese employees took a big risk leaving a large Japanese firm to go to work for a small American one. For many American firms, the difficulty of hiring good Japanese staff is often the major barrier to success in Japan.

The third important factor in Mentor's success is that top management in Oregon allows the Japanese operation to be run as a Japanese company. The company keeps only one American in Japan to bridge the gap in accounting practices. (*Oregon Business,* December 1988, copyright MEDIAmerica, Inc. 1988.)

As can be seen in Figure 8, office and electrical machinery are the largest categories of U.S. exports to the Pacific Rim. While Japan, Korea, and Taiwan are the leading Asian markets, and have been receiving much attention in the trade press as new markets for U.S. products, the other Pacific Rim nations also present good prospects for U.S. companies. As these countries have received less cov-

Figure 8. Key U.S. Exports to the Pacific Rim, 1989, Total: $101.2 Billion
(Source: U.S. Department of Commerce)

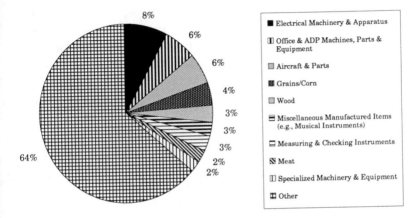

erage, we have included a detailed section on doing business in the ASEAN Nations and Hong Kong later in this chapter.

North America

The North American leg of the Triad is currently the most important region for the United States. Canada and Mexico are the United States' first and third largest trade partners, respectively (Japan is second). Table 3 outlines key economic statistics of the three countries which comprise the North American Triad region.

Table 3. North American Key Economic Data, 1988 (US$ billions)

Country	GDP	Exports	Imports
United States	4,847.3	315.3	458.7
Canada	435.9	111.4	112.2
Mexico	176.7	20.7	18.9
Total North America	**5,459.9**	**447.3**	**589.8**

Source: The World Bank

The North American market has seen increased integration with the implementation of the U.S.–Canada Free Trade Agreement (FTA) starting in 1987, which is discussed in detail below. The North American market was further integrated by the Mexican–U.S. Framework Agreement. While not as comprehensive as the U.S.–Canada FTA, this marks an important first step toward improved economic relations between the two countries. The U.S. Department of Commerce hopes to formalize an extensive trade agreement patterned after the U.S.–Canada FTA with Mexico and expand it to include the rest of Latin America in a free trade pact covering the Western Hemisphere by the year 2010.

With the advent of the FTA, U.S. companies have increased access to their largest trade partner. About 22 percent of total U.S. exports in 1989 went to Canada, while about 75 percent of total Canadian exports were to the United States. According to the U.S. Department of Commerce, best export prospects for U.S. firms include auto parts and accessories, computers and peripherals, and building materials and supplies. Figure 9 shows the composition of U.S. exports to Canada.

Figure 9. Key U.S. Exports to Canada, 1989, Total: $78.6 Billion
(Source: U.S. Department of Commerce)

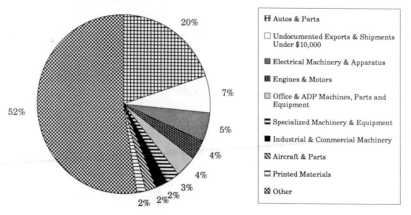

20%

7%

52%

5%

4%

4%

3%

2% 2%2%

Ⅲ Autos & Parts

☐ Undocumented Exports & Shipments Under $10,000

▨ Electrical Machinery & Apparatus

▩ Engines & Motors

▨ Office & ADP Machines, Parts and Equipment

▱ Specialized Machinery & Equipment

■ Industrial & Commercial Machinery

▨ Aircraft & Parts

▱ Printed Materials

▨ Other

Case Study

Several years ago, a medium-sized Ontario company that produces wool, cotton, and synthetic fiber hosiery for men and women, decided to tackle the huge market south of the Canadian border. They first researched the market and conducted a thorough analysis of competitors and potential distribution channels in the United States. The company concluded that the volume demands of major retail chains would far exceed current production capacity.

The hosiery company developed a distribution strategy of selling through manufacturer's representatives to independent retailers and catalog houses, avoiding the volume problems that selling to major chains would create. Orders are met by a weekly shipment to a single FOB point in the United States and transhipped by parcel post or courier. This approach allows the company to achieve manageable export volumes without requiring the level of investment necessary to support traditional distribution approaches.

With the right strategy, small- and medium-sized firms on either side of the border can tap into the potential on the other side. (From *Woods Gordon*, Canada–U.S. Free Trade Agreement, Newsletter Number Four, November 1988.)

The effect of trade agreements is illustrated by Figure 10, reflecting the growth in U.S. exports to Canada and Mexico resulting from the recent trade agreements.

Mexico is currently liberalizing its trade policies to open internal markets by slashing tariffs, reducing the number of items subject to import licensing, and establishing standard cost, insurance, freight (c.i.f.) values as the basis for customs evaluation. U.S. market integration with Mexico is on the rise, especially in border industries mostly due to the innovative *maquiladora* industry structure. In a *maquiladora*, the United States or other foreign company sends com-

Figure 10. U.S. Exports to Canada and Mexico, 1984–1989
(Source: U.S. Department of Commerce)

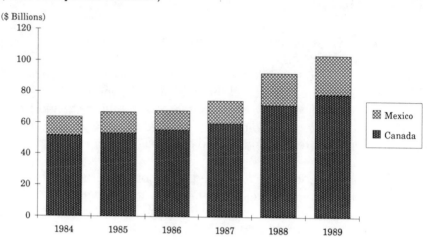

ponents, raw materials, and equipment duty-free to Mexico where the final product is then assembled and exported. This allows foreign companies to take advantage of the low labor rates in Mexico.

Case Study

American Yazaki Parts may be the largest and most active Japanese *maquiladora* in Mexico near the Texas border. Its five plants in Juarez manufacture wire harnesses for Ford, Mazda, Honda, Nissan, and Toyota plants in the United States. The Toshiba American, Inc. plant is also interesting because of its high degree of automation, with computers controlling and executing much of the initial assembly work.

The maquiladora program was originally intended to strengthen U.S.–Mexican industrial relations. However, in recent years, the program has attracted companies from other nations, particularly the Japanese, who have been aggressive in taking advantage of the benefits of maquiladoras.

Case Study (Continued)

By the end of 1987, there were a total of 1,300 maquiladora plants. "The Japanese maquilas increased in number from 39 to 52 in less than a year, and the trend shows no sign of abating. In fact, the relatively small number of Japanese maquilas is partially explained by the fact that the companies currently in Mexico are large corporations. Medium- and small-sized corporations are expected to follow soon," according to Elsie Echeverri-Carroll, economist with the Bureau of Business Research at the University of Texas at Austin who authored a report on the growth of Japanese maquilas.

The recent increase in Japanese maquiladoras is directly related to the growth of Japanese investment in the United States. Production in Mexico represents a means of avoiding roadblocks in the U.S. market. "Economic measures such as yen revaluation and restrictions on Japanese exports to the American market appear to be the main reason for the existence of Japanese maquiladoras," says Ms. Echeverri-Carroll.

Japanese companies mention three other reasons for maquiladora participation. The first is cost. Low wages are the magnet for labor-intensive manufacturing operations for such goods as electronic components, auto parts and furniture (three of the top five types of businesses engaged in maquiladoras). The second reason is proximity to U.S. markets and customers. The third reason involves public relations and politics. The Japanese feel that North American production, linked to U.S. production, gives them an advantage in protectionism and restrictive trade legislation issues. Even though the companies are of Japanese ownership and are located in Mexico, they create jobs in the United States. (*Journal of Commerce*, October 25, 1989.)

Figure 11 illustrates categories of U.S. exports to Mexico.

Figure 11. U.S. Exports Mexico, 1989, Total: $25 Billion
(Source: U.S. Department of Commerce)

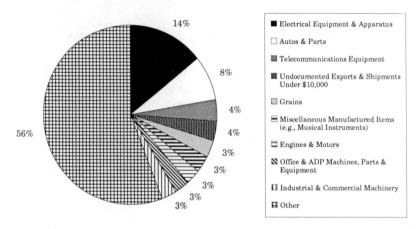

The United States is, however, the key market of the North American region. The United States is the world's largest importer and, with a population of about 244 million and $4.5 trillion in GDP, offers a huge, wealthy market for foreign goods. Domestic U.S. companies are currently experiencing increasing competition for market share as new countries seek to enter their market. Many foreign companies see large investment as a way to enter the U.S. market and avoid protectionism. Figure 12 shows the increasingly large numbers of foreign firms, particularly European, establishing a presence in the United States.

THE EUROPEAN COMMUNITY'S "PROJECT 1992"*

Sometime during 1988, American business and government leaders appeared suddenly to awaken to the growing integration of the European market. Due to be implemented by the end of 1992, the

---

* An earlier version of this article appeared in the *Economic Development Review* (Volume 7, Number 4, Fall 1989). This revised version is included with the permission of the editor and the American Economic Development Council.

Figure 12. Cumulative Foreign Direct Investment in the U.S.
(Source: U.S. Department of Commerce)

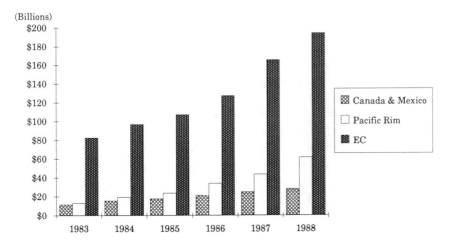

"Single Market Initiative," "Project 1992," or "EC92," is designed to create the largest trading area in the world—a Europe "free of restrictions on the movement of goods... persons, services, and capital." [*Completing the Internal Market*, White Paper from the Commission to the European Council, COM(85) 310 final, Brussels, 14 June 1985, paragraph 4.] This section examines what is occurring in Europe, what the prospects appear to be for 1992, what some of the implications are for the United States, and how a number of U.S. firms are adjusting their strategies in response.

Background of the European Community and "1992"

A number of observers have suggested that in the 1992 program we are witnessing the birth of a "United States of Europe." Others believe that nationalist pressures will prevent the European Community from amounting to much more than a free trade zone. The fact is that major changes have already taken place within the European Community, and that—despite disagreement in some areas—there seems to be substantial commitment from all parties to implementation of the Single Market Initiative.

The EC was created by the Treaty of Rome, which came into effect in 1958. The original six member countries were Belgium, France, Italy, Luxembourg, the Netherlands, and West Germany. Substantial economic integration has always been a key objective of the EC. However, little progress was achieved towards that goal for more than a quarter century.

Over the years the membership of the EC has doubled from the original six, with the entry of Denmark, Ireland, and the United Kingdom in 1973, Greece in 1981, and Spain and Portugal in 1986. From the viewpoint of progress toward a true common market, however, undoubtedly the most significant milestones in the Community's history to date occurred in 1985 and 1986–1987.

1985 saw the publication of the White Paper *Completing the Internal Market* by the EC Commission under Lord Cockfield, then President. In the White Paper, Lord Cockfield detailed the remaining obstacles to true integration of the European marketplace and outlined some 300 specific measures needing to be implemented in order to dismantle internal trade barriers and create a single market by the end of 1992.

One of the key obstacles to European market integration, however, had not been in trade barriers but in the workings of the EC itself. The problem was that Community procedures required that such directives have the *unanimous* consent of the Council of Ministers, the EC's ultimate decision-making body. Naturally, differing levels of economic development, conflicting national priorities, and historical and cultural differences all combined to make unanimity an impossibly cumbersome mechanism for such an ambitious legislative program as proposed in the White Paper.

The Single European Act changed this. The key procedural innovation of the Act was to replace unanimous consent with a system of "qualified (i.e., weighted) majority" voting in the Council of Ministers for most (but not all) matters. As expected, the effect of this has been to greatly accelerate the pace of legislation.

An integrated European Community would be the only economy in the world that could compare in sheer magnitude to the United States. Consider the statistics in Table 4.

Table 4. Comparative EC and U.S. Market Statistics, 1988

Statistic	EC	U.S.
Population	325 million	246 million
Gross Domestic Product	$4.61 trillion	$4.49 trillion
Civilian Labor Force	140 million	122 million
Unemployment Rate	10.4%	5.5%
Per Capita GDP	$14,169	$19,681
Imports (% of GDP)	$1,072 b (23.3%)	$459 b (10.2%)
Exports (% of GDP)	$1,052 b (22.8%)	$315 b (7.0%)

Source: The World Bank

The EC has a population one-third greater than the United States, and a labor force fifteen percent greater. The GDP of the two economies differs by less than five percent. Unemployment has been a more persistent problem in the EC than in the United States, but fell from nearly twelve percent in 1987 to about ten percent by the end of 1988.

The final two lines of Table 4 illustrate perhaps the most important difference between the European Community and the United States, at least as far as our relative competitive position in world trade is concerned. The EC is clearly a far more "trade intensive" economy: In proportion to GDP, the EC imports nearly twice as much and exports well over *three times* as much as the United States. *European firms on the whole simply have far more experience in international trade than their American counterparts.*

What is the 1992 Initiative?

The European Community's "Project 1992" or "Single Market Initiative" aims to create a single integrated European market by removing all obstacles to the free movement of people, goods, services, and capital by the end of 1992.

It is important to recognize that a full-blown single market will not suddenly come into being at midnight on December 31, 1992. On the one hand, some effects have already been felt and other measures will be phased in well before that date. Customs documentation required for the transport of goods within the EC, for example, has already been dramatically reduced. On the other hand, full implementation of some measures is bound to extend beyond the 1992 deadline, even given the wholehearted cooperation of member countries.

In developing its 1992 program, the European Community has recognized some stark realities. One of these was economic stagnation—growth in the EC economies was failing to keep pace with that of the United States and Japan, let alone that of newly industrialized "tigers" like South Korea and Taiwan. Between 1980 and 1987 the EC created only one million new jobs, as compared to 18 million in the United States, and economic growth fell to 1.7 percent per year.

At the same time it was becoming clear that the EC was at a competitive disadvantage compared to its trading partners. High production and administrative costs made it difficult for European companies to compete on the basis of price, while lagging R&D efforts curtailed the role of technological innovation in opening new markets... or keeping old ones.

Behind these ills lay a simple fact: the fragmentation of the European market. Looked at as a whole, the EC appeared to be a vast and wealthy market, with a population of over 320 million consumers and total "national" income rivaling that of the United States. However, it was very difficult for any company to operate successfully throughout that market. Import duties and tariffs were not the problem; they had been eliminated for intra-Community trade by the end of the 1960s. But more subtle and complex trade barriers remained. Except perhaps for industries like oil and automobiles, fragmentation of the European market has been such that few European competitors in any sector commanded more than a five percent market share.

According to the EC Commission, the removal of various trade barriers is supposed to give the EC's GDP a boost of two percent or more, while improved economies of scale and intensified competition are projected to add another two to four percent. The total GDP impact of $200–300 billion or more would be enough to bridge the GDP gap between the European Community and the United States as it stood in 1987.

There are three types of trade barriers targeted for removal:

Physical barriers are essentially border controls that interfere with the free movement of persons and goods from country to country. Project 1992 is supposed to mean unrestricted freedom for citizens to travel and work within the EC, simplified transit documentation, elimination of border safety checks for vehicles, and other measures to make travel and commerce in the EC more like that in the United States.

Technical barriers consist primarily of product standards, laws restricting capital movements, and government procurement regulations. Traditionally each European country has developed its own standards covering everything from the content of food products to the color of a computer's visual display. Of all the obstacles to free trade in the Community, it is product standards, testing requirements and other such technical barriers that have the greatest potential to limit access to the EC market for foreign goods.

It is important to recognize that the EC is *not* attempting to replace all national technical standards with comprehensive Euro-standards. To do so would have entailed arguing among countries to impose standards that would most benefit its domestic producers. The approach that the EC has adopted is "mutual recognition" of national standards, meaning broadly that if a product is good enough to be sold in one EC country, it's good enough for the rest.

It is not likely that mutual recognition will completely eliminate the use of standards to exclude imports and protect domestic competitors. Some observers expect attempts to legislate interpretations of safety and environmental issues that will benefit local interests.

Fiscal barriers are differences in national tax structures that threaten to distort trade and investment patterns within the Community as other types of barriers are dismantled. Most of the controversy surrounds indirect taxation—value-added tax (VAT) and excise taxes.

All EC countries impose VAT, a sort of national sales tax. VAT is levied at every step in the chain of transactions: from the purchase of raw materials, components, subassemblies, and so on to the final purchase by the consumer. The vendor at each stage claims a refund or credit for the VAT paid on cost of goods sold, so only the end purchaser ultimately bears the burden of the tax. VAT is also collected on imports including, at present, imports from other EC countries.

The VAT system poses two problems for the Single Market Initiative. First, with the elimination of border controls there will have to be some kind of EC–level clearing house for VAT collected on sales from one country to another. This system has not yet been designed. Second, VAT rates will have to be brought into line throughout the Community. The "harmonization" or "approximation" of VAT rates has proven to be one of the most contentious issues the EC Commission has had to deal with. It is necessary because it is feared that great differences in rates would distort trading patterns or make it impossible to remove border controls.

Excise taxes, in contrast, are imposed only on a limited number of products, but they vary even more widely than VAT. Some examples: Taxes on pure alcohol range from about $1.50 per gallon in Greece to over $100 per gallon in Denmark; France's 71 percent tax on cigarettes is more than twice as high as the U.K.'s 34 percent. At this point the Commission will not even attempt to align excise taxes throughout the Community.

Progress to Date and Outstanding Issues

As suggested above, the European Community faces many difficult issues in putting the 1992 program into place. Nevertheless no one should underestimate the progress that has been achieved. As of mid-1989 about half the nearly 300 directives had been approved by the Council of Ministers, at least in principle. Compromises have been reached on some issues like indirect taxation which at one time seemed extremely intractable. In other areas, however, conflicts remain or are even escalating.

Recently, differences among EC heads of state over the direction and extent of the Community's integration have been widely reported in the United States as well as Europe. The June 1989 summit conference in Madrid is an example, with Margaret Thatcher and François Mitterrand trading barbs over each other's commitment to coordination of monetary and economic affairs. To some extent such disagreements are merely manifestations of age-old rivalries. More important, however, are the truly substantive technical problems that arise in some areas, and the different views within the Community of what European integration can and should encompass.

First, there remains some question as to whether the Community has the **political will** to fully implement the 1992 program. The EC Commissioners and other officials are themselves committed and are learning to work together more effectively. Polls consistently show that business people throughout the European Community firmly support the Single Market Initiative. Nevertheless there will inevitably remain narrow interest groups which will resist implementation of the 1992 program.

An area that promises to provide one of the severest tests of this political will is **public procurement**. EC governments from the federal down to the local levels spend over US$600 billion per year on public procurement, when purchases by "basic services" or utilities are included. National procedures and regulations generally discriminate against foreign products and vendors, and protect domestic firms from competition. Although the goal of the EC Commission is that 80 percent of public procurement contracts within the Community should be awarded through open tender, the present reality is far short of that target: Only about two percent by value of contracts go to bidders from other countries, even other EC countries. Even under the Commission's current proposals, procurement by basic services—energy, telecommunications, and the like—would be excluded from open competition. The Commission now looks likely to have a less vigorous and powerful enforcement role than it had hoped. Unfortunately the excluded sectors also are not subject to scrutiny under General Agreement on Tariffs and Trade (GATT), leaving few openings for bringing international pressure to bear.

While it is outside of the scope of the 1992 program, **economic and monetary union (EMU)** was the single hottest area of controversy in the EC. Presently the major European currencies, with the notable exception of the British pound sterling, are linked by the European Monetary System or EMS. The central bank of each EMS country is committed to holding the exchange rate of its currency within a defined trading range through market intervention, interest rate adjustments, and other means. The EC is looking to this system to provide a stable basis for trade and to reduce inflation, and there is some evidence that it has worked.

Already a trade-weighted basket of EC currencies, the European Currency Unit or ECU, is being widely adopted as a convenient unit of account for financial reports and commercial transactions, as well as for official EC budgeting and accounting as originally intended. But the ECU is still just an abstraction: You may be able to get a business loan denominated in ECUs, but you can't carry them around in your pocket.

Britain also appears to be at odds with most of the other member states in another area that, like economic and monetary union, transcends the 1992 program—the so-called **social dimension** of the European Community. The "social dimension" is the European Commission's catchall phrase for a range of measures, "the core of which is a proposed charter of fundamental social rights." (*The Economist*, July 8, 1989) A related issue of concern to business people is a proposed European Company Statute that includes provisions for worker participation in management.

Impact on US. Businesses and Other Trading Partners

The U.S.–EC relationship is the dominant axis of world trade. When the sales of U.S. companies' European subsidiaries and European companies' U.S. subsidiaries are included, the partnership represents some 15 percent of global trade—over $1 trillion a year. Although exports account for only about ten percent of America's share of this trade flow, as our merchandise trade deficit continues to reflect, U.S. exports to the EC showed a healthy 30 percent increase in 1988. What effect will the accelerating change taking place there have on American firms in future years?

Strategically it is important to be alert to both offensive and defensive implications of the single market. From the offensive viewpoint, it is obvious that any company with pretensions to world-class status cannot ignore the world's biggest market. Beyond this, however, some American business people argue that U.S. companies may have a competitive edge over local companies in the new European market. Two advantages enjoyed by many U.S. firms have been cited in particular:

- A number of U.S. companies have been operating in Europe for years. They may actually be better prepared to address the European market as a whole than their local competitors—both in their organizational and operational structure and in having a European perspective rather than a French or a German one.
- By the time they reach out overseas, most U.S. companies already know how to compete in an open market that has a population of hundreds of millions and spans an entire continent. Relatively few European firms have that experience.

The above is not to understate the difficulties of entering and doing business in Europe's complex, multicultural market. There are certainly pitfalls as well as possible benefits in extrapolating U.S. business experience to any foreign environment. The point is that American business people need not feel that they are necessarily at a disadvantage in Europe, because the single European market is as new to Europeans as it is to us. But *what* is new is different in the two cases—to the Europeans it is the size, openness and competitiveness of the market; to Americans it is its cultural and linguistic diversity, fragmentation, unfamiliar social institutions, and so on.

There are a wide range of alternatives to penetrate the European market, from exporting to various modes of direct investment. In many cases choosing the right kind of "strategic alliance" with a European partner can help make the most out of both American experience and local knowledge. Many European firms are eager to ally themselves with U.S. companies, for the sake of marketing or technical expertise or to gain access to U.S. markets in return for guidance into Europe.

Looking at defensive issues, the point bears repeating that with a large, integrated home market as a base, established EC-wide firms will be poised to attack other markets more aggressively. At the same time, European firms which are, for the first, time facing real competition in their once-protected domestic markets are anxiously seeking to establish footholds abroad. Just as Americans are looking with increased interest at the world's largest market, the European Community, so are many of these European companies focusing their attention on the second largest, the United States.

Case Study

An example of a strategy that is both offensively and defensively motivated is that of an American company we will call Auto Components, Inc., or ACI. Traditionally ACI has done a majority of its business with General Motors. The key to its success with GM has been to work closely with GM's design engineers from early in the product development cycle. In this way ACI has been able to lock out competitors and ensure that its components meet GM's standards for quality, performance, fit, and cost. GM is of course a true multinational; it has major manufacturing operations in Europe and Australia, as well as in North America, and sources its components and materials locally to a great extent. To date, ACI had exported only in minor quantities, and was not a supplier to GM outside the United States and Canada. In the increasing globalization of the automobile industry—with producers increasingly offering international models, rather than cars designed only for a single market—ACI saw a potential threat as well as an opportunity. The opportunity was of course to become a supplier to Opel, GM's subsidiary in Europe, and perhaps eventually to other European auto manufacturers also. The threat was that a competing component manufacturer would establish with Opel the same sort of relationship ACI had with GM in Detroit, and would use that foothold to attack ACI's own position in the United States. ACI's response was to search out and acquire a small engineering and prototyping company close to Opel's headquarters near Frankfurt, West Germany. If their strategy works as planned, ACI will gradually open up a major new market, while at the same time protecting its domestic base.

Something of a paradox faces would-be American marketers in Europe. On the one hand, it is the prospect of the "single market" of over 320 million consumers that rightly attracts their attention. On the other hand, sellers of consumer goods and services (and to some extent industrial products as well) ignore at their peril the fact that the EC is made up of 12 independent nations speaking nine major languages plus a host of less widely used tongues and dialects—

Basque, Catalan, Gaelic, and Flemish, to name a few. Consumer preferences differ widely across Europe, which will be the case long after 1992: The fact that it becomes easier and cheaper for a Frenchman to buy German wines doesn't mean that he will do so.

So the U.S. consumer-products company eyeing the EC market is often faced not merely with the need to modify its products and its promotional approach for a "European" market, but to adapt them to a number of *national* markets. Obviously this is an expensive process; it demands that the company carefully analyze and prioritize markets within the EC, and make only those product modifications which promise to be cost-justified. In industrial markets, too, companies generally must be prepared to undertake the considerable expense of translating parts lists, operating manuals, and so forth, into major European languages. In several cases we have seen, potential European buyers have interpreted American firms' failure to provide local-language sales and reference materials as a lack of commitment to their markets.

Pricing is another marketing-related issue that raises problems internationally which are unfamiliar to many U.S. companies. There is a delicate trade-off between pricing exports in U.S. dollars versus local currency. U.S. dollar pricing removes exchange risk as a threat to the value of individual export orders, but may cut down on sales volume for two reasons: (i) The importer/distributor may himself be unwilling to bear the exchange risk, and (ii) The end user may turn away from the imported product if the price goes up in local currency terms due to a rise in the value of the dollar. Possible compromises include denominating prices in the ECU, which is likely to be more stable in relation to the dollar than any single EC currency.

The phrase "fortress Europe" has been widely used to sum up outsiders' fears of a more protectionist Europe after 1992. These fears have subsided to a large extent, but there remain some potentially crucial areas of ambiguity in the EC's external trade relationships. Furthermore, in a few particular cases, the Community has taken steps that clearly have a negative impact on the United States and which may be harbingers of more restrictive actions to come. Many of these issues are complex technical matters.

For example, American companies have dealt with **local content** requirements for many years in Canada, Mexico, and other markets. These have meant, for example, that if General Motors wanted to sell cars in Canada, it had to assemble them there and incorporate a minimum of Canadian parts and labor. Complex **rules of origin** are something of a new wrinkle in this area. European countries have imposed import **quotas** and so-called **"voluntary"** export restraints (VERs) in the past, particularly on Japan, but the United States has not been notably affected by these measures. The greatest part of the EC's trade fears still focus on Japan, but lately American firms have been catching some of the fallout. In one 1989 case earlier this year the EC claimed that the Japanese photocopier company, Ricoh, was trying to evade export restraints by shipping to the Community from its U.S. subsidiary; the EC ruled that the copiers were not really of U.S. origin and were in violation of the restraints. Ricoh will now have to put more U.S. components into its copiers if it wants to ship them to the EC as U.S. products , so this ruling may be seen as somewhat beneficial to the United States.

Consumer electronics, textiles, footwear, and ceramics were recently cited by a U.S. government international economist as sectors in which EC import restrictions aimed at other trading partners could hit U.S. exporters.

One strategy for avoiding some of these problems is to establish a direct **physical presence** in the European Community and thus hope to qualify for national treatment as an EC company. The overt signs at this time are that an EC-resident subsidiary of a U.S. company will indeed be entitled to national treatment throughout the Community, except perhaps in sensitive areas like public procurement. There have been vague suggestions, however, that there be some kind of test of the amount or kind of investment to be met in order to qualify for national treatment. Although there seems to be no present cause for alarm over this issue, it is one that bears watching.

Case Study

One small U.S. company almost learned a very difficult lesson about local content and rules of origin. The company, which manufactures and designs integrated circuits for a large U.S. computer manufacturer, has annual sales of approximately $12 million and sold approximately 50 percent of its products to this one computer manufacturer. Unbeknownst to the company, the computer manufacturer was then taking the integrated circuits and shipping them to their plant in Spain for assembly into computers.

Case Study (Continued)

In February 1989, the EC adopted new rules governing semiconductors and country of origin. The new rules modify the interpretation of the term "last substantial change." These requirements specify that a significant portion of the semiconductor wafer manufacturing process must occur in Europe for the products to be classified of European origin. The Semiconductor Industry Association has lobbied both Congress and the European Commission in Brussels to modify and/or clarify the ruling on the basis that such a ruling will in essence discriminate against all imported chips.

The computer manufacturer subsequently approached the small company and warned that it would probably have to cancel its orders for U.S.-made integrated circuits because of the new ruling requiring local content.

Extremely concerned about losing 50 percent of their sales, the company sought help in developing some strategies on how they could continue to supply this crucial client and yet meet the tough requirements imposed by the European Commission. Ultimately, the company entered into a licensing agreement whereby certain transfers of technology occurred in Europe which thus enabled the computer manufacturer to continue to utilize the expertise of the integrated circuit manufacturer.

The intent of the ruling might have been to encourage more sophisticated work and R&D to occur in Europe, in essence, however, this may have a significant impact on U.S. manufacturers who are attempting to sell their chips in the European Community. It has been acknowledged that the European Community's level of sophistication in semiconductor manufacturing significantly lags behind that in the United States and Japan. All imported chips will now be subject to higher tariffs, and thus be placed at a competitive disadvantage.

Currently, Motorola is one of the few major U.S. chip manufacturers with a completely integrated production facility in Scotland. The semiconductor country of origin ruling has caused Fujitsu to announce that it plans to set up a $580 million dollar integrated semiconductor facility in the United Kingdom.

The 1992 Environment: Key Questions for Your Business To benefit from the increase in trading opportunities throughout Europe, businesses need to understand exactly what it all means with respect to the following key areas, as they move into the new trade era:

- **Marketing Considerations.** Will the elimination of tariff barriers allow you to compete in a market that was previously closed to you? When will this occur?

  What other companies are located close enough to compete economically in your markets? How strong are they? What must you do to compete with them? What barriers might hinder them from entering your market?

  What price advantages will the Single Market give to the competition in the national EC markets? When will the elimination of tariff barriers allow new competitors to enter? How will you compete?

  How does your product quality compare to that of the potential competition?

  What changes do you need to make to your marketing and selling activities to compete with other firms? How will your advertising, packaging, sales force, distribution, customer service, product and/or service line and other components of the marketing mix be affected?

- **Supply Considerations.** Will you now have access to less expensive or higher quality raw materials? What supply benefits will accrue to your competitors?

  Will less costly capital equipment or more advanced technology be available to you and your competitors?

- **Operating Considerations.** How effective are your research and development, purchasing, production, information systems, and marketing capabilities, in relation to potential competitors from other EC countries?

  How good is your productivity in relation to the potential competition?

  How do your material costs, wage rates, and overhead cost structures compare to those of your potential competition?

Is there an opportunity for your company to consolidate its European operations and reduce its overhead?

Will your planning, control, and costing systems provide the decision-making support needed to compete effectively?

Do you have adequate capacity to meet increased product demand?

- **Regulations.** Will changes in existing product standards, arising from the 1992 legislation, allow you to enter markets more quickly, or on a less costly basis?

Will certain institutional barriers such as quotas, technical standards, pollution or safety regulations, still inhibit access to new markets, or limit access to customers by potential competitors?

- **Taxation.** What effect will 1992 have on direct and indirect taxes, and how will these changes affect the prices of products to the final customer?

Will differences in the national tax systems give rise to opportunities for relocation of operations or reorganization of corporate structure, as a result of 1992?

Meeting the Challenge: a Three-Step Approach

To meet the challenge of the Single European Market, you should not wait until 1992, the date by which the Commission of the European Community has chosen to create Europe's Single Market. You should act now—your competitors will have already begun their plans for the Single Market.

Your response should include three basic steps:

I.   Assess the impact and opportunities created by the Single Market.
II. Develop strategies to address your company's opportunities and weaknesses.
III. Implement your plan.

I. Assess the Impact and Opportunities

You will need to analyze a large number of factors in order to determine the opportunities and impact of 1992 on your business. These will include:

- **Management.** Coping with trade in Europe is, above all, a management challenge. To enter new markets and meet new competition, you will need to consider

  - Your company's management strengths and skills, and those of competitors;

  - Knowledge of new technology and management tools; and

  - Use of productivity, quality, and employee motivation programs.

- **Competition.** Increased competition will result in all twelve countries. You will require information about

  - Your competitor's capacity utilization;

  - Their suppliers and raw material costs;

  - Their productivity and product quality;

  - Their interest in, and ability to, enter new markets; and

  - EC regulations affecting competitors from other parts of the world.

- **Regulatory Matters.** Doing business in the other Member States will require familiarity with regulatory affairs as they apply to your markets. How will the following affect you?

  - Reduction in market entry costs arising from changes to standards;

  - Labor law;

  - Environment law; and

  - Product liability law.

- **Suppliers.** 1992 may affect your suppliers, and consequently, the prices you pay for your materials and capital equipment. What effect will the following have on your operations?

  - The removal of barriers to imports;

  - Rules of origin; and

  - Exchange rates.

- **The Cost of Financing.** The Single European Market could have an impact on the cost of financing. You may wish to consider

  - The relative cost and availability of financing in different countries; and

- Increased competition among financial institutions and its effect on the cost and availability of financing.

- **Corporate Tax Considerations.** The 1992 and future Commission initiatives will affect the future formulation of tax policy because, in the absence of trade barriers, each country's tax rates must remain competitive with those in the other countries to maintain tax revenues, investment and jobs. Therefore, in planning, you need to consider

  - The differential among tax rates in EC countries, and the effect of this differential on your competitiveness; and

  - The extent to which this differential may change over time.

- **VAT and Excise Duties.** The Commission has proposals to harmonize rates of VAT and excise duties. This will have the effect of reducing or increasing the cost of goods and services.

- **Distribution.** Distribution considerations are important in analyzing potential new market opportunities, both in terms of channels and physical distribution. Consider

  - The importance of price in sourcing;

  - Availability of distributors, and their competitiveness, productivity, and marketing capabilities;

  - Freight costs relative to competitors;

  - The importance of delivery frequency and reliability;

  - Customer service requirements and possibilities; and

  - The potential for forming strategic alliances with foreign companies.

- **The Customer.** 1992 opens up opportunities for obtaining new customers, for both you and your competitors. Consider

  - The Single Market's impact on customer attitudes to sourcing, investment, expansion and location;

  - Its impact on prices to customers in other European countries; and

  - the importance of pricing in sourcing.

- **Government Procurement.** 1992 will improve access to government procurement contracts (estimated to account for over ten percent of GDP in the average Member State). You will need to consider the effect of

- Access by foreign competitors to public contracts;
- New opportunities for access to foreign public contracts; and
- Changes in public procurement rules.

II. Establish Strategies

Once you have assessed the impact of 1992, you will need to prepare a strategic response to the opportunities and challenges identified. Success in the European Single Market demands effective and efficient management, and the creative use of current technology. Your possible strategic options for attacking 1992 will include one or more of the following:

- Operating and overhead cost reduction;
- Developing new products or markets;
- Mergers, acquisitions, and divestitures;
- Plant location;
- Customer service requirements;
- Improved sourcing;
- Financial restructuring; and
- Application of new technologies.

III. Implementation

Finally, you must implement your 1992 strategy. This will require a major ongoing commitment by top management.

A time-based implementation plan is essential. The plan must be monitored continuously over a period of months and years. It must also be adjusted in response to unforeseen developments, including legislative and competitive moves.

The implications of 1992 are extremely complex and many Commission initiatives have yet to be negotiated. Thus, top management's hands-on attention will be needed over the long-term to ensure successful adaptation to the new European market.

In Conclusion: Reason for Optimism

No U.S. company of any size is likely to be unaffected by the integration of the European market. EC92 holds out the potential of a huge market that the United States is only beginning to exploit, and it represents a new environment in which powerful global competitors will be born, and from which they will reach into every market in the world, most definitely including our own.

Such radical change always engenders fear, and fear in the international trade community too often leads to defensiveness and protectionism. American diplomatic and economic relations with the Community are good. On balance there is much reason for optimism that the Single Market Initiative will result in massive new opportunities for U.S.–EC trade and investment.

Numerous government and private sector organizations in the United States now offer information and other services to support companies' moves into Europe. We advise companies that are not already in the European market to evaluate their opportunities *now*— don't wait until 1992 to come up with a plan; it may be too late.

Companies should determine just which directives will affect their products, markets, or operations, and set up a system for tracking these directives through the EC bureaucracy and national governments. Where directives threaten to have a negative impact, large companies may lobby the EC Commission or legislature directly, while smaller firms may work through their government or industry representatives to seek changes. Finally, it is important for companies to take a hard-headed look at their internal resources and what it is going to take to develop a sound EC92 strategy. Where internal resources fall short in areas like market research, international tax issues, distribution strategies, and so on, companies should be looking to develop their capabilities or augment them with outside professional assistance.

THE ASEAN NATIONS AND HONG KONG*

The business and popular press has devoted a great deal of attention in recent years to the large economies of North Asia—China, Japan,

---

*Article reprinted from *Export Today*, with the permission of the editor.

South Korea, and Taiwan. The awesome demographics and age-old mystique of China continue to fascinate Westerners, while the remarkable industrial development and export success of Japan, South Korea, and Taiwan are viewed with envy and alarm.

To some extent this focus on North Asia has tended to overshadow the lesser-known countries to the south. Those American companies that do look to Hong Kong and the ASEAN countries — Brunei, Indonesia, Malaysia, the Philippines, Singapore, and Thailand—are typically more concerned with sourcing raw materials and components or with low-cost production for other markets. But these countries represent a host of market opportunities in their own right. Their combined population of 314 million is close to that of the European Economic Community, and Southeast Asia's combined Gross Domestic Product of approximately $270 billion, though only some five to six percent of the United States or the EEC, makes it a region of considerable (and growing) economic significance.

Behind these regional statistics lie tremendous disparities. Indonesia's nearly 180 million people are dispersed over some 6,000 of the country's 13,677 islands; per capita income is under $500 a year. Singapore's 2.6 million citizens inhabit a single island of only 240 square miles, but are the wealthiest in Asia after Japan.** 95 percent of Thais are Buddhist, 92 percent of Filipinos are Christian (85 percent are Roman Catholic), and 87 percent of Indonesians Muslims... making it by far the largest Muslim nation in the world.

Such unique national characteristics make for interesting market niches. Few Americans would suppose that Hong Kong, with its thousands of squatters and "boat people" living in squalor, also has the world's highest ratio of Rolls Royces to population. Or that Malaysia, officially a Muslim nation, has the greatest per capita consumption of cognac of any country, as well as more Mercedes-Benz automobiles for its size than any country but West Germany.

** To be precise, it is Brunei, a sultanate of about 2,200 square miles on the northwest coast of Borneo, that has the region's highest per capita national income at over $13,000 per year. The population of Brunei is under 250,000, however, and the wealth generated by the country's oil and gas exports is in fact held predominantly by the ruling family. Though not a significant consumer market, it is nevertheless true that Brunei has spent lavishly on public-works projects, some of which offer opportunities to foreign bidders.

Statistics like these demonstrate that there are attractive marketing opportunities in a number of Southeast Asian countries:

- For many consumer products, the large population itself suggests opportunities—even if only one percent of the population use a product, that's over three million consumers.

- For luxury goods, it is clear that there are wealthy and status-conscious individuals in all the countries of Southeast Asia who are eager to buy imported products with prestigious brand names.

- Makers of industrial products should recognize that the countries of Southeast Asia are investing heavily to maintain economic growth rates two to three times those of the OECD countries.

- Providers of technical services should be aware that large-scale development projects in Indonesia, Malaysia, the Philippines, and Thailand often utilize American engineering, consulting, and other skills.

Foreign Presence and Business Climate

Both European and American multinational corporations (MNCs) have long been involved in Southeast Asia. In many cases, as with the British in Malaysia and Singapore, and the Dutch in Indonesia, strong commercial ties have remained even after former colonies have gained independence. American MNCs are relative newcomers, and are more likely to have manufacturing or sourcing operations in this region than marketing and distribution. But the fact that MNCs are well established in much of Southeast Asia does not mean that they have locked up every opportunity that exists in the region. Just as in the United States, there are often market niches that the major corporations are unaware of, or that they do not consider big enough to merit their attention. In practice, as discussed below, the presence of European or American MNCs may be helpful to the smaller company seeking to enter a Southeast Asian market.

Depending on the form of market entry sought, there may be factors other than basic demographics which make a particular Southeast Asian country attractive. Many of these countries offer incentives, grants, and loan programs which are second to none in the world. For example, Singapore provides incentive programs which include tax holidays, investment credits, and reimbursement for a substantial portion of employee training costs (both in Singapore and outside of Singapore), and also shelters income gained from re-export activities. Additional incentives may be available in industries, like Information Technology, that the Singapore government has targeted for strategic development.

Hong Kong, on the other hand, offers one of the lowest corporate tax rates in the world and is truly a free trade zone. Employment passes are easy for American businesspeople to obtain, unlike in many Pacific Rim countries. It is possible to set up operations in Hong Kong in a very short period of time and use the colony as a base to serve the larger Southeast Asian market.

These kinds of pro-business policies, together with the capacity of the regional market to consume goods and services, and the various government tax incentives, make Southeast Asia extremely attractive for many companies.

There is a widespread perception that companies go to Southeast Asia to take advantage of low labor costs, but this is much less a factor today than in the past. For example, Singapore, the world's leading producer of computer disk drives, has a serious shortage of skilled workers in the electronics sector, and is reluctant to grant work permits to more workers from Malaysia to alleviate the shortage; as a consequence, wages for test engineers and other jobs have been bid up to high levels. In Hong Kong, concerns about the colony's future after 1997, when it reverts to the rule of the People's Republic of China, have led many highly trained and employable workers to emigrate to Canada and Australia; employers here, too, have been forced to resort to high wages to retain key personnel.

While it is true that wages are lower in Indonesia, Malaysia, the Philippines, and Thailand, one must appreciate that labor cost is determined not by wages alone, but by productivity as well. These countries may indeed offer a cost advantage to labor-intensive operations, but training costs are likely to be relatively high, and the language barrier may be an obstacle in seeking to raise productivity to expected standards.

Labor unions are not generally a major problem in Southeast Asian countries, but there are exceptions. Foreign-owned enterprises in the Philippines have been the target of union pressure, to a far greater extent than domestic companies. In one recent case a U.S. multinational planning to close down a factory in Manila felt it necessary to offer a severance payment of 2 ½ months' pay for every year of service in order to minimize the risk of sabotage and other disruptions.

The quality of infrastructure is another area where there are vast disparities among Southeast Asian countries, and in many cases from site to site within a given country. Port and telecommunications facilities are of a world-class standard in both Hong Kong and Singapore, as are banking and other services. Facilities are generally good in West (Peninsular) Malaysia as well, but poor telephone and telex service, an unreliable power supply, and/or horrendous urban traffic congestion can be serious problems in other countries in the region.

In some of the less developed countries within Southeast Asia, such as Indonesia, Malaysia, and Thailand, U.S. companies may find a ready market for products and technologies which are approaching the end of their life cycle in North America and Europe. The reason is that many of these products continue to fit the needs of industries that are still at a relatively basic level in these countries. In telecommunications, for example, the OECD countries are rapidly moving to all-digital systems—indeed, this trend is clear even in Southeast Asia, where Singapore will be one of the first countries in the world to install a complete fiber-optic network. Countries like Indonesia, on the other hand, cannot afford the huge capital investment required to upgrade to state-of-the-art systems, and are faced with the need to procure large amounts of analog equipment to maintain their old-technology networks. In agriculture and other traditional industries, too, proven "low-tech" equipment is often better suited to the needs and maintenance capabilities of these countries than the complex machinery employed in the West.

Thus, the Southeast Asian countries offer a full spectrum of demand for goods and services at different levels of price, quality, and sophistication. As a result, Southeast Asia presents a wide range of opportunities that many companies may be overlooking as a result of the attention that other Pacific Rim countries receive.

Viewed as a whole, as shown in Table 5 and Figure 13, a three-tiered market may be distinguished in Southeast Asia:

- The first tier includes Hong Kong and Singapore. These are small but highly developed economies that compare with the other Newly Industrialized Countries (NICs) like South Korea and Taiwan in their infrastructure and capacity to absorb the latest tech-

Table 5. U.S. Exports to Southeast Asia (US$ Millions)

Country	1985	1986	1987	1988	1989
Brunei	51	202	93	78	63
Hong Kong	2,786	3,030	3,983	5,687	6,304
Indonesia	795	946	767	1,059	1,256
Malaysia	1,539	1,730	1,897	2,142	2,875
Philippines	1,379	1,363	1,599	1,878	2,206
Singapore	3,476	3,380	4,053	5,768	7,353
Thailand	849	936	1,544	1,962	2,292
Total	**10,875**	**11,587**	**13,936**	**18,574**	**22,349**

Source: U.S. Department of Commerce

nology in both industrial and consumer goods and services. Despite having less than three percent of the region's population, Hong Kong and Singapore together account for some 60 percent of U.S. exports to Southeast Asia. These countries are often used as headquarters sites for regional operations.

Figure 13. U.S. Exports to Southeast Asia (US$ Millions)
(Source: U.S. Department of Commerce)

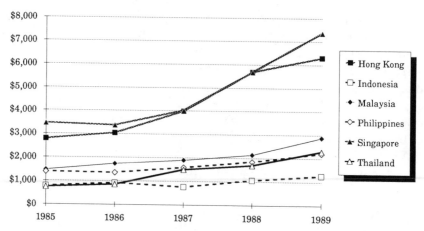

- The second tier includes Malaysia and Thailand, with populations of 17 and 55 million, respectively, and which are rapidly advancing toward the status of NICs while still retaining large undeveloped sectors. Both countries have increasing levels of per capita national income, and are investing heavily in industrial development. They also receive significant grants and loans for infrastructure development from international funding agencies such as the World Bank and Asian Development Bank. These countries are significant consumer and industrial markets in their own rights, and are often selected as off-shore manufacturing sites by U.S. and European MNCs.

- Although the volume of U.S. exports to the Philippines, a former American colony, might suggest that it belongs in the second tier, for the purposes of market assessment it is probably more useful to place it in a third category along with Indonesia. Both countries have large , poor populations and, to a greater extent than others in the group under consideration, face fundamental economic problems. In the case of Indonesia, the basic problem is to diversify away from reliance upon oil and gas exports as a source of foreign exchange and growth. For the Philippines the task is to restructure and rebuild the economy following the ravages of the Marcos years. 1988 per capita GDP was estimated at $476 for Indonesia and $654 for the Philippines.

Some Pragmatic Suggestions

Within Southeast Asia, then, there are markets for almost every variety of product and service that is offered by American companies. From this point of view American businesses should consider Southeast Asia just as seriously when looking for overseas markets as Europe, Canada, or other more familiar areas of the world. But doing business in Southeast Asia is indeed different from doing business elsewhere. Following are some pragmatic suggestions for approaching Southeast Asian markets:

1. *Review the market potential of the region as a whole and by country, based on imports of products or services similar to your own.* This information can be obtained from the Department of Commerce.

2. *Look at who the competitors are and determine how well established they are.* For example, the large Hong Kong trading companies and many of the Commonwealth trading companies already have developed roots within Southeast Asia and make for a formidable degree of competition. Do not overlook, either, the Japanese trading companies that have moved into Southeast Asia rather strongly. For this stage of market evaluation you may wish to retain an international consulting firm and/or travel to the region for a first-hand look.

3. *The fact that a trading company offering products that apparently compete with yours may already be entrenched in a given market is not necessarily a negative.* Your product may be viewed as complementary to an existing product line, especially if it has special applications or features. If your product does have a competitive advantage in terms of features or price, it may be possible to negotiate with the trading company to distribute your product through its established channels. This can be a far faster route to market penetration than attempting direct sales in an unfamiliar market, or seeking to build up your own network of distributors. The knowledge of the market you gain by indirect distribution through an established agent will put you in a better position should you later elect to enter the market directly. This brings us to our next point.

4. *Be careful about entering into any kind of distribution or joint venture agreement, especially where you are not familiar with the people you are doing business with.* Southeast Asia is notorious for individuals representing themselves as directors of 15 or 20 companies that in fact are mere shells with little or no capital or personnel behind them. Though their business cards can appear very impressive, they in fact do not represent strong organizations you would wish to be your business partners. Thus a background check by a bank, accounting firm, or law firm is well worth your while before entering into any such agreement. Another point to bear in mind is to preserve your future freedom of action by strictly defining and limiting the scope and duration of any agreement. We have seen cases in which American businesses granted exclusive 20- or 30-year distribution rights to a loosely defined

"East Asian" market in return for a single up-front payment. The appointed distributors then recouped their investment several times over by selling sub-distributorships in individual countries. In fact the prime "distributors" never had any intention to invest the resources necessary to promote the products in question. A company trying to recover from such a short-sighted error faces having to buy back the rights to distribute its own products, for considerably more than it originally received for the distribution license!

5. *Evaluate all of the available incentives and allowances, tax breaks, grants and loan programs carefully before deciding to set up an operation in Southeast Asia.* Get guarantees of these in writing. Government brochures designed to attract investment may present these as if they are granted as a matter of course. In fact they are generally subject to negotiation. The time when you have negotiating leverage is *before* you make a commitment. It is not unusual for companies to find that incentives they had counted on on the basis of brochures subtly vaporize when operations have already started if not nailed down in advance.

6. *Consider the protection of your trademarks, copyrights, and patents.* Although in recent years new laws have been passed in Southeast Asian countries to strengthen protection of intellectual property rights, enforcement is still a question. U.S. trade officials, for example, remain concerned about effective copyright and patent protection in Thailand, and suspension of GSP treatment for Thai exports to the United States—the country's largest export market—has been threatened. Thus, seeking advice from a well established international law firm on how best to protect your products, trade secrets, good name and market identity is advice well taken.

Conclusion

It has been noted that we are likely to be entering "the century of the Pacific Rim." Recently much attention has been diverted by other watershed developments in international business, particularly the European Economic Community's 1992 Single Market

Initiative. But the shift of economic power to the Pacific Rim continues nonetheless.

Within the Pacific Rim, Japan, China, South Korea, and Taiwan have held the spotlight. Southeast Asia is a market with more consumers than the United States and Canada combined, dynamic economic growth, a hunger for foreign products of many kinds, and, in a number of cases, enlightened policies favoring foreign investment. Yet this region remains largely unknown to American business.

UNITED STATES–CANADA FREE TRADE AGREEMENT (FTA)

The United States and Canada are each other's major trading partner. In recognition of this and to better promote trade, on January 1, 1989, the United States and Canada formed the world's largest free trade area, stretching from the Arctic Circle to the Rio Grande.

U.S. exports to Canada reached $70 billion in 1988, just slightly less than exports to the entire European Community. At the same time, Canada supplies about 20 percent of U.S. imports. The U.S. purchases approximately 78 percent of Canada's exports. In 1987, the two countries exchanged goods and services totaling $166 billion and bilateral direct investment totaled $79 billion. (Source: Department of Commerce—*Business America*, January 30, 1989, page 2.)

Tariff Phase-Out Schedule

While 73 percent of U.S. exports to Canada were duty free prior to the FTA, over the next ten years, all remaining tariffs will be phased out. Goods are classified into three categories. For goods in Category A, all tariffs were removed beginning January 1, 1989. Category B tariffs will be removed over a period of five years with a twenty percent reduction per year. Tariffs on items in Category C will be removed over a ten year period, at a rate of ten percent per year. Table 6 outlines examples of products in each of these categories.

Table 6. Tariff Categories and Examples

Category A	Category B	Category C
Computers	Printed matter	Apparel
Animal Feed	Paints	Rail Cars
Bourbon Whiskey	Chemicals	Pleasure Craft
Electronic Calculators	Furniture	Tires
Telephone Sets	Paper and Paper Products	Steel
Fur Coat/Leather	After-Market Auto Parts	Pre-fabricated
Skis/Motorcycles	Printing Machinery	buildings
Ice/Roller Skates		Most Agricultural Products

Rules of Origin

U.S. companies considering exporting to Canada who wish to take advantage of preferential tariff treatment must pay close attention to the *rules of origin and certificate of origin regulations*. The primary purpose of the rules of origin is to ensure that the product has been produced or substantially enhanced either in the United States or in Canada. Goods that are wholly produced in the United States or Canada will qualify for preferential treatment. Goods which are composed of imported input, but which have been changed in ways which are physically and commercially significant, will also be eligible for preferential tariff treatment. However, it is the exporter's responsibility to ensure that the goods have been sufficiently altered. In addition, the regulations require that fifty percent of the direct cost of processing be American or Canadian or a combination of the two.

When shipped to the United States, many imported products are classified according to a tariff schedule and assigned an identification number in accordance with the Harmonized System of tariff classifications and statistical coding. In essence, the rules require that the item which was imported be sufficiently transformed so as to be classified under a different classification when exported to Canada. For example, many companies may import screws, nuts and bolts from third countries. When such items are shipped into the United States they are classified by a statistical coding according to the Harmonized system. Most manufacturers will then take those nuts, bolts, and screws and assemble them into items such as television sets or other consumer products. When the U.S. exporter ships that television set or consumer appliance to Canada, the product enters the country under a new product statistical classification. Therefore, those bolts, nuts or screws have been sufficiently transformed so as to lose their identity as screws, nuts or bolts because they became a sub-component in the consumer product.

The U.S. exporter should also be aware that goods that are further processed in a third country before being shipped to their final destination will not qualify for preferential treatment, such as goods produced by U.S. or Canadian-owned *maquiladora* operations in Mexico. Goods which are shipped through a third country are also not eligible for FTA treatment unless they have remained under customs control and have only undergone unloading, reloading, or any other handling operation to preserve them in good condition.

Exporters are responsible for determining the eligibility of their goods for preferential tariff treatment and for providing the importer with the certificate of origin. The Canadian importer must have a valid exporter's certificate of origin from the U.S. exporter which certifies that the goods in question meet the FTA rules of origin. Exporters may provide importers with certificates of origin for a product line, a product, or an individual shipment and certificates can be obtained which apply to more than a single shipment.

Because of the complexity of the rules of origin, specific questions on the certificate of origin and related topics as they apply to U.S. exports to Canada should be addressed to Canada Customs and Excise, National Hotline, 800-267-6626. General questions can also be addressed to the U.S. Department of Commerce, Office of Canada, Room 3033, Washington, DC 20230, telephone 202-377-3101.

Government Procurement

The Free Trade Agreement expands the size of United States and Canadian federal government procurement projects which will be open to fair competition among suppliers from both countries. The value of new contracts open to U.S. firms as a result of the FTA is estimated at $500 million annually. U.S.–Canadian suppliers will be eligible to compete for government contracts in excess of $25,000. However, companies should be aware that there are exemptions for projects that are classified as national security. In the past, the Canadian federal government granted domestic products a minimum price differential of ten percent. Lowering the threshold by which U.S. manufacturers will able to compete for Canadian government contracts is especially valuable to small and medium-sized firms.

Professional Services

In the professional services sector, efforts are underway for professional organizations to permit mutual recognition and professional accreditation and licensing. For example, standards are now being developed for professional engineers and architectural services.

Finally, in another area, the Free Trade Agreement streamlines border crossing procedures for business visitors, professionals, traders and investors.

Best Export Prospects

For U.S. businesses considering exports to Canada, the Department of Commerce has identified the following industry sectors as having the most promise:

- Medical Equipment: Approximately 78 percent of all medical equipment sold in Canada is of U.S. origin. 1992 estimated sales should total $2 billion. With mutual recognition of technical standards, this should become a high growth area.

- Household Furniture: The United States currently exports approximately $124 million worth of furniture to Canada. The removal of tariffs makes U.S. furniture more cost competitive with foreign imports. The U.S. Department of Commerce has identified high-end living room and ready-to-assemble furniture as the most promising.

- Sports Equipment: Canada currently imports $420 million of sports equipment from the United States. This is expected to continue to be a high growth area.

- Building Materials and Products: U.S. exports account for 62 percent of all products sold in Canada. Growth rate of eight percent per annum is expected in the next four years.

- Computers and Peripherals: U.S. exports account for 80 percent of the marketplace in Canada and U.S. imports in 1987 were valued at $1.75 billion. It has been estimated that the annual growth rate for microcomputers will continue at a rate of 25 percent per annum for the next two to three years.

THE GENERAL AGREEMENT ON TARIFFS AND TRADE (GATT)

The General Agreement on Tariffs and Trade (GATT) was initially established in 1948 with 23 countries as signatories. Its basic aim is to liberalize world trade and provide agreed-upon rules for international business. Today, over 94 countries are signatories to the GATT. While the Agreement itself is a complicated document, the international business person should be aware of some of its fundamental principles and aims. First, under the famous "most favored nation" clause, the agreement seeks to promote trade on the basis of non-discrimination. Under this clause, member countries are obligated to treat each other as favorably as they do any country in the application and administration of import and export duties and charges.

A second basic principle is that, if a country chooses to give protection to a domestic industry, it should be provided through the customs tariff and not through other commercial barriers. Each country establishes a tariff schedule which is publicly available. Third, the GATT provides a forum for consultation, conciliation, and dispute settlement between countries. For example, the United States recently threatened to bring action against the European Community for its ban on U.S. beef produced with hormones. The forum of choice was the GATT Council which examines such disputes and may recommend remedial action. The GATT Council meets annually to explore a variety of issues and topics. Some of these issues include trade in meat, trade in dairy products, and anti-dumping practices.

The GATT's country membership is approximately two-thirds developing countries. One primary concern of these countries is that they have access to foreign markets.

The most recent round of negotiations, commonly referred to as the Uruguay Round, was launched in Geneva in September, 1986. During the negotiations, which last approximately four years, the 94 member countries discuss trade issues which have been identified as causing "friction." The U.S. government's agenda for the Uruguay Round included further tariff reductions, greater facilitation of agricultural trade, trade in services, and the elimination of certain non-tariff measures.

Non-Tariff Barriers

With respect to the non-tariff measures, the GATT has increasingly turned its attention to the distorting effects on world trade of non-tariff measures. Some of these issues include subsidies and counter-vailing measures.

All governments around the world seek to promote economic development of domestic industries. In some countries, and in some particular industries, subsidies are a way of providing domestic assistance. However, what may be of assistance to one domestic industry may cause trade distorting harm to an export. As a result, the GATT has attempted to establish guidelines as to when subsidies and countervailing measures may be imposed by a particular country.

Technical Barriers to Trade

This section of the GATT attempts to provide guidelines as to when countries may justifiably adopt technical regulations or standards, for reasons of safety, health, consumer and environmental protection, or other purposes. Many countries have claimed that Japan in particular has been guilty of implementing stringent standards that favor domestic industries and keep out foreign imports. This area continues to be an issue for trade friction among many countries.

Government Procurement

It is the intent of the signatories to GATT to increase international competition in bidding for government procurement contracts. The

United States is seeking greater transparency in the rules and regulations for bidding on such contracts, especially among the developing countries.

Revised GATT Anti-Dumping Rules   "Dumped" goods are broadly defined as imports which are sold at prices below those charged by the producer in his domestic market. In the Tokyo Round, which concluded in 1980, new rules were developed which established the conditions under which anti-dumping duties may be imposed as a defense against dumped imports. In the United States, the International Trade Commission (ITC) is the regulatory body responsible for hearing claims by U.S. industries who believe they have been harmed by foreign imports in the United States. The number of cases that have been filed before the ITC has increased dramatically within the last five years. Currently, the roster of complaints against various industry products exceeds over 80 cases.

New Issues of the Uruguay Round

Under the Uruguay Round, the United States has included as part of its negotiating agenda the following items:

- Development of regulations as they relate to professional services in international trade;
- Intellectual property rights; and
- Trade related investment measures.

Services   The export of technical professional services is a recent phenomena. With the growth of information technology, especially as it relates to computer systems and software, there has been a greater demand for U.S. companies to provide such services overseas. However, the mechanisms by which such services may be provided has not been clarified. Indeed, most U.S. companies have encountered a vast array of regulatory systems which may hinder their ability to conduct such business, prevent them from doing such business or require them to train so many local people as to make the delivery of such services not feasible.

Intellectual Property Rights   One of the key issues for the United States in the Uruguay Round is the implementation of more stringent intellectual property protection rules. The United States is concerned with developing regulations which provide uniform, substantive standards for protection among all 94 country members; an effective means for enforcement among all 94 country members; and an effective and expeditious dispute settlement process. This promises to be one of the most contentious points in the Uruguay negotiations. However, the United States is using it as leverage against other countries who wish to obtain greater access to U.S. markets via reduced tariffs. For more detailed information on intellectual property protection, see the following section of this chapter.

Trade-Related Investment Measures (TRIMs)   With respect to TRIMs, the United States has complained that foreign governments have imposed such stiff restrictions on local investment as to create significant barriers to doing business in that country. For example, it is not unusual for many developing countries to require a foreign company to hire a certain percentage of local employees, purchase a certain percentage of goods from local suppliers, or require that the ownership of the local company be with a local partner as the majority holder. This is a technique that is used widely both in Southeast Asia as well as in the Caribbean and South American countries. It is expected that many developing countries will resist interference in what they perceive as domestic control of investments. However, given the developing countries' thirst for more sophisticated technology, the United States may be able to obtain some concessions. This issue has served as a disincentive for many U.S. companies to doing business overseas.

Further information on the progress of the GATT negotiations can be obtained from the United States Chamber of Commerce in Washington, D.C. or trade associations.

INTELLECTUAL PROPERTY PROTECTION

The United States' legal system of intellectual property rights (IPRs) serves several important functions in the development and marketing of U.S. products overseas. For example, the U.S. patent system allows and encourages businesses to invest in much needed re-search and development. Upon the development of new products, the developer can apply for and be awarded a patent which gives the company or person exclusive ownership interest in the product. Such interests can translate into commercial value either through the sale of products or through royalty payments, if the patent holder grants a license to allow others to manufacture the products.

Throughout this section, we will use the term "intellectual property rights" to refer to a grouping of different types of pro-prietary protection. The following definitions are useful terms for reference.

Definitions

- A U.S. *patent* grants an inventor an exclusive right to make, use, and sell the patented product or process for a period of 17 years. Patents protect the idea as well as the process. The most important aspect of these rights is that the patented invention can be made, used, or sold only with the authorization of the patent owner.

- A U.S. *trademark* describes any work, name, or symbol which is used in trade and business to distinguish a product from other similar goods (e.g., Pepsi). Trademark laws are used to prevent others from making a product with a confusingly similar mark.

- *Copyright* protects the writings of an author against illegal or un-authorized copying of literary, dramatic, musical, and artistic work. The protection afforded under copyright laws has recently been extended to cover computer software, including manuals. Unlike patent protection, the idea expressed in the text is not pro-tected from use by third parties.

- *Mask work* describes a new type of intellectual property, pro-tected by the Semiconductor Chip Protection Act of 1984. It is, in essence, the design of an electrical circuit, the pattern of which is transferred and fixed in a semiconductor chip during the manu-facturing process.

- *Trade secrets* refers to any formula, pattern, device or compilation of information used in one's business, which is held in confidence by the owner. The concept of trade secrets can, in some jurisdictions, be interpreted to include the concept of know-how. The trade secret must have some commercial value and the owner must take appropriate steps to protect the secret.

- *Intellectual property* is a general term which describes inventions or other discoveries which have a commercial value, are proprietary in nature, and may have been registered with government authorities for sale or use by their owner. Such terms as patent, trademark, copyright, or mask works fall under the category of Intellectual Property.

Most industrialized nations, including Western Europe, Japan, Canada, and the United States, have strong systems of intellectual property protection. These legal systems extend to the granting of such rights as well as to the enforcement of such rights. However, *many countries do not see the need to have strong protection for intellectual property rights, and this can have serious consequences for the U.S. business going overseas.*

The newly industrialized countries—mostly those in the Pacific Rim and Latin America—have become international trade competitors of U.S. businesses. They either have inadequate laws or they fail to effectively enforce them. A weekly business magazine carried a report about a Hong Kong computer book store making available unauthorized copies of Lotus 1-2-3™ for $45.00 *(Business Week,* May 22, 1989, page 87).

Before a new-to-export business dismisses these problems as something "only the big boys" are worried about, consider three significant problems that a small to medium-sized U.S. business might encounter.

First, U.S. manufacturers are losing market share and encountering both volume and price competition from illegally traded or unauthorized goods that are sold around the world and in the U.S. In February 1988, the U.S. International Trade Commission completed a study which estimated that in one year (1986) U.S. businesses lost from $43 billion to $61 billion as a result of counterfeit goods being sold in place of legitimately manufactured goods *(Journal of Commerce,* February 29, 1988). The illegal products cut across industry sectors ranging from computer software to designer clothing, hair care products, and automobile parts.

In a recent study of film piracy in 58 foreign countries conducted by the Motion Picture Export Association of America, it was estimated that illegal copies cost the U.S. industry $740 million annually in lost revenues. While piracy is a widespread practice internationally, it was found to be particularly troublesome in several countries, headed by Saudi Arabia (losses of $75 million), Turkey ($45 million), and Egypt ($37 million). In a separate survey, the International Intellectual Property Alliance discovered losses of $35 million dollars for U.S. companies as a result of motion picture piracy in South Korea. In addition, the Philippines and Indonesia have been cited as major outposts of video piracy.

A second source of losses for U.S. firms stems from the loss of payment of royalties or remittances from the licensing and assignment of patent rights, trademarks, and copyrights. The industries which benefit from payment of royalties pursuant to copyright laws calculate that they lose more than $1.3 billion per annum *(Business America*, September 25, 1989, page 3).

In the arena of patent licensing fees, it is estimated that U.S. firms received $6.1 billion from legitimate overseas licensing and the assignment of patent rights *(Business America*, September 25, 1989, page 3).

The third area where U.S. firms are harmed by inadequate intellectual property protection is the disincentive to invest in costly R&D. This is especially true for industries where R&D costs are great, but the product itself can be inexpensively reproduced, such as drugs and computer software. Software executives estimate that piracy has cost them between $100 to $400 million a year in revenue losses. (Source: *Washington Post*, April 1989.) The pharmaceutical industry has been particularly hard hit. It can take ten years and $125 million to $160 million to get a new pharmaceutical product on the market, but a chemist can often easily copy a pharmaceutical. If not legally protected, the original developer of the product can be driven from the market by unauthorized products, oftentimes sold at significantly lower costs.

Because of the billions of dollars at stake, the United States has taken steps to strengthen intellectual property laws. Since 1983, Congress has passed 14 laws to strengthen intellectual property rights. Passage of the Semiconductor Chip Works Act has attempted to provide statutory protection for new and emerging technologies.

On the international level, the United States recently became a signatory to an international treaty, the Berne Convention for the Protection of Literary and Artistic Works. And, in multilateral negotiations currently being conducted pursuant to the General Agreement on Tariffs and Trade, the United States is leading the effort to institute intellectual property regulations amongst all 97 member countries.

The United States has been most successful in assisting U.S. exporters through bilateral negotiations. By threatening to impose trade sanctions on foreign imports from a particular country into the United States, the United States has been able to negotiate concessions from the exporting country that they would implement stronger intellectual property rights protection as well as enforcement mechanisms. In late 1988, President Reagan denied Thailand duty free treatment of $165 million worth of goods because of lax enforcement of intellectual property laws. The United States recently signed an agreement with Singapore to curb its once-rampant film piracy industry. In addition, the United States also reached an agreement with Taiwan in 1989 to provide protection for U.S. audio/visual works.

For the U.S. business going overseas, protection of the company's proprietary products is usually one of the last items on the checklist, if at all. This can be a costly mistake.

A company's proprietary product should be viewed as the company's most valuable asset. The name of the company, any registered trademarks or product trade names, trade secrets, and so forth, are all valuable assets which the new to export business should use care not to inadvertently "give away" or overlook.

For example, if you are considering entering into a distribution agreement with a potential overseas distributor, will that distributor have the right to use your company's name in advertising and marketing materials? Will that right be specified in the distribution agreement? Often, it is not. In some countries, a distributor may be required to register the name of your company because it is serving as your company's agent. Is it your intent for that foreign distributor to "own or have some sort of vested interest in" your company's name? If not, those terms should also be specified in the distribution agreement.

Another key point: Do not assume that U.S. registered intellectual property rights extend any legal protection to your company in a foreign country. Depending upon domestic laws and the scope of international treaties to which the host country and the United States may be signatories, reciprocity may or may not be available. For example, now that the United States is a signatory to the Berne Convention, you might assume that copyrighted materials registered in the United States would receive protection in another country which is also a signatory to that treaty. This may not be the case depending upon local laws and enforcement policies. We would urge you to consult with competent legal counsel to ascertain whether your company needs to make a separate filing in the foreign country in which you wish to conduct business.

With respect to the patent protection, patents generally need to be registered in each country in which you seek protection. Japan has its own system for registration, as do most of the East Asian countries. U.S. businesses should be aware that the processing time for a patent application can be as long as in the United States (approximately two to three years), if not longer. Therefore if you believe your patented product may be marketed overseas, you should seriously consider instituting concurrent filings in a number of other countries so that the period of review and granting of patent rights can proceed in a timely fashion. The United States is a member of the Patent Cooperative Treaty which allows concurrent review of patent applications. Other countries which are signatories to the Treaty include: Barbados, Austria, Belgium, Finland, most of Northern Europe, Japan, South Korea, Sweden, and the United Kingdom.

In addition, the European Patent Convention permits a single European patent application to be filed in English in the Munich, Germany office. If a patent is granted, patent protection is extended in the following countries: Austria, Belgium, France, West Germany, Italy, Lichtenstein, Luxembourg, Netherlands, Sweden, Switzerland, and the United Kingdom.

Another reason for significant concern about properly registered trademarks or trade names, copyrights, or patented materials is to allow border checks by customs officials. If your product has not been properly registered in the country in which it may be manufactured or distributed, and counterfeits are subsequently exported, customs officials may not be able to stop the bogus products. Unless the product has been registered in that country, customs officials are generally not empowered to stop the counterfeited material.

In the Omnibus Trade Bill of 1988, U.S. customs officials are empowered to stop counterfeit goods entering the United States. However, underlying that statutory authority is the assumption that the legal owner of the intellectual property right has properly registered such interests with U.S. government officials. For $190, U.S. companies can file a request for U.S. Customs Service to lookout for imported products that might violate their copyright and trademark rights. Under the federal Fraud Priority Program, the Customs Service has seized products valued at $30 million. To obtain further information, companies should contact: Value, Special Programs, and Admissibility Branch (ORR), U.S. Customs Service, Washington, DC 20229, (202) 566-5765.

Another reason U.S. businesses should be vigilant in guarding their intellectual property rights stems from the problem of product liability and loss of goodwill. Certain automobile manufacturers of components have had problems with counterfeit goods bearing the name of the company embossed or engraved on the components. The counterfeit goods were sold and purchased by innocent customers who assumed the products were genuine. Subsequent accidents resulted from the faulty components which resulted in the legitimate owner being sued. While liability for the faulty product may be minimized, the loss in goodwill and litigation costs might have been avoided.

Here are some helpful hints to keep in mind regarding IPRs and international markets:

- Consult with competent legal counsel about registering your tradename and trademarks in the United States and potential overseas markets.

- Make sure your written materials, such as manuals, and so forth, are copyrighted in the United States.

- Confer with your attorney about the need for concurrent patent filings in overseas markets.

- If you have trade secrets which are important to the company's manufacturing or process, take appropriate steps to ensure confidentiality.

SECTION 2

REGIONAL OVERVIEWS
AND COUNTRY DATA

Section 2 offers overviews of eight regions and individual country data sheets for key countries. Data sheets for individual countries in the regions covered in this section can be found immediately after each regional overview. Data sheets for countries not in these regions are included in Other Country Data.

EUROPEAN COMMUNITY

As discussed in Section I (see pages 6–7 and pages 19–37), the European Community represents a large and diverse market for U.S. businesses. In the course of writing this book, an extremely important development occurred which is likely to affect the workings of the EC. This is the economic reunification of West and East Germany; full political unification is due by the end of 1990.

West Germany had the largest population and economy of the EC prior to reunification. West German businesses have been actively taking advantage of the new market opportunities in East Germany. U.S. companies that have been active in West Germany should be in a strong position to do likewise.

The assimilation of East Germany will enhance Germany's dominant position within the community, increasing its population by over 27 percent to 67 million and raising GDP some 17 percent to over $1.4 billion. (*The Economist*, European Community Survey, July 7, 1990, p. 15.)

BELGIUM

Basic Data

Population (mid-1988):   9.9 million
Area (sq. kilometers):   37 thousand
Languages: Flemish (Dutch),
                           French

Key Economic Data

GDP (1988): $153.8 billion
Real GDP Growth 1980-88:   1.4%
GDP/Capita (1988): $15,536
Exchange Rate: $1 = 33.6825
                               Franc

Foreign Trade

Total Exports (1988): $88.9 billion
Total Imports (1988): $91.0 billion
Imports from U.S. (1989): $8.6 billion*
                           (*includes
                           Luxembourg)

Key Contacts

American Embassy Commercial Section
27 Boulevard du Regent
B-1000 Brussels, Belgium
APO New York 09667-1000
Tel: 32-2-513-3830
Telex:846-21336

American Chamber of Commerce in
    Belgium
Avenue des Arts 50, Boite 5
B-1040, Brussels, Belgium
Tel: 32-2-513-67-70/9
Telex: 64913 AMCHAM B

Embassy of Belgium Commercial Section
3330 Garfield Street, NW
Washington, DC 20008
Tel: (202) 333-6900
Telex: 89 566 AMBEL WSH

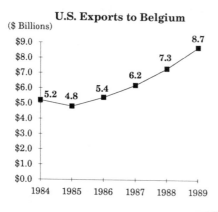

U.S. Exports to Belgium
($ Billions)

Leading Imports from U.S. 1989

Tobacco
Aircraft, Parts and Equipment
ADP and Office Machines
Internal Combustion Piston Engines
Coal
Pearls and Gemstones
Alcohols and Derivatives
Plastics (in primary forms)
Automobile Parts and Accessories
Engineering Plant and Equipment

DENMARK

Basic Data

Population (mid-1988):	5.1 million
Area (sq. kilometers):	43 thousand
Language:	Danish

Key Economic Data

GDP (1988):	$90.5 billion
Real GDP Growth 1980-88:	2.2%
GDP/Capita (1988):	$17,750
Exchange Rate:	$1 = 6.2320 Krone

Key Contacts

American Embassy Commercial Section
Dag Hammarskjolds Alle 24
2100 Copenhagen, Denmark
APO New York 09170
Tel: 45-1-423-144
Telex:22216

Embassy of Denmark Commercial Section
3200 Whitehaven Street, NW
Washington, DC 20008
Tel: (202) 234-4300
Telex: 089525 DEN EMB WSH

Foreign Trade

Total Exports (1988):	$27.8 billion
Total Imports (1988):	$26.5 billion
Imports from U.S. (1989):	$1.0 billion

U.S. Exports to Denmark
($ Billions)

Leading Imports from U.S. 1989

Aircraft, Parts and Equipment
Coal
ADP and Office Machines
Telecommunications Equipment
Printed Matter
Measuring Instruments
Tobacco
ADP and Office Machine Parts
Veneers, Plywood and Particle Board
Est. of Shipments Valued Under $1,501

FEDERAL REPUBLIC OF GERMANY
(West Germany)

Basic Data

Population (mid-1988):	61.3 million
Area (sq. kilometers):	249 thousand
Language:	German

Key Economic Data

GDP (1988):	$1.2 trillion
Real GDP Growth 1980-88:	1.8%
GDP/Capita (1988):	$19,605
Exchange Rate:	$1 = 1.6360 Deutsche Mark

Foreign Trade

Total Exports (1988):	$322.6 billion
Total Imports (1988):	$248.9 billion
Imports from U.S. (1989):	$16.9 billion

Key Contacts

American Embassy Commercial Section
Deichmanns Ave.
5300 Bonn 2, FRG
APO New York 09080
Tel: 49-228-3391
Telex:885-452

American Chamber of Commerce
Rossmarkt 12, Postfach 100 162
D-6000 Frankfurt
Main 1
Federal Republic of Germany
Tel: 49-69-28-34-01
Telex: 418679 ACC D

Embassy of the FRG Commercial Section
4645 Reservoir Road, NW
Washington, DC 20007
Tel: (202) 298-4000
Telex: 8 9481 DIPLOGERMA WSH

U.S. Exports to West Germany

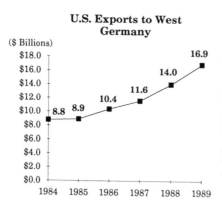

($ Billions)

8.8 8.9 10.4 11.6 14.0 16.9
1984 1985 1986 1987 1988 1989

Leading Imports from U.S. 1989

Aircraft, Parts and Equipment
ADP and Office Machines
ADP and Office Machine Parts
Measuring Instruments
Arms and Ammunition
Engines and Motors
Valves
Automobiles and Other Vehicles
Pulp and Waste Paper
Automobile Parts and Accessories

FRANCE

Basic Data

Population (mid-1988):	55.9 million
Area (sq. kilometers):	547 thousand
Language:	French

Key Economic Data

GDP (1988):	$949.4 billion
Real GDP Growth 1980-88:	1.8%
GDP/Capita (1988):	$16,984
Exchange Rate:	$1 = 5.4935 Franc

Foreign Trade

Total Exports (1988):	$161.7 billion
Total Imports (1988):	$176.7 billion
Imports from U.S. (1989):	$11.6 billion

Key Contacts

American Embassy Commercial Section
2 Avenue Gabriel
75382 Paris Cedex 08
Paris, France
APO New York 09777
Tel: 33-1-42-96-12-02
Telex:650221 AMEMB

American Chamber of Commerce
21, Avenue George V
F-75008 Paris, France
Tel: 33-1-47-23-70-28
Fax: 33-1-47-20-18-62

Embassy of France Commercial Section
4101 Reservoir Road, NW
Washington, DC 20007
Tel: (202) 944-6000
Telex: 248320 FRCC UR

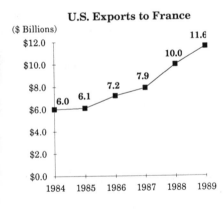

U.S. Exports to France
($ Billions)

Year	Value
1984	6.0
1985	6.1
1986	7.2
1987	7.9
1988	10.0
1989	11.6

Leading Imports from U.S. 1989

Engines and Motors
Aircraft, Parts and Equipment
ADP and Office Machines
ADP and Office Machine Parts
Measuring Instruments
Valves
Coal
Automobiles and Other Vehicles
Works of Art and Antiques
Gold

GREECE

Basic Data

Population (mid-1988):	10.0 million
Area (sq. kilometers):	132 thousand
Language:	Greek; English and French widely understood

Key Economic Data

GDP (1988):	$40.9 billion
Real GDP Growth 1980-88:	1.4%
GDP/Capita (1988):	$4,090
Exchange Rate:	$1 = 161.85 Drachma

Foreign Trade

Total Exports (1988):	$5.4 billion
Total Imports (1988):	$11.9 billion
Imports from U.S. (1989):	$706 million

Key Contacts

American Embassy Commercial Section
91 Vasilissis Sophias Blvd.
10160 Athens, Greece
APO NY 09255
Tel: 30-1-721-2951
Telex:21-5548

American-Hellenic Chamber of Commerce
16 Kanari Street, 3rd Floor
106 74 Athens, Greece
Tel: 30-1-18-385/36-36-407
Telex: 223063 AMCH GR

Embassy of Greece Commercial Section
2221 Massachusetts Avenue, NW
Washington, DC 20008
Tel: (202) 667-3168
Telex: 64479

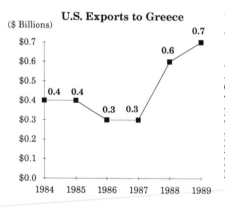

U.S. Exports to Greece
($ Billions)

Leading Imports from U.S. 1989

Arms and Ammunition
Aircraft, Parts and Equipment
Oilseed and Oleaginous Fruit
Telecommunications Equipment
Pulp and Waste Paper
Wood and Railway Sleepers of Wood
Residual Petroleum Products
Medicinal Products
Ferrous Waste and Scrap
Measuring Instruments

IRELAND

Basic Data

Population (mid-1988):	3.5 million
Area (sq. kilometers):	70 thousand
Language:	Irish (Gaelic), English

Key Economic Data

GDP (1988):	$27.8 billion
Real GDP Growth 1980-88:	1.7%
GDP/Capita (1988):	$7,948
Exchange Rate:	$1 = 1.66905 Pound (punt)

Foreign Trade

Total Exports (1988):	$18.7 billion
Total Imports (1988):	$15.6 billion
Imports from U.S. (1989):	$2.5 billion

Key Contacts

American Embassy Commercial Section
42 Elgin Road
Ballsbridge
Dublin, Ireland
Tel: 353-1-688-777
Telex:93684

American Chamber of Commerce
20 College Green
Dublin 2, Ireland
Tel: 353-1-793-733/1-793-402
Telex: 31187 UCIL EI

Embassy of Ireland Commercial Section
2234 Massachusetts Avenue, NW
Washington, DC 20008
Tel: (202) 462-3939
Telex: 64160 HIBERNIA 64160
440419 HIBERNIA 440419

U.S. Exports to Ireland
($ Billions)

Leading Imports from U.S. 1989

ADP and Office Machine Parts
ADP and Office Machines
Valves
Organic Chemicals
Aircraft, Parts and Equipment
Medicinal Products
Animal Feed
Electrical Switches
Engines and Motors
Live Animals

ITALY

Basic Data

Population (mid-1988):	57.4 million
Area (sq. kilometers):	301 thousand
Language:	Italian

Key Economic Data

GDP (1988):	$828.8 billion
Real GDP Growth 1980-88:	2.2%
GDP/Capita (1988):	$14,440
Exchange Rate:	$1 = 1199.00 Lira

Foreign Trade

Total Exports (1988):	$128.6 billion
Total Imports (1988):	$135.5 billion
Imports from U.S. (1989):	$7.2 billion

Key Contacts

American Embassy Commercial Section
Via Veneto 119/A
00187 Rome, Italy
APO New York 09794
Tel: 39-6-46741
Telex:622322 AMBRMA

American Chamber of Commerce
Via Cantu 1
20123 Milano, Italy
Tel: 39-2-86-90-611
Telex: 352128 AMCHAM I

Embassy of Italy Commercial Section
1601 Fuller Street, NW
Washington, DC 20009
Tel: (202) 328-5500
Telex: 90-4076 ITALY EMB WSH

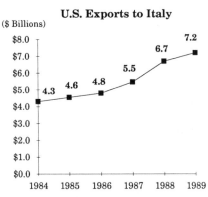

U.S. Exports to Italy
($ Billions)

Leading Imports from U.S. 1989

Aircraft, Parts and Equipment
Coal
ADP and Office Machines
Pulp and Waste Paper
Measuring Instruments
ADP and Office Machine Parts
Medicinal Products
Valves
Wood and Railway Sleepers of Wood
Telecommunications Equipment

THE NETHERLANDS

Basic Data

Population (mid-1988):   14.8 million
Area (sq. kilometers):   37 thousand
Language: Dutch

Key Economic Data

GDP (1988): $228.3 billion
Real GDP Growth 1980-88:   1.6%
GDP/Capita (1988): $15,425
Exchange Rate: $1 = 1.8441
                           Guilder

Foreign Trade

Total Exports (1988): $103.2 billion
Total Imports (1988): $99.7 billion
Imports from U.S. (1989): $11.4 billion

Key Contacts

American Embassy Commercial Section
Lange Voorhout 102
The Hague, Netherlands
APO New York 09159
Tel: 31-70-62-49-11
Telex:(044) 31016

American Chamber of Commerce
Carnegieplein 5
2517 KJ The Hague, Netherlands
Tel: 31070-65-98-08/9
Telex: 18138

Embassy of the Netherlands Commercial
    Section
4200 Linnean Avenue, NW
Washington, DC 20008
Tel: (202) 244-5300
Telex: 248366 via WU 89494

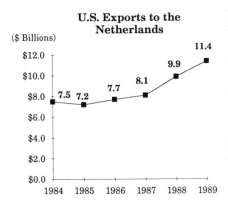

U.S. Exports to the Netherlands
($ Billions)

Leading Imports from U.S. 1989

Aircraft, Parts and Equipment
ADP and Office Machines
ADP and Office Machine Parts
Oilseed and Oleaginous Fruit
Animal Feed
Hydrocarbons and Derivatives
Engines and Motors
Measuring Instruments
Coal
Arms and Ammunition

PORTUGAL

Basic Data

Population (mid-1988):	10.3 million
Area (sq. kilometers):	92 thousand
Language:	Portuguese

Key Economic Data

GDP (1988):	$41.7 billion
Real GDP Growth 1980-88:	0.8%
GDP/Capita (1988):	$4,048
Exchange Rate:	$1 = 143.70 Escudo

Foreign Trade

Total Exports (1988):	$10.2 billion
Total Imports (1988):	$16.0 billion
Imports from U.S. (1989):	$926 million

Key Contacts

American Embassy Commercial Section
Avenida das Forcas Armadas
1600 Lisbon, Portugal
APO New York 09678-0002
Tel: 351-2-726-6600
Telex:12528 AMEMB

American Chamber of Commerce
Rua de D. Estefania, 155, 5 Esq.
Lisbon 1000, Portugal
Tel: 351-1-57-25-61/82-08
Telex: 42356 AMCHAM P

Embassy of Portugal Commercial Section
2125 Kalorama Rd., NW
Washington, DC 20008
Tel: (202) 328-8610
Telex: 64399 PORT EMB P

U.S. Exports to Portugal ($ Billions)

Leading Imports from U.S. 1989

Aircraft, Parts and Equipment
Animal Feed
Oilseed and Oleaginous Fruit
Maize
Coal
ADP and Office Machines
ADP and Office Machine Parts
Telecommunications Equipment
Valves
Wheat

SPAIN

Basic Data

Population (mid-1988): 39 million
Area (sq. kilometers): 505 thousand
Languages: Castilian Spanish, Catalan, Basque

Key Economic Data

GDP (1988): $340.3 billion
Real GDP Growth 1980-88: 2.5%
GDP/Capita (1988): $8,726
Exchange Rate: $1 = 100.41 Peseta

Foreign Trade

Total Exports (1988): $40.5 billion
Total Imports (1988): $60.4 billion
Imports from U.S. (1989): $4.8 billion

Key Contacts

American Embassy Commercial Section
Serrano 75
Madrid, Spain
APO New York 09285
Tel: 34-1-276-3400
Telex:27763

American Chamber of Commerce
Avda. Diagonal 477
08036 Barcelona, Spain
Tel: 34-3-321-81-95/6
Fax: 34-3-321-81-97

Embassy of Spain Commercial Section
2700 15th Street, NW
Washington, DC 20009
Tel: (202) 265-0190
Telex: 89 2747 SPAIN WSH

U.S. Exports to Spain

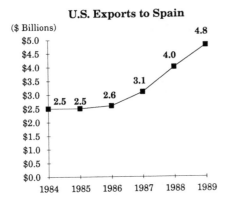

($ Billions)

Leading Imports from U.S. 1989

Aircraft, Parts and Equipment
Oilseed and Oleaginous Fruit
ADP and Office Machines
Coal
Tobacco
Measuring Instruments
Ferrous Waste and Scrap
ADP and Office Machine Parts
Maize
Animal Feed

UNITED KINGDOM

Basic Data

Population (mid-1988):	57.1 million
Area (sq. kilometers):	245 thousand
Languages:	English, Welsh, Scottish Gaelic

Key Economic Data

GDP (1988):	$702.4 billion
Real GDP Growth 1980-88:	2.8%
GDP/Capita (1988):	$12,301
Exchange Rate:	$1 = 1.8110 Pound Sterling (£)

Foreign Trade

Total Exports (1988):	$145.0 billion
Total Imports (1988):	$189.5 billion
Imports from U.S. (1989):	$20.9 billion

Key Contacts

American Embassy Commercial Section
24/31 Grosvenor Square
London W1A 1AE, England
Box 40
FPO New York 09509
Tel: 44-1-499-9000
Telex:266777

American Chamber of Commerce
75 Brook Street
London W1Y 2Eb, United Kingdom
Tel: 44-1-493-03-81
Telex: 23675 AMCHAM

Embassy of the United Kingdom
  Commercial Section
3100 Massachusetts Avenue, NW
Washington, DC 20008
Tel: (202) 462-1340
Telex: 892384 WSH
892380 WSH

U.S. Exports to the United Kingdom

($ Billions)

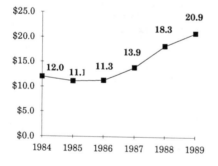

Leading Imports from U.S. 1989

Aircraft, Parts and Equipment
ADP and Office Machines
ADP and Office Machine Parts
Engines and Motors
Valves
Telecommunications Equipment
Works of Art and Antiques
Est. of Shipments Valued Under $1,501
Gold
Electrical Apparatus

EASTERN EUROPE AND THE SOVIET UNION

During the final months of writing this book, dramatic changes in Eastern Europe caused numerous revisions to this section. It is beyond anyone's ability to predict with certainty the ultimate outcome of these changes. In witnessing the business response to the developing situation in Eastern Europe, however, we are confident in stating that the business implications, while still unclear, hold great promise for U.S. exports.

The desire for economic reform has been expressed in one form or another by citizens of all of the countries of Eastern Europe and the Soviet Union. But the pace and extent of reform varies greatly by country. In the Soviet Union, for example, there is presently strong debate regarding what should be the nature and degree of economic and political reform. Poland has made substantial reforms in pricing, privatization and the liberalization of its trade regime and exchange rates. Romania, on the other hand, has made no significant change in its economic policies. Table 6 summarizes the extent of change for a number of these countries.

Foreign business response to the new situation has also varied greatly by country. For example, by April 1, 1990, there were

Table 6. Economic Reform in Central and Eastern Europe

	Price Reform	Priviti- zation	Capital Market	Trade Lib- eralization	Exchange Rate
Hungary	+	+	+	+	+
Poland	++	+	+	+	++
Czechoslovakia	0	0	0	0	+
Yugoslavia	+	+	0	+	++
Romania	0	0	0	0	0
Bulgaria	0	0	0	+	+

++Substantial reform
+Some reform
0 No significant change
Source: "Building Free Market Economies in Central and Eastern Europe: Challenges and Realities," The Institute of International Finance, April 1990, p. 36.

over 1,500 joint ventures registered in the Soviet Union between foreign companies and Soviet entities. Of these, slightly over 170, or just over 10 percent, were with U.S. companies. However, only about 200 of all the joint ventures are actually operational; the rest exist solely on paper. U.S. companies have also shown interest in Hungary, Poland, and Czechoslovakia, but relatively little in Romania and Bulgaria.

In general, there are three types of U.S. companies becoming active in Eastern Europe. The first is large Fortune 100 companies. For example, Gillette reportedly has agreed to establish a large razor manufacturing facility in the Soviet Union. The second type is entrepreneurs of East European descent. For example, a small U.S. computer company whose owner was originally from Hungary established a joint venture with a Hungarian ministry. The owner intends to relocate to Hungary to manage the joint venture. Finally, there are a number of small, specialized companies that have found a particular niche in business with East Europe.

As shown in Table 7 below:

Table 7. Eastern Europe Key Economic Data, ($ Billions)

Country	GDP*	Exports**	Imports**
USSR	$2,535.0	$107.7	$96.0
Poland	276.3	26.0	24.3
East Germany	207.2	30.8	31.0
Yugoslavia	154. 1	11.4	12.6
Czechoslovakia	154.0	23.5	23.9
Romania	126.0	12.5	10.6
Hungary	92.0	9.6	9.8
Bulgaria	68.0	16.8	16.9
Albania†	2.8	0.4	0.4
Eastern Europe Total	**$3,615.4**	**$238.7**	**$225.5**

* GDP data are for 1988
** Export and Import data are for 1987
† Data for Albania are estimates for 1986
Source: Central Intelligence Agency

- The Soviet economy dominates the region with a 1988 GDP* of $2.5 trillion. The next largest economy is Poland, with a GDP of $276 billion, followed by East Germany, with a GDP of $207 billion.

- Eastern European countries as a whole trade very little with non-socialist countries. The Soviet Union's trade with non-socialist countries represents a mere 0.7 percent of total GDP.

U.S. Exports to Eastern Europe

From 1980 to 1987, U.S. exports to Eastern Europe, excluding the Soviet Union and Yugoslavia, declined every year (except 1983–84, when they grew slightly) from a high of $2.3 billion in 1980 to a low of $720 million in 1987. Over the past two years, however, total U.S. exports to the countries of Eastern Europe have increased to a total of $1.0 billion in 1989, as shown in Figure 14.

---

*Accurate data regarding the economies of Eastern Europe and the Soviet Union have been very difficult to obtain. This is especially true regarding the basic measurement of GDP. Table 7, and Figures 14 and 15 present data from a number of sources, but may not be 100% accurate, due to different reporting criteria used by Eastern European countries.

Figure 14. U.S. Exports to Eastern Europe, 1989 ($ Millions)
(Source: U.S. Department of Commerce)

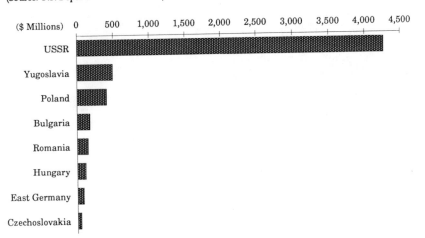

Exports to the Soviet Union have shown growth from 1986 to 1989, reaching $4.3 billion in 1989—a 54 percent increase over 1988 levels.

As Figures 15 and 16 indicate, U.S. exports to both the Soviet Union and the rest of Eastern Europe are comprised mainly of agricultural commodities.

- In 1989, 68 percent of U.S. exports to the Soviet Union consisted of grains. This category is followed by animal feed (nine percent) and fertilizers (six percent). These figures underscore the enormous pressures on the Soviet Union to meet domestic food demands.

- Exports to Eastern Europe were of a slightly different composition. U.S. exports of grains represented 18 percent of total 1989 exports. This category is followed by aircraft and parts (13 percent), coal (eight percent), and animal hides and skins (seven percent).

The Eastern Bloc countries are now seeking to overhaul their economies by improving domestic production and efficiency, and encouraging more exports. The Soviet Union has expressed its intention to integrate its economy into the world economy. A key component of this goal is to make its exports more competitive in the

Figure 15. Key U.S. Exports to the USSR, 1989, (Total = $4.3 billion)
(Source: U.S. Department of Commerce)

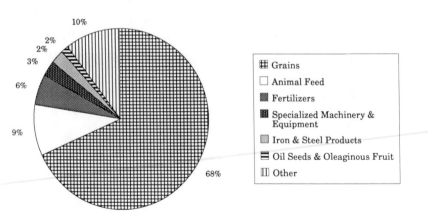

Figure 16. Key U.S. Exports to Eastern Europe (not including Yugoslavia), 1989, (Total = $1.0 Billion)
(Source: U.S. Department of Commerce)

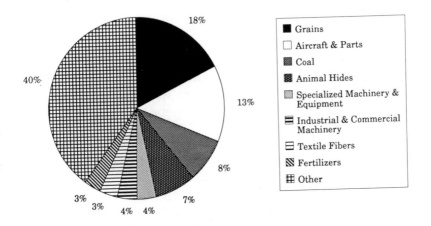

world market. This development has several important ramifications for U.S. businesses:

- Opportunities will exist for U.S. exports of machinery, transportation equipment, and capital goods for machine-building industries, timber and chemicals industries, the agro-industrial sector, light industry, and consumer durables production.

- The Soviet Union has been negotiating with GATT officials, with the possibility of full Soviet participation in the Agreement.

- Attempts are being made to streamline the Soviet bureaucracy with regard to foreign trade. For example, some Soviet enterprises, entities, and industrial cooperatives are now authorized to carry out import-export transactions with government permission.

It is important, however, to be cautious of viewing Eastern Europe as an "open economy." Soviet leaders have stated that they intend to continue to conduct the majority of their foreign trade (60 percent) with other socialist countries, and that trade in important products (including fuel, metal and food) shall remain the prerogative of specialized foreign trade agencies.[1] In other Eastern Euro-

---

[1]Ippolit Dioumoulen, Ministry for Foreign Economic Relations, in "Basic Reform of the USSR's Foreign Economic Complex," *European Affairs*, Autumn, 1989, pp. 42–44.

pean countries, the state may want to retain control of industries deemed vital to the national interest. The extent of state involvement in the economy is likely to vary by country.

U.S. Investment in Eastern Europe

Changes in investment laws in Eastern Europe during the 1980s make U.S. investment and joint ventures with Eastern European partners much more feasible for foreign companies:

- Regulations introduced in 1988 in the Soviet Union have removed stipulations that 51 percent of any joint venture be retained on the Soviet side and that the head of a joint venture must be a Soviet national. Moreover, a 1987 agreement on mutual protection of capital investments protects foreign investment from being subject to requisition, nationalization or jurisdictional confiscation. New regulations enacted in 1989 further clarify joint venture issues.

- Prior to the 1980s, Eastern European countries seriously restricted the inflow of foreign capital. Most of these countries now have lists of sectors in which foreign equity participation is encouraged. In Hungary, for example, all sectors are open to joint venture operations; priority areas include: electronics and electrical equipment, robot technology and computers; pharmaceutical products; equipment and machinery for the chemical industries, and the production of specific herbicides and pesticides. In Poland , foreign equity participation is allowed in all sectors except small-business ventures, the defense industry, transportation, and insurance.

GERMAN DEMOCRATIC REPUBLIC
(East Germany)

Basic Data

Population (mid-1989):	16.7 million
Area (sq. kilometers):	108 thousand
Language:	German

Key Economic Data

GDP (1988):	$207.2 billion
Real GDP Growth 1980-88:	3.9%
GDP/Capita (1988):	$12,400
Exchange Rate:	$1 = 1.6360 Deutsche Mark

Key Contacts

American Embassy-Berlin
1080 Berlin
Neustaedtische Kirchstrasse 4-5
USBER Box E; Berlin GDR
APO New York 09742
Tel: 37-2-2202741
Telex: 112479 USEMB DD

Embassy of German Democratic Republic
1717 Massachusetts Avenue, N.W.
Tel: (202) 232-3134
Telex: 649-1073

Foreign Trade

Total Exports (1988):	$30.8 billion
Total Imports (1988):	$31.0 billion
Imports from U.S. (1989):	$94 million

U.S. Exports to East Germany
($ Billions)

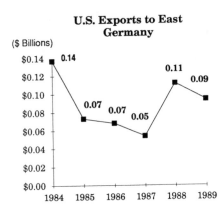

Leading Imports from U.S. 1989

Maize
Industrial Machinery
Barley
Ships, Boats and Floating Structures
Photographic Equipment
Measuring Instruments
Inorganic Chemicsls
ADP and Office Machines
Automobiles and Other Vehicles
Meat

HUNGARY

Basic Data

Population (mid-1989):	10.6 million
Area (sq. kilometers):	93 thousand
Language:	Hungarian

Key Economic Data

GDP (1988):	$92 billion
Real GDP Growth 1984-88:	1.1%
GDP/Capita (1988):	$8,670
Exchange Rate:	$1 = 64.3544 Forint

Foreign Trade

Total Exports (1987):	$9.6 billion
Total Imports (1987):	$9.8 billion
Imports from U.S. (1989):	$122 million

Key Contacts

American Embassy Commercial
   Development Center
V. Szabadsag Ter 12
Budapest, Hungary
APO New York 09213
Tel: 36-1-126-450
Telex: 227136 USCDCH

American Chamber of Commerce
Dozsa Gyorgy ut 84-A
1068 Budapest VI, Hungary
Tel: 36-1-428-753
Fax: 122-8890

Embassy of Hungarian People's Republic
3910 Shoemaker Street, NW
Washington, DC 20008
Tel: (202) 362-6730
Fax (202) 966-8135

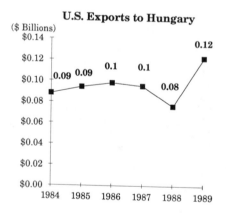

U.S. Exports to Hungary
($ Billions)

Leading Imports from U.S. 1989

Nonelectrical Machinery
Internal Combustion Piston Engines
Tractors
Automobile Parts and Accessories
Fertilizers
Measuring Instruments
Machine tools
Tobacco
Organic Chemicals
Glass

POLAND

Basic Data

Population (mid-1989):	38.4 million
Area (sq. kilometers):	313 thousand
Language:	Polish

Key Economic Data

GDP (1988):	$276.3 billion
Real GDP Growth 1984-88:	3.6%
GDP/Capita (1988):	$7,187
Exchange Rate:	$1 = 9500 Zloty

Key Contacts

American Embassy-Warsaw
Aleje Ujazdowskle 29/31
c/o American Consulate General (WAW)
Warsaw, Poland
APO New York, NY 09213
Tel: 48-22-283041
Telex: 813304 AMEMB PL

Embassy of Polish People's Republic
2640 16th Street, NW
Washington, DC 20009
Tel: (202) 234-3800
Telex: 089480 POLMISSION WHS

Foreign Trade

Total Exports (1987):	$26.0 billion
Total Imports (1987):	$24.3 billion
Imports from U.S. (1989):	$414 million

U.S. Exports to Poland

($ Billions)

Leading Imports from U.S. 1989

Aircraft, Parts and Equipment
Fertilizers
Cotton Textile Fibers
Automobile Parts and Accessories
Animal Hides and Skins
Oil (not crude)
Measuring Instruments
Tobacco
Pulp and Waste Paper
Engines and Motors

USSR

Basic Data

Population (mid-1989):   288.7 million
Area (sq. kilometers):   22.4
Language: Russian; at
                          least 18 other
                          major
                          languages

Key Economic Data

GDP (1988): $2.5 trillion
Real GDP Growth 1984-89: 3%
GDP/Capita (1988): $8,802
Exchange Rate: $1 = .5887
                          Ruble

Key Contacts

American Embassy–Moscow
Ulitsa Chaykovskogo 19/21/23
Moscow, USSR
APO NY 09862
Tel: 7-096-252-24-51
Telex: 413160 USGSO SU

Embassy of the Union of Soviet Socialist
    Republics
1125 16th Street, NW
Washington, DC 20036
Tel: (202) 628-8548

Foreign Trade

Total Exports (1987): $107.7 billion
Total Imports (1987): $96.0 billion
Imports from U.S. (1989): $4.3 billion

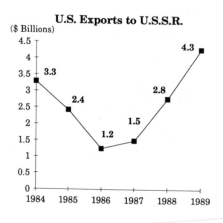

U.S. Exports to U.S.S.R.
($ Billions)

Leading Imports from U.S. 1989

Maize
Wheat
Animal Feed
Fertilizers
Cereals
Oilseed and Oleaginous Fruit
Iron Flat-rolled Products
Iron and Steel Tubes
Engineering Plant and Equipment
Measuring Instruments

YUGOSLAVIA

Basic Data

Population (mid-1989):	23.8 million
Area (sq. kilometers):	256 thousand
Language:	Serbo-Croatian, Slovene, Macedonian

Key Economic Data

GDP (1988):	$154.1 billion
Real GDP Growth 1984-87:	0.65%
GDP/Capita (1988):	$6,470
Exchange Rate:	$1 = 11.52 Dinar

Key Contacts

American Embassy–Belgrade
Kneza Milosa 50
American Consulate General
Belgrade, Yogoslavia
APO New York 09213
Tel: 38-11-645-655
Telex: 11529 AMEMB YU

Embassy of the Socialist Federal Republic of Yugoslavia
2410 California Avenue, NW
Washington, DC 20008
Tel: (202) 462-6566
Telex: YWI 89440 or RCA 248558

Foreign Trade

Total Exports (1987):	$11.4 billion
Total Imports (1987):	$12.6 billion
Imports from U.S. (1989):	$252 million

U.S. Exports to Yugoslavia

Leading Imports from U.S. 1989

Coal
Aircraft, Parts and Equipment
Engineering Plant and Equipment
Copper
Oilseed and Oleaginous Fruit
Industrial Machinery
Commercial Vehicles
Organic Chemics
ADP and Office Machine Parts
Measuring Instruments

EUROPEAN FREE TRADE ASSOCIATION (EFTA)

The recent emphasis on the integration of the European Community in 1992 has thrust another European trading bloc, the European Free Trade Association, or EFTA, into the shadows. The EFTA countries, however, still offer opportunities to U.S. businesses. All of the EFTA countries rank among the wealthiest nations in the world as measured by per capita GDP. EFTA differs greatly from the EC in that it is a loose free trade association, without the political goals and mechanisms of the EC. But EFTA's apolitical stance may be changing: at least four of its six members are considering eventually joining the EC.

EFTA nations are also carefully assessing how to remain competitive in Europe after 1992. Switzerland, for example, is investing heavily in the EC and harmonizing Swiss business law with EC business law to assure continued access to the EC market. All six countries will use their membership in EFTA and in the GATT to obtain access to the Community after 1992.

EFTA consists of six countries: Austria, Finland, Iceland, Norway, Sweden and Switzerland. EFTA nations purchased a total of $11.1 billion in U.S. exports in 1989, led by Switzerland and Sweden.

Table 8 illustrates the economic size of the EFTA countries. The six EFTA nations had a combined 1989 GDP of $705 billion, about 18

Table 8. EFTA Key Economic Data, ($ Billions)

Country	GDP*	Exports**	Imports**
Sweden	190	49.9	45.8
Swittzerland	175	50.6	56.3
Austria	126	28.1	36.6
Finland	116	21.6	20.9
Norway	93	22.5	23.2
Iceland	5	1.4	1.6
EFTA Total	**705**	**174.1**	**184.4**

*Data are from 1989
**Data are from 1988
Source: The World Bank; The Economist Intelligence Unit, The Economist

percent of the GDP of the EC. Although trade (both imports and exports) equal 17 percent of the trade of the EC, U.S. exports to these nations are increasing. In 1989, Switzerland led the EFTA countries in imports from the U.S. with $4.9 billion. Figure 17 shows the relative size of U.S. exports to EFTA.

Figure 17.   U.S. Exports to EFTA, 1989, (Total = $11.1 billion)
(Source: U.S. Department of Commerce)

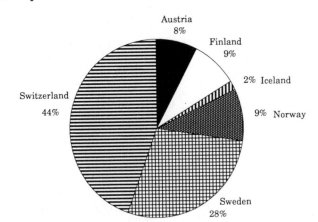

AUSTRIA

Basic Data

Population (mid-1988):	7.5 million
Area (sq. kilometers):	84 thousand
Language:	German

Key Economic Data

GDP (1989):	$126 billion
Real GDP Growth 1980-88:	1.7%
GDP/Capita (1989):	$16,800
Exchange Rate:	$1 = 11.5285 Shilling

Foreign Trade

Total Exports (1988):	$28.1 billion
Total Imports (1988):	$36.6 billion
Imports from U.S. (1989):	$873 million

Key Contacts

American Embassy-Vienna
Boltmanngasse 16
A-1091 Vienna, Austria
APO NY 09108
Tel: 43-222-31-55-11
Telex: 114634

American Chamber of Commerce
Porzellangasses 35
A-1090 Vienna, Austria
Tel: 43-222-31-57-51
Fax: 43-222-31-57-52/15

Embassy of Austria
2343 Massachusetts Avenue, NW
Washington, DC 20008
Tel: (202) 483-4474
Telex: 440010

U.S. Exports to Austria
($ Billions)

Leading Imports from U.S. 1989

Aircraft, Parts and Equipment
Printed Matter
ADP and Office Machines
Medicinal Products
Measuring Instruments
Automobiles and Other Vehicles
ADP and Office Machine Parts
Est. of Shipments Valued Under $1,501
Telecommunications Equipment
Automobile Parts and Accessories

FINLAND

Basic Data

Population (mid-1988):   5 million
Area (sq. kilometers):   337 thousand
Language: Finnish, Swedish

Key Economic Data

GDP (1989): $116 billion
Real GDP Growth 1980-88:   2.8%
GDP/Capita (1989): $23,200
Exchange Rate: $1 = 3.8300
                                Markka

Key Contacts

American Embassy–Helsinki
Itainen Puistotie 14A
SF-00140
Helsinki, Finland
APO NY 09664
Tel: 358-0-17-1931
Telex: 121644-USEMB SF or 125541
(Commercial Section)

Embassy of Finland
3216 New Mexico Ave, NW
Washington, DC 20016
Tel: (202) 363-2430
Fax: (202) 363-8233

Foreign Trade

Total Exports (1988): $21.6 billion
Total Imports (1988): $20.9 billion
Imports from U.S. (1989): $969 million

U.S. Exports to Finland

($ Billions)

Leading Imports from U.S. 1989

Automobiles and Other Vehicles
Aircraft, Parts and Equipment
ADP and Office Machines
Ships, Boats and Floating structures
ADP and Office Machine Parts
Est. of Shipments Valued Under $1,501
Telecommunications Equipment
Measuring Instruments
Crude Minerals
Valves

ICELAND

Basic Data

Population (mid-1989):   248 thousand
Area (sq. kilometers):   103 thousand
Language: Icelandic

Key Economic Data

GDP (1989): $5.0 billion
Real GDP Growth 1981-87:   6.6%
GDP/Capita (1987): $21,660
Exchange Rate: $1 = 53
                            Króna

Key Contacts

American Embassy
Laufasvegur 21
Reykjavik, Iceland
FPO NY 09571-0001
Tel: 354-1-29100
Telex: USEMB IS 3044

Embassy of Iceland
2022 Connecticut, NW
Washington, DC 20008
Tel: (202) 265-6653
Telex: RCA 248596 ICEX

Foreign Trade

Total Exports (1988): $1.4 billion
Total Imports (1988): $1.6 billion
Imports from U.S. (1989): $179 million

U.S. Exports to Iceland

Leading Imports from U.S. 1989

Aircraft, Parts and Equipment
Tobacco
Est. of Shipments Valued Under $1,501
Measuring Instruments
Engines and Motors
Automobiles and Other Vehicles
Coal
Crustaceans
Cereal and Flour Preparations
ADP and Office Machines

NORWAY

Basic Data

Population (mid-1988):	4.2 million
Area (sq. kilometers):	324 thousand
Language:	Norwegian

Key Economic Data

GDP (1989):	$93 billion
Real GDP Growth 1980-88:	3.8%
GDP/Capita (1989):	$22,142
Exchange Rate:	$1 = 6.2905 Krone

Key Contacts

American Embassy Commercial Section
Drammensveien 18
Oslo 2, Norway
APO NY 09085
Tel: 47-2-44-85-50
Telex: 78470

Embassy of Norway
2720 34th Street, NW
Washington, DC 20008
Tel: (202) 333-6000
Telex: 89-2374 NORAMB WSH

Foreign Trade

Total Exports (1988):	$22.5 billion
Total Imports (1988):	$23.2 billion
Imports from U.S. (1989):	$1.0 billion

U.S. Exports to Norway
($ Billions)

Leading Imports from U.S. 1989

Aircraft, Parts and Equipment
ADP and Office Machines
Engineering Plant and Equipment
Telecommunications Equipment
Measuring Instruments
Automobiles and Other Vehicles
Engines and Motors
Oilseed and Oleaginous Fruit
Est. of Shipments Valued Under $1,501
ADP and Office Machine Parts

SWEDEN

Basic Data

Population (mid-1988):   8.3 million
Area (sq. kilometers):   450 thousand
Language: Swedish

Key Economic Data

GDP (1989): $190 billion
Real GDP Growth 1980-88:   1.7%
GDP/Capita (1989): $22,891
Exchange Rate: $1 = 5.9460 Krona

Key Contacts

American Embassy
Strandvagen 101
S-115 27 Stockholm, Sweden
Tel: 46-8-783-5300
Telex: 12060 AMEMB S

Embassy of Sweden
600 New Hampshire Avenue, NW,
   Suite 1200
Washington, DC 20037
Tel: (202) 944-5600
Telex: 89 2724 SVENSK WSH

Foreign Trade

Total Exports (1988): $49.9 billion
Total Imports (1988): $45.8 billion
Imports from U.S. (1989): $3.1 billion

U.S. Exports to Sweden
($ Billions)

Leading Imports from U.S. 1989

Aircraft, Parts and Equipment
ADP and Office Machines
Automobiles and Other Vehicles
Engines and Motors
ADP and Office Machine Parts
Measuring Instruments
Est. of Shipments Valued Under $1,501
Automobile Parts and Accessories
Telecommunications Equipment
Works of Art and Antiques

SWITZERLAND

Basic Data

Population (mid-1988):	6.5 million
Area (sq. kilometers):	41 thousand
Languages:	German, French, Italian, Romansch

Key Economic Data

GDP (1989):	$175 billion
Real GDP Growth 1980-88:	1.9%
GDP/Capita (1989):	$26,923
Exchange Rate:	$1 = 1.3895 Franc

Foreign Trade

Total Exports (1988):	$50.6 billion
Total Imports (1988):	$56.3 billion
Imports from U.S. (1989):	$4.9 billion

Key Contacts

American Embassy
Jubilaeumstrasse 93
3005 Bern, Switzerland
Tel: 41-31-437011
Telex: 845-912603

Swiss-American Chamber of Commerce
Talacker 41
8001 Zürich, Switzerland
Tel: 41-1-211-24-54
Telex: 813448 IPCO CH

Embassy of Switzerland
2900 Cathedral Ave., NW
Washington, DC 20008
Tel: (202 745-7900
Telex: 440055

U.S. Exports to Switzerland

($ Billions)

Leading Imports from U.S. 1989

Works of Art and Antiques
Gold
Aircraft, Parts and Equipment
ADP and Office Machines
Automobiles and Other Vehicles
Pearls and Gemstones
Measuring Instruments
Organic Chemicals
Engines and Motors
Jewelry

PACIFIC RIM

Japan is, of course, the dominant economic force in this region. As the United States' second largest trading partner, Japan is a significant supplier to the U.S. as well as a major market for savvy (and patient) U.S. exporters. (For more information on Japan, please refer to pages 7–13 of Section 1.)

Other Pacific Rim countries of significance to the U.S. include the "Four Tigers": South Korea, Hong Kong, Taiwan, and Singapore. These countries have led the Pacific Rim's rapid export-led economic development. With a combined GDP of $248.7 billion and total exports of $175.1 billion, these four nations account for over 31% of total exports from the Pacific Rim.

These nations relied heavily on their well-trained, low-cost labor force to gain their foothold in the world export market. Recently, however, rising labor costs as well as deliberate moves by some of their governments have prompted a shift from the production and export of relatively low-cost, low-technology manufactured goods (such as footwear and apparel) into the production of more expensive high-technology goods (such as computers and semiconductors) and services.

As has been the case with Japan, successes in the export market have also translated into trade surpluses with the U.S., which provides the single largest market for their exports. Moves on the part of the U.S. to reduce its trade deficit have led to trade conflicts between the U.S. and the Four Tigers.

The Pacific Rim is covered in more detail in Section 1 (see pages 7–13). This dynamic region includes the ASEAN countries (see pages 37–46), which are important to U.S. businesses both as markets and sources of materials and components.

AUSTRALIA

Basic Data

Population (mid-1988):   16.5 million
Area (sq. kilometers):   7.7 million
Language: English, native
                          languages

Key Economic Data

GDP (1988): $246 billion
Real GDP Growth 1980-88: 3.3%
GDP/Capita (1988): $14,909
Exchange Rate: $1 = .7979
                          Dollar

Foreign Trade

Total Exports (1988): $25.3 billion
Total Imports (1988): $29.3 billion
Imports from U.S. (1989): $8.3 billion

Key Contacts

American Embassy Commercial Section
Moonah Pl.
Canberra, A.C.T. 2600, Australia
APO San Francisco 96404
Tel: 061-62-705000
Telex: 62104 USAEMB

American Chamber of Commerce
Level 2, 39-41 Lower Fort Street
Sydney, N.S.W., 2000 Australia
Tel: 612-241-1907
Telex: 72729 ATTIAU

Embassy of Australia Commercial Section
1601 Massachusetts Ave., NW
Washington, DC 20036
Tel: (202) 797-3201
Telex: WU 892621

U.S. Exports to Australia

($ Billions)

Leading Imports from U.S. 1989

Aircraft, Parts and Equipment
ADP and Office Machines
ADP and Office Machine Parts
Automobile Parts and Accessories
Est. of Shipments Valued Under $1,501
Engineering Plant and Equipment
Internal Combustion Piston Engines
Measuring Instruments
Printed Matter
Telecommunications Equipment

BRUNEI DARUSSALAM

Basic Data

Population (mid-1989):	345 thousand
Area (sq. kilometers):	6 thousand
Languages:	Malay, English, Chinese

Key Economic Data

GDP (1987):	$3.1 billion
Real GDP Growth 1982-86:	0.4%
GDP/Capita (1987):	$13,663
Exchange Rate:	$1 = 1.8305 Dollar

Key Contacts

American Embassy
P.O. Box 2991
Bandar Seri Begawan, Brunei
Tel: 673-2-29670
Telex: BU 2609 AMEMB

Embassy of Brunei
2600 Virginia Avenue, NW Suite 300
Washington, DC 20037
Tel: (202) 342-0159
Telex: 6491071 BRUDC

Foreign Trade

Total Exports (1987):	$2.1 billion
Total Imports (1987):	$800 million
Imports from U.S. (1989):	$63 million

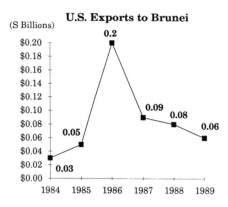

U.S. Exports to Brunei
(S Billions)

Leading Imports from U.S. 1989

Aircraft, Parts and Equipment
Engineering Plant and Equipment
Mechanical Handling Equipment
Telecommunications Equipment
Measuring Instruments
Arms and Ammunition
Est. of Shipments Valued Under $1,501
Industrial Machinery
Works of Art and Antiques
Heating and Cooling Equipment

HONG KONG

Basic Data

Population (mid-1988):	5.7 million
Area (sq. kilometers):	1 thousand
Languages:	Chinese (Cantonese), English

Key Economic Data

GDP (1988):	$44.8 billion
Real GDP Growth 1980-88:	7.3%
GDP/Capita (1988):	$7,864
Exchange Rate:	$1 = 7.7700 Dollar

Foreign Trade

Total Exports (1988):	$63.2 billion
Total Imports (1988):	$63.9 billion
Imports from U.S. (1989):	$6.3 billion

Key Contacts

American Consulate General
26 Garden Road
Hong Kong
Box 30
FPO San Francisco 96659-0002
Tel: 852-5-239011
Telex: 63141 USDOC HX

American Chamber of Commerce
1030 Swire Road
Hong Kong
Tel: 852-5-260165
Telex: 83664 AMCC HX

Embassy of Britain/Hong Kong Office,
Commercial Section
3100 Massachusetts Avenue, NW
Washington, DC 20008
Tel: (202) 898-4591
Telex: 440484 HK WSH UY

U.S. Exports to Hong Kong
($ Billions)

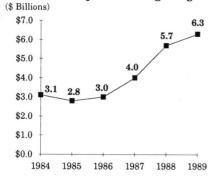

Leading Imports from U.S. 1989

Valves
Gold
Tobacco
Aircraft, Parts and Equipment
Pearls and Gemstones
ADP and Office Machines
ADP and Office Machine Parts
Telecommunications Equipment
Paper and Paperboard
Fruit and Nuts

REPUBLIC OF INDONESIA

Basic Data

Population (mid-1988):	174.8 million
Area (sq. kilometers):	1.9 million
Languages:	Malay (Bahasa Indonesia), English, Dutch, local dialects

Key Economic Data

GDP (1988):	$83.2 billion
Real GDP Growth 1980-88:	5.1%
GDP/Capita (1988):	$476
Exchange Rate:	$1 = 1842 Rupiah

Foreign Trade

Total Exports (1988):	$19.7 billion
Total Imports (1988):	$15.7 billion
Imports from U.S. (1989):	$1.3 billion

Key Contacts

American Embassy Commercial Section
Medan Merdeka Salatan 5
Jakarta, Indonesia
APO San Francisco 96356
Tel: 62-21-360-360
Telex: 44218 AMEMB JKT

American Chamber of Commerce
The Landmark Centre
2nd Floor, Suite 2204
Jl. Jendral Sudirman
Jakarta, Indonesia
Tel: 62-21-578-0656
Telex: 62822 LAMARK IA

Embassy of Indonesia Commercial Section
2020 Massachusetts Avenue, NW
Washington, DC 20036
Tel: (202) 775-5200
Telex: 248287

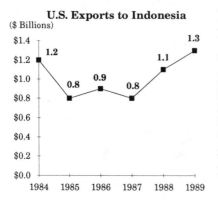

U.S. Exports to Indonesia
($ Billions)

Leading Imports from U.S. 1989

Cotton Textile Fibers
Aircraft, Parts and Equipment
Engineering Plant and Equipment
Pulp and Waste Paper
Manmade Fibers
Plastics (in primary forms)
Oilseed and Oleaginous Fruit
Additives for Mineral Oils
Wheat
Metallic Salts

JAPAN

Basic Data

Population (mid-1988):	122.6 million
Area (sq. kilometers):	378 thousand
Language:	Japanese

Key Economic Data

GDP (1988):	$2.8 trillion
Real GDP Growth 1980-88:	3.9%
GDP/Capita (1988):	$23,195
Exchange Rate:	$1 = 147.55 Yen

Foreign Trade

Total Exports (1988):	$264.8 billion
Total Imports (1988):	$183.3 billion
Imports from U.S. (1989):	$44.6 billion

Key Contacts

American Embassy Commercial Section
10-1 Alasaka, 1-chome
Minato-ku (107)
Tokyo, Japan
APO San Francisco 96503
Tel: 81-3-224-5000
Telex: 2422118 AMEMB

American Chamber of Commerce
Fukide Building, #2
1-21 Toranomon, Minato-ku
4-Chome
Tokyo (105), Japan
Tel: 03-433-5381
Telex: 2425104 KYLE J

Embassy of Japan Commercial Section
2520 Massachusetts Avenue, NW
Washington, DC 20008
Tel: (202) 234-2266
Fax: (202) 939-6700

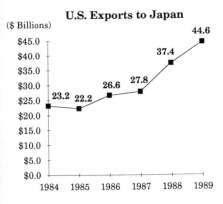

U.S. Exports to Japan
($ Billions)

23.2, 22.2, 26.6, 27.8, 37.4, 44.6

1984 1985 1986 1987 1988 1989

Leading Imports from U.S. 1989

Aircraft, Parts and Equipment
ADP and Office Machines
Wood
Maize
ADP and Office Machine Parts
Valves
Measuring Instruments
Fish
Works of Art and Antiques
Aluminum

REPUBLIC OF KOREA
(South Korea)

Basic Data

Population (mid-1988):	42.1 million
Area (sq. kilometers):	98 thousand
Language:	Korean

Key Economic Data

GDP (1988):	$171.3 billion
Real GDP Growth 1980-88:	9.9%
GDP/Capita (1988):	$4,078
Exchange Rate:	$1 = 710.43 Won

Foreign Trade

Total Exports (1988):	$60.7 billion
Total Imports (1988):	$51.8 billion
Imports from U.S. (1989):	$13.5 billion

Key Contacts

American Embassy Commercial Section
82 Sejong-Ro; Chongro-ku
South Korea
APO San Francisco 96301
Tel: 82-2-732-2601
Telex: AMEMB 23108

American Chamber of Commerce
Room 307, Chosun Hotel
Seoul, Korea
Tel: 82-2-753-6471
Telex: 23745 or 28432 CHOSUN

Embassy of Korea Commercial section
2320 Massachusetts Ave., NW
Washington, DC 20008
Tel: (202) 939-5600
Fax: (202) 797-0595

U.S. Exports to South Korea
($ Billions)

Leading Imports from U.S. 1989

Aircraft, Parts and Equipment
Valves
Animal Hides and Skins
Maize
Industrial Machinery
Pulp and Waste Paper
Cotton Textile Fibers
Ferrous Waste and Scrap
ADP and Office Machines
Hydrocarbons and Derivatives

MALAYSIA

Basic Data

Population (mid-1988):   16.9 million
Area (sq. kilometers):   330 thousand
Languages: Malay (Bahasa
                          Melayu), English,
                          Chinese dialects,
                          Tamil

Key Economic Data

GDP (1988): $34.7 billion
Real GDP Growth 1980-88:   4.6%
GDP/Capita (1988): $2,052
Exchange Rate: $1 = 2.7020
                              Ringgit or dollar

Foreign Trade

Total Exports (1988): $20.8 billion
Total Imports (1988): $16.6 billion
Imports from U.S. (1989): $2.9 billion

Key Contacts

American Embassy Commercial Section
376 Jalan Tun Razak
P.O. Box 10035
50400 Kuala Lumpur, Malaysia
Tel: 6-03-248-9011
Telex: FCSKL MA 32956

American Chamber of Commerce
15.01, 15th Floor
Amoda, Jalan Imbi
55100 Kuala Lumpur, Malaysia
Tel: 6-03-248-2407/2540
Telex: MA 32956 FCSKL

Embassy of Malaysia Commercial Section
2401 Massachusetts Avenue, NW
Washington, DC 20008
Tel: (202) 328-2700
Telex: 440119 MAEM UI

U.S. Exports to Malaysia

Leading Imports from U.S. 1989

Valves
Aircraft, Parts and Equipment
Measuring Instruments
ADP and Office Machine Parts
Paper and Paperboard
Industrial Machinery
ADP and Office Machines
Inorganic Chemicals
Ferrous Waste and Scrap
Telecommunications Equipment

NEW ZEALAND

Basic Data

Population (mid-1988):	3.3 million
Area (sq. kilometers):	269 thousand
Languages:	English, Maori

Key Economic Data

GDP (1988):	$39.8 billion
Real GDP Growth 1980-88:	2.2%
GDP/Capita (1988):	$12,060
Exchange Rate:	$1 = .5928 Dollar

Foreign Trade

Total Exports (1988):	$8.8 billion
Total Imports (1988):	$7.3 billion
Imports from U.S. (1989):	$1.1 billion

Key Contacts

American Embassy Commercial Section
29 Fitzherbert Terrace, Thorndon
Wellington, New Zealand
P.O. Box 1190
FPO San Francisco 96690-0001
Tel: 64-4-722-068
Telex: NZ 3305

American Chamber of Commerce
O.O. Box 3408
Wellington, New Zealand
Tel: 04-727549
Telex: 3514 INBUSMAC NZ

Embassy of New Zealand Commercial Section
37 Observatory Circle, NW
Washington, DC 20008
Tel: (202) 328-4800
Telex: 8 9526 TOTARA WSH

U.S. Exports to New Zealand
($ Billions)

Leading Imports from U.S. 1989

Aircraft, Parts and Equipment
ADP and Office Machines
Est. of Shipments Valued Under $1,501
ADP and Office Machine Parts
Telecommunications Equipment
Measuring Instruments
Petroleum Products
Ethylene Polymers
Engines and Motors
Fertilizers

PEOPLE'S REPUBLIC OF CHINA

Basic Data

Population (mid-1988):	1.1 billion
Area (sq. kilometers):	9.6 million
Languages:	Mandarin, Cantonese, Shanghainese, Fuzhou, Hokkien-Taiwanese, other dialiects

Key Economic Data

GDP (1988):	$272.3 billion
Real GDP Growth 1980-88:	10.3%
GDP/Capita (1988):	$247
Exchange Rate:	$1 = 4.7221 Yuan

Key Contacts

American Embassy Commercial Section
Xiu Shui Bei Jie 3
10060 Beijing, PRC
Box 50
FPO San Francisco 96655
Tel: 86-1-532-3831
Telex: AMEMB CN 22701

American Chamber of Commerce in China
c/o General Electric (USA) China Co.
Jian Guo Men Wal; International Club
Beijing, People's Republic of China
Tel: 86-1-5322491/5322559
Fax: 86-1-5127345

Embassy of the People's Republic of China
2300 Connecticut Avenue, NW
Washington, DC 20008
Tel: (202) 328-2500
Telex: 44038

Foreign Trade

Total Exports (1988):	$47.5 billion
Total Imports (1988):	$55.2 billion
Imports from U.S. (1989):	$5.8 billion

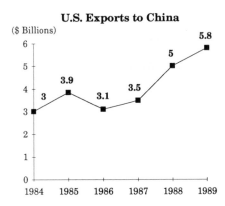

U.S. Exports to China
($ Billions)

Leading Imports from U.S. 1989

Wheat
Aircraft, Parts and Equipment
Fertilizers
Cotton Textile Fibers
Measuring Instruments
Wood
Organic Chemicals
Industrial Machinery
ADP and Office Machines
Engines and Motors

PHILIPPINES

Basic Data

Population (mid-1988):   59.9 million
Area (sq. kilometers):   300 thousand
Languages: Tagalog (Filipino), English, local dialects

Key Economic Data

GDP (1988): $39.2 billion
Real GDP Growth 1980-88:   0.1%
GDP/Capita (1988): $654
Exchange Rate: $1 = 23.00 Peso

Foreign Trade

Total Exports (1988): $7.1 billion
Total Imports (1988): $8.2 billion
Imports from U.S. (1989): $2.2 billion

Key Contacts

American Embassy Commercial Section
395 Buenida Avenue
Extension Makati
Manila, the Philippines
APO San Francisco 96528
Tel: 63-2-818-6674
Telex: 22708 COSEC PH

American Chamber of Commerce
P.O. Box 1578 MCC
Manila, the Philippines
Tel: 63-2-818-7911
Telex: (ITT) 45181 AMCHAM PH

Embassy of the Philippines Commercial Section
1617 Massachusetts Avenue, NW
Washington, DC 20036
Tel: (202) 483-1414
Telex: 44 0059 AMBPHIL

U.S. Exports to the Philippines
($ Billions)

Leading Imports from U.S. 1989

Valves
Wheat
Aircraft, Parts and Equipment
Paper and Paperboard
ADP and Office Machine Parts
Telecommunications Equipment
Est. of Shipments Valued Under $1,501
Plastics (in primary forms)
Heating and Cooling Equipment
Electric Switches

REPUBLIC OF SINGAPORE

Basic Data

Population (mid-1988):	2.6 million
Area (sq. kilometers):	1 thousand
Languages:	Chinese, (Mandarin), Malay, Tamil, English

Key Economic Data

GDP (1988):	$23.9 billion
Real GDP Growth 1980-88:	5.7%
GDP/Capita (1988):	$9,184
Exchange Rate:	$1 = 1.8125 Dollar

Foreign Trade

Total Exports (1988):	$39.2 billion
Total Imports (1988):	$43.8 billion
Imports from U.S. (1989):	$7.4 billion

Key Contacts

American Embassy Commercial Section
30 Hill Street
Singapore 0617
FPO San Francisco 96699
Tel: 65-338-0251
Telex: RS 42289 AMEMB

American Business Council
Scotts Road, #16-07
Shaw Center
Singapore 0922
Tel: 65-235-0077
Telex: 50296 ABC SIN

Embassy of Singapore Commercial Section
1824 R Street, NW
Washington, DC 20009
Tel: (202) 667-7555
Telex: 440024 SING EMB

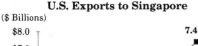

U.S. Exports to Singapore

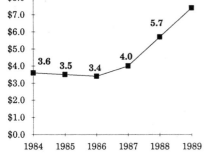

($ Billions)

Year	Value
1984	3.6
1985	3.5
1986	3.4
1987	4.0
1988	5.7
1989	7.4

Leading Imports from U.S. 1989

Valves
Aircraft, Parts and Equipment
ADP and Office Machine Parts
ADP and Office Machines
Musical Instruments
Engines and Motors
Engineering Plant and Equipment
Measuring Instruments
Electrical Switches
Electrical Machinery

REPUBLIC OF CHINA
(Taiwan)

Basic Data

Population (mid-1988):	20.2 million
Area (sq. kilometers):	35,980
Languages:	Chinese (Mandarin), Taiwanese

Key Economic Data

GDP (1988):	$118.9 billion
Real GDP Growth 1980-88:	7.2%
GDP/Capita (1988):	$5,886
Exchange Rate:	$1 = 26.72 New Taiwan Dollar

Foreign Trade

Total Exports (1988):	$60.4 billion
Total Imports (1988):	$44.6 billion
Imports from U.S. (1988):	$11.3 billion

Key Contacts

American Institute in Taiwan
7 Lane 134
Hsin Yi Road
Section 3
Taipei, Taiwan R.O.C.
Tel: 886-2-709-2000
Telex: 23890 USTRADE

American Chamber of Commerce
Room 1012–Chia Hsin Bldg. Annex
96 Chung Shan N. Rd., Section 2
P.O. Box 17-277
Taipei, Taiwan, R.O.C.
Tel 886-2-551-2515
Telex: 27841 AMCHAM

Coordination Council for North American
   Affairs
4201 Wisconsin Avenue, NW
Washington, DC 20016
Tel: (202) 686-6400
Telex: 440292

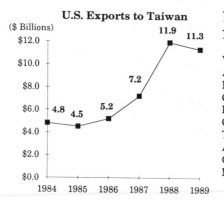

U.S. Exports to Taiwan
($ Billions)

Leading Imports from U.S. 1989

Valves
Automobiles and Other Vehicles
Maize
Oilseed and Oleaginous Fruit
Hydrocarbons and Derivatives
Oil (not crude)
Telecommunications Equipment
ADP and Office Machines
Carboxylic Acids
Measuring Instruments

THAILAND

Basic Data

Population (mid-1988):	54.5 million
Area (sq. kilometers):	514 thousand
Language:	Thai

Key Economic Data

GDP (1988):	$58 billion
Real GDP Growth 1980-88:	6.0%
GDP/Capita (1988):	$1064
Exchange Rate:	$1 = 25.64 Baht

Foreign Trade

Total Exports (1988):	$15.8 billion
Total Imports (1988):	$17.9 billion
Imports from U.S. (1989):	$2.3 billion

Key Contacts

Commercial Section
Shell Building, "R" Floor
140 Wireless Road
Bangkok, Thailand
APO San Francisco 96346
Tel: 66-2-252-5040
Telex: 20966 FCSBKK

American Chamber of Commerce
P.O. Box 11-1095
140 Wireless Road
7th Floor, Kian Gwan Bldg.
Bangkok, Thailand
Tel: 66-2-251-9266
Telex: 82828 KGCOM TH

Embassy of Thailand Commercial Section
2300 Kalorama Road, NW
Washington, DC 20008
Tel: (202) 483-7200
Telex: 892535

U.S. Exports to Thailand

($ Billions)

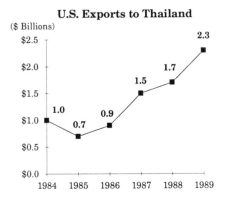

Leading Imports from U.S. 1989

Valves
Aircraft, Parts and Equipment
Arms and Ammunition
Cotton Textile Fibers
Pearls and Gemstones
Telecommunications Equipment
Engines and Motors
Iron
ADP and Office Machine Parts
Tobacco

NORTH AMERICA

The markets of Canada and Mexico are among the most important for U.S. businesses. Canada and Mexico rank first and third among U.S. trading partners. (see pages 13–18.) The United States—Canada Free Trade Agreement has highlighted and contributed to the importance of U.S.–Canadian trade. Discussions are presently underway for a similar agreement between the U.S. and Mexico. In fact, the idea for a Free Trade Agreement covering the U.S. , Canada, and Mexico, or even the whole Western Hemisphere is being discussed.

CANADA

Basic Data

Population (mid-1988):	26 million
Area (sq. kilometers):	10 million
Languages:	English, French

Key Economic Data

GDP (1988):	$435.9 billion
Real GDP Growth 1980-88:	3.3%
GDP/Capita (1988):	$16,765
Exchange Rate:	$1 = 1.1565 Dollar

Key Contacts

American Embassy Commercial Section
100 Wellington Street
Ottawa, Ontario
Canada, K1P 5T1
Tel: (613) 238-5335
Telex: 0533582

Embassy of Canada Commercial Section
501 Pennsylvania Avenue, NW
Washington, DC 20001
Tel: (202) 682-1740
Telex: 89644 DOMCAN A WSH

Foreign Trade

Total Exports (1988):	$111.4 billion
Total Imports (1988):	$112.2 billion
Imports from U.S. (1989):	$78.6 billion

U.S. Exports to Canada

Leading Imports from U.S. 1989

Automobile Parts and Accessories
Automobiles and Other Vehicles
Est. of Shipments Valued Under $1,501
Commercial Vehicles
Valves
Internal Combustion Piston Engines
ADP and Office Machines
Aircraft, Parts and Equipment
Shipments Valued Under $10,000
ADP and Office Machine Parts

MEXICO

Basic Data

Population (mid-1988):	83.7 million
Area (sq. kilometers):	2.0 million
Language:	Spanish

Key Economic Data

GDP (1988):	$176.7 billion
Real GDP Growth 1980-88:	0.5%
GDP/Capita (1988):	$2,111
Exchange Rate:	$1 = 2853.0 Peso

Foreign Trade

Total Exports (1988):	$20.7 billion
Total Imports (1988):	$18.9 billion
Imports from U.S. (1989):	$24.9 billion

Key Contacts

American Embassy Commercial Section
Paseo de la Reforma 305
Mexico 5 D.F., Mexico
P.O. Box 3085
Laredo, TX 78044
Tel: 522-211-0042
Telex: 017-73-091 or 017-75-685

American Chamber of Commerce
Lucerna 78-4
Mexico, D.F., Mexico
Tel: (905) 705-0995
Fax: (905) 535-3166

Embassy of Mexico Commercial Section
2829 16th Street, NW
Washington, DC 20009
Tel: (202) 234-6000
Telex: 90 4307 OCCMEX

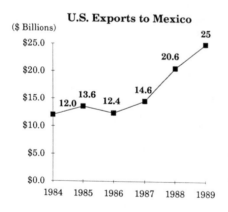

U.S. Exports to Mexico
($ Billions)

Leading Imports from U.S. 1989

Automobile Parts and Accessories
Telecommunications Equipment
Electrical Switches
Equipment for Distributing Electricity
Est. of Shipments Valued Under $1,501
Electrical Machinery
Valves
Measuring Instruments
Internal Combustion Piston Engines
ADP and Office Machine Parts

SOUTH AMERICA*

South America's debt crisis and its ramifications for the entire world financial network continue to receive trememdous press coverage. Nine South American countries (Argentina, Bolivia, Brazil, Chile, Colombia, Ecuador, Peru, Uruguay and Venezuela) are among the world's seventeen most highly indebted countries! Yet, lurking behind this crisis are many new and promising political and economic developments.

The World Bank classifies the fourteen countries of South America as middle-income countries. Thus, most, if not all south American countries have reached an income level conducive to the importation of industrial goods and services, and in some cases, luxury items.

This "middle-income" category tells us very little, however, about differences among these nations' economies. Breaking it down further, we find tremendous disparities. At one end of the spectrum lies Bolivia with a GDP per capita of $625. At the other end is Venezuela with a GDP per capita of $3,391. As can be seen in Table 9:

- Brazil is the largest economy in South America, with a GDP of $323.6 billion. Brazil is also the largest trading nation in the region. Argentina is the second largest economy, with a GDP of $79.4 billion. Of the larger countries in the region, Bolivia has the smallest economy, with a GDP of $6.0 billion.

- While trade is important to all South American economies, this importance varies by country. Exports make up a relatively small percentage of GDP in Brazil, Argentina and Peru, ranging from 10–11 percent of GDP. In comparison, exports in Venezuela and Chile comprise 16 and 32 percent, respectively, of GDP.

South America enjoyed tremendous economic growth during the 1960s and early 1970s. However, economic and political problems, including the rise of military governments, civil uprisings, regional conflicts, and the oil price shocks of the 1970s led to a marked slowdown in economic growth.

---

*Trade statistics in this section include figures for Guyana and Suriname, which are discussed in the Overview Section on the Caribbean Basin.

Table 9. South America Key Economic Data, 1988, ($ Billions)

Country	GDP	Exports	Imports
Brazil	$323.6	33.7	14.7
Argentina	79.4	9. 1	5.3
Venezuela	63.8	10.2	11.6
Colombia	39.1	5.3	4.5
Peru	25.7	2.7	2.8
Chile	22. 1	7.1	4.8
Ecuador	10.3	2.2	1.7
Uruguay	6.7	1.4	1.2
Paraguay	6.0	0.9	0.9
Bolivia	4.3	0.5	0.7
French Guiana*	2.0	0.04	0.3
Suriname**	1.2	0.3	0.3
Guyana**	0.3	0.2	0.3
Falkland Islands**	0.06	0.01	0.01
South American Total	**$582.6**	**$73.6**	**$48.8**

*Data are for 1985
**Data are for 1987
(Source: The World Bank; Central Intelligence Agency)

- **Slow Rates of Economic Growth.** During the period 1980-88, South American economies grew at an average rate of 1.2 percent. Bolivia was the hardest hit of all countries, suffering from a negative growth rate of –1.6 percent per year, while Uruguay experienced a negative growth rate of –0.4 percent per year and Argentina –0. 2 percent per year.

- **High Rates of Inflation, at Times Even Hyper-Inflation.** During the same period (1980–88), most South American countries experienced high, often extreme, rates of inflation, ranging from an exorbitant rate of over 600 percent in Bolivia to 21 percent in Paraguay and Chile. Venezuela, which enjoyed a relatively stable rate of inflation of 11 percent per year through 1987, is beginning to experience the inflation woes of its neighbors, with its 1989 inflation rate estimated at 85 percent.

- **Latin American Debt Crisis.** After years of runaway borrowing to finance large-scale industrial growth during the 1970s, Latin American countries faced a debt crisis during the 1980s. In 1985, Peru announced that debt service payments would not exceed 10 percent of export revenues. In 1987, Brazil announced a moratorium on debt service payments. Developments such as these are forcing the entire financial community to look carefully at the causes of this crisis and come up with creative, long-term solutions.

  Total public and private external debt ranges from $2.5 billion for Paraguay to $123.9 billion for Brazil. More significant than the amount of the total debt is the ability of each country to service, or continue to make payments, on its debt. Debt service is typically measured as a percentage of a country's total exports of goods and services. This measure is used because debt service is paid in hard currency, which is obtained through exports. Of all South American countries, Peru has the lowest debt service-to-exports ratio (13 percent); Chile, Paraguay, and Ecuador have ratios of about 21 percent; Argentina has an astonishing 45 percent ratio.

U.S. Exports To South America

During the 1980s, U.S. exports to South America ranged from a high of $17.4 billion in 1980 to a low of $10.5 billion in 1983. Since 1983, however, U.S. exports have increased, reaching $14.5 billion in 1989.

- Historically, Brazil has been the largest South American importer of U.S. goods. In 1988, Venezuela became the largest importer of U.S. goods and services, with imports totalling $4.6 billion, compared with Brazil's $4.3 billion. But in 1989 U.S. exports to Venezuela fell back to $3.0 billion (a decrease of 34 percent) while exports to Brazil increased to $4.8 billion, once again making Brazil the largest South American importer of U.S. goods and services.

- As Figure 18 shows, the largest importers of U.S. goods, after Brazil and Venezuela, are Colombia ($1.9 billion), Chile ($1.4 billion), Argentina ($1.0 billion), Peru ($690 million) and Ecuador ($641 million).

Figure 18. U.S. Exports to South America, 1989, ($ Millions)
(Source: U.S. Department of Commerce)

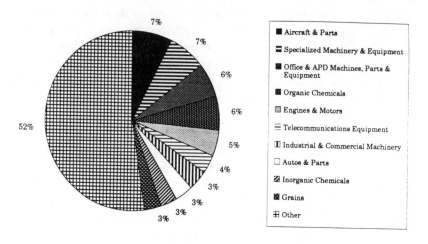

South America imports a great variety of goods from the U.S.
Figure 19 illustrates several patterns to U.S.–South American trade:

- Industrial equipment and goods from the U.S. constitute the major categories of South American imports from the U.S. Imports in this area include aircraft, spacecraft and parts (seven percent of total

Figure 19. Key U.S. Exports to South America, 1989, (Total = $14.5 billion)
(Source: U.S. Department of Commerce)

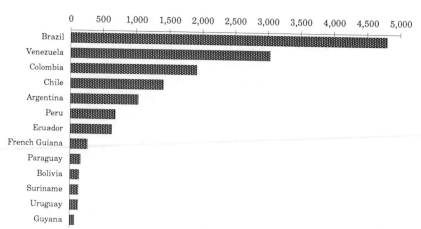

imports), specialized machinery and equipment (seven percent), and office and automatic data processing machines (six percent).

- Mechanical equipment, such as internal combustion engines (five percent), and automobiles, tractors and parts (three percent), is another major area of imports.

- Imports of grains and cereals from the U.S. represent a mere three percent of the total , largely because South American countries are major producers of grains and other agricultural products.

U.S. Investment in South America

South America has long been the target of foreign investment by U.S. multinational companies who recognized opportunities for lower-cost production due to lower labor costs and attractive investment laws, and for forays into South American markets. U.S. multinationals have traditionally invested largely in the areas of mining, manufacturing and agriculture.

In all, South America represents a favorable business and investment climate due for the following reasons:

- The relatively well-developed infrastructure in each country.

- The high level of education of South Americans and the availability of skilled workers and managers.

- In recent years, almost all countries have enacted legislation and investment codes containing attractive incentives for U.S. companies due to the slow rates of economic growth.

While South American countries generally tend to be pro-business, there are differences:

- Wage rates tend to differ markedly between countries.

- Certain sectors are protected in specific countries. For example, the oil industries of Venezuela and Argentina are controlled by national oil companies. The mining sector in Argentina, however, is highly concessionary toward foreign investors.

Issues to be aware of include:

- High level of unionization.
- The continuing risk of political instability.
- Inflationary pressures.

ARGENTINA

Basic Data

Population (mid-1989):	31.5 million
Area (sq. kilometers):	2.8 million
Language:	Spanish

Key Economic Data

GDP (1988):	$79.4 billion
Real GDP Growth 1980-88:	–0.2%
GDP/Capita (1988):	$2,521
Exchange Rate:	$1 = 5140 Austral

Foreign Trade

Total Exports (1988):	$9.1 billion
Total Imports (1988):	$5.3 billion
Imports from U.S. (1989):	$1.0 billion

Key Contacts

American Embassy Commercial Section
4300 Columbia
1425 Buenos Aires, Argentina
APO Miami 34034
Tel: 54-1-744-7611
Telex: 18156 AMEMB AR

American Chamber of Commerce
Av. Pte. Roque Saenz Pena 567, P6
1352 Buenos Aires, Argentina
Tel: 54-1-331-3436
Telex: 390-21139 BOSBK AR

Embassy of Argentina Commercial Section
1600 New Hampshire Avenue, NW
Washington, DC 20009
Tel: (202) 939-6400
Telex: 89-2537 EMBARG WSH

U.S. Exports to Argentina

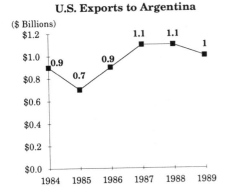

($ Billions)

Leading Imports from U.S. 1989

Organic Chemicals
ADP and Office Machines
ADP and Office Machine Parts
Engineering Plant and Equipment
Aircraft, Parts and Equipment
Inorganic Chemicals
Synthetic Resins, Rubber and Plastics
Automobile Parts and Accessories
Measuring Instruments
Coal

BRAZIL

Basic Data

Population (mid-1988):	144.4 million
Area (sq. kilometers):	8.5 million
Language:	Portuguese

Key Economic Data

GDP (1988):	$323.6 billion
Real GDP Growth 1980-88:	2.9%
GDP/Capita (1988):	$2,241
Exchange Rate:	$1 = 64.838 Cruzeiro

Foreign Trade

Total Exports (1988):	$33.7 billion
Total Imports (1988):	$14.7 billion
Imports from U.S. (1989):	$4.8 billion

Key Contacts

American Embassy Commercial Section
Avenida das Nocoes, Lote 3
Brasilia, Brazil
APO Miami 34030
Tel: (061) 223-0120
Telex: 061-1091

American Chamber of Commerce
C.P. 916, Praca Pio X-15, 5th Floor
20,040 Rio de Janeiro, RJ–Brazil
Tel: 55-21-203-2477
Telex: 391-2134084 AMCH BR

Embassy of Brazil Commercial Section
3006 Massachusetts Avenue, NW
Washington, DC 20008
Tel: (202) 745-2700
Telex: 440371 BRASMB or 89430 BRASMB

U.S. Exports to Brazil

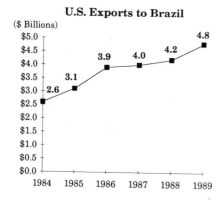

($ Billions)

Leading Imports from U.S. 1989

Aircraft, Parts and Equipment
Telecommunications Equipment
Organic Chemicals
Coal
ADP and Office Machine Parts
Internal Combustion Piston Engines
Automobile Parts and Accessories
ADP and Office Machines
Electrical Equipment
Measuring Instruments

CHILE

Basic Data

Population (mid-1988):	12.8 million
Area (sq. kilometers):	757 thousand
Language:	Spanish

Key Economic Data

GDP (1988):	$22.1 billion
Real GDP Growth 1980-88:	1.9%
GDP/Capita (1988):	$1,726
Exchange Rate:	$1 = 286.27 Peso

Foreign Trade

Total Exports (1988):	$7.1 billion
Total Imports (1988):	$4.8 billion
Imports from U.S. (1989):	$1.4 billion

Key Contacts

American Embassy Commercial Section
Edificio Codina
Agustinas 1343
Santiago, Chile
APO Miami 34033
Tel: 56-2-710133
Telex: 240062 USA CL

Chilean-American Chamber of Commerce
Av. Americo Vespicio Sur 80, 9 Piso
4131 Correo Central
Santiago, Chile
Tel: 56-2-484140
Telex: 392-340260 PBVTR CK

Embassy of Chile Commercial Section
1732 Massachusetts Avenue, NW
Washington, DC 20036
Tel: (202) 785-1746
Telex: 89-2663 EMBACHILE WSH

U.S. Exports to Chile

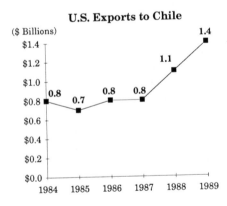

($ Billions)

Leading Imports from U.S. 1989

Engineering Plant and Equipment
Fertilizers
ADP and Office Machines
Est. of Shipments Valued Under $10,000
Resins, Rubber and Plastics
Organic Chemicals
Inorganic Chemicals
Automobile Parts and Accessories
Mechanical Equipment
Internal Combustion Piston Engines

COLOMBIA

Basic Data

Population (mid-1988):   31.7 million
Area (sq. kilometers):   1.1 million
Language: Spanish

Key Economic Data

GDP (1988): $39.1 billion
Real GDP Growth 1980-88:   3.4%
GDP/Capita (1988): $1,233
Exchange Rate: $1 = 496.25
                             Peso

Foreign Trade

Total Exports (1988): $5.3 billion
Total Imports (1988): $4.5 billion
Imports from U.S. (1989): $1.9 billion

Key Contacts

American Embassy Commercial Section
Calle 38, No. 8-61
P.O. Box A.A. 3831
Bogota, Colombia
APO Miami 34038
Tel: 57-1-285-1300
Telex: 44843

Colombian-American Chamber of
   Commerce
Apartado Aereo 8008
Calle 35, No. 6-16
Bogota, Colombia
Tel: 57-1-285-7800
Telex: 396-43326/45411 CAMC CO

Embassy of Colombia Commercial Section
2118 LeRoy Place, NW
Washington, DC 20008
Tel: (202) 387-8338
Telex: 197 624 COLE UT

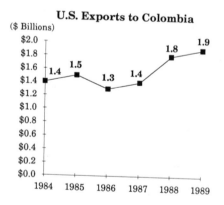

U.S. Exports to Colombia
($ Billions)

Leading Imports from U.S. 1989

Organic Chemicals
Resins, Rubber and Plastics
Engineering Plant and Equipment
Internal Combustion Piston Engines
Aircraft, Parts and Equipment
Fertilizers
Oilseed and Oleaginous Fruit
ADP and Office Machines
Est. of Shipments Valued Under $10,000
Wheat

PERU

Basic Data

Population (mid-1988):	20.7 million
Area (sq. kilometers):	1.3 million
Languages:	Spanish, Quechua, Aymara

Key Economic Data

GDP (1988):	$25.7 billion
Real GDP Growth 1980-88:	1.1%
GDP/Capita (1988):	$1240
Exchange Rate:	$1 = 98500 Inti

Foreign Trade

Total Exports (1988):	$2.7 billion
Total Imports (1988):	$2.8 billion
Imports from U.S. (1989):	$690 million

Key Contacts

American Embassy Commercial Section
Corner Avenidas Inca Garcilaso de la Vega
   y España
Lima 100, Peru
P.O. Box 1995
APO Miami 34031
Tel: 51-14-338-000
Telex: 25212 PE(USEMBGSO)

American Chamber of Commerce in Peru
Av. Ricardo Palma 836
Miraflores
Lima 18, Peru
Tel: 51-14-47-9349
Telex: 394-21165 BANKAMER

Embassy of Peru Commercial Section
1700 Massachusetts Avenue, NW
Washington, DC 20036
Tel: (202) 833-9860
Telex: 197675 LEPRU UT

U.S. Exports to Peru

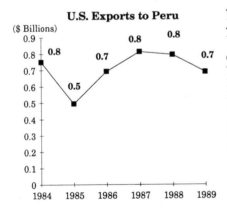

Leading Imports from U.S. 1989

Oil (not crude)
Wheat
Rice
Engineering Plant and Equipment
Internal Combustion Piston Engines
Aircraft, Parts and Equipment
Mechanical Handling Equipment
Maize
Fertilizers
Nitrogen Compounds

VENEZUELA

Basic Data

Population (mid-1988):	18.8 million
Area (sq. kilometers):	912 thousand
Language:	Spanish

Key Economic Data

GDP (1988):	$63.8 billion
Real GDP Growth 1980-88:	0.9%
GDP/Capita (1988):	$3,393
Exchange Rate:	$1 = 49.00 Bolivar

Foreign Trade

Total Exports (1988):	$10.2 billion
Total Imports (1988):	$11.6 billion
Imports from U.S. (1989):	$3.0 billion

Key Contacts

American Embassy Commercial Section
Avenida Francisco de Miranda and Avenida
  Principal de la Floresta
P.O. Box 62291
Caracas 1060-A, Venezuela
APO Miami 34037
Tel: 58-2-284-7111
Telex: 25501 AMEMB VE

Venezulean-American Chamber of
  Commerce and Industry
Torre Credival, Piso 10
2da. Avenida de Campo Alegre
Caracas 1010-A, Venezuela
Tel: 58-2-32-49-76
Telex: 395-23627 VACCI VC

Embassy of Venezuela Commercial Section
2445 Massachusetts Avenue, NW
Washington, DC 20008
Tel: (202) 342-2214
Telex: 440071

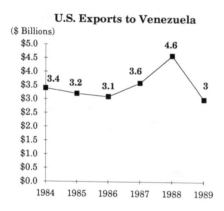

U.S. Exports to Venezuela
($ Billions)

Leading Imports from U.S. 1989

Engineering Plant and Equipment
Oil (not crude)
Wheat
Cereals
ADP and Office Machines
Automobile Parts and Accessories
Animal Feed
Telecommunications Equipment
Industrial Machinery
Internal Combustion Piston Engines

THE CARIBBEAN BASIN

In 1984 the U.S. Congress passed legislation aimed at improving economic conditions in Central America and the Caribbean. The Caribbean Basin Initiative (CBI) encourages the economic diversification and development of the region by providing preferential access to the U.S for many products from CBI beneficiary nations. Currently, twenty-two countries are designated CBI beneficiaries; another six may claim eligibility. (See below for a full list of CBI countries.) Critics feared that the CBI would result in a flood of imports in the U.S. market and a significant trade imbalance. In fact, U.S. exports to the region have actually increased by 44 percent between 1984–1989 and the U.S. trade deficit with the region has been replaced by a trade surplus.

The region covered by CBI is diverse and small compared with other countries in Latin America. The region can be broken down into four categories:

- **Larger Mainland Central American Countries.** This category includes Costa Rica, El Salvador, Guatemala, Honduras, Nicaragua and Panama. The largest economy belongs to Guatemala, with 1989 GDP of $8.1 billion. All of these countries are classified as lower-middle-income, with GDP per capita ranging from $840 in Honduras to $1,529 in Costa Rica. Costa Rica is considered the most politically stable of these countries. As a result, it has been successful in attracting foreign investment to its export-related sectors.

  All five countries are Spanish-speaking and the majority of their populations are Roman Catholic. While small in comparison with other Latin American countries, these countries are quite large compared with the other countries in the Caribbean Basin.

- **Smaller Mainland Countries.** This category consists of Belize, Suriname, and Guyana. GDP per capita varies significantly among these three countries: Guyana is the poorest of the three with GDP per capita of $450; Belize has a GDP per capita of $1,438; Suriname's GDP per capita is $2,800. All three countries' economies are dominated by the agricultural sector. They export mainly tropical fruits, such as pineapples and bananas, to the U.S.

- **Larger Island Nations.** This category is comprised of the Dominican Republic, Trinidad and Tobago, Jamaica, Barbados and Haiti. The Dominican Republic and Haiti each form one-half of the island of Hispaniola. The Dominican Republic has the largest economy among the island nations with GDP of $4.7 billion in 1988. Barbados enjoys the highest GDP per capita in this category ($5,405). Haiti is the poorest country with a GDP per capita of $360. These countries' economies are dominated by tourism, petroleum, food processing, and textile production.

- **Smaller Island Nations.** This category includes the remaining island nations, including the Leeward and Windward Islands, which are comprised of Antigua and Barbuda, Dominica, Grenada, St. Lucia and St. Vincent. The economies of these countries are very small, ranging from Turks and Caicos Islands (GDP of $15 million) to the Netherlands Antilles (GDP of $1.2 billion). These islands are largely dependent on tourism.

Table 10 helps to demonstrate the vast differences in economic power of Caribbean nations.

Recent major trends in the region have included:

- **Increased Political Stability.** The Caribbean Basin is historically an impoverished region and one that suffered from political instabilities and continual economic crises. Recently, however, there has been a general decline in challenges to current political systems, and the governments of the different countries have been working together to achieve political stability in the entire region. Glaring exceptions have been Panama, Nicaragua, El Salvador and Haiti.

- **Slow, Even Negative, Rates of Economic Growth.** With the exception of Costa Rica, between 1980 and 1988, the countries in the region experienced slow rates of economic growth. An extreme case is Trinidad and Tobago, whose economy experienced an annual negative growth rate of 6.1 percent! However, since 1984, most countries have achieved some growth. In 1988, growth rates of individual countries were between 2.5 percent and 3.5 percent. This moderate growth is expected to continue.

Table 10. Caribbean Basin Key Economic Data, 1988, ($ Billions)

Country	GDP	Exports	Imports
Guatemala	$8. 1	$1.1	$1.5
Panama	5.5	2.4	2.8
El Salvador	5.5	0.6	1.0
Costa Rica	4.7	1.3	1.4
Dominican Republic	4.6	0.9	1.6
Trinidad and Tobago	4.4	1.2	1.2
Honduras	3.9	0.9	0.9
Nicaragua	3.2	0.2	0.8
Jamaica	3.2	0.8	1.4
Haiti	2.5	0.2	0.3
Bahamas*	2.3	0.3	1.0
Barbados*	1.4	0.2	0.5
Netherlands Antilles**	1.2	0.08	1. 1
Suriname*	1.2	0.3	0.3
Guyana*	0.3	0.2	0.3
Cayman Islands**	0.3	0.002	0. 1
Leeward & Windward Islands	0.2	0.03	0.3
Belize*	0.2	0.1	0. 1
Turks and Caicos Islands***	0.02	0.003	0.03
Caribbean Basin Total	**$52.7**	**$10.8**	**$16.6**

*Data are from 1987
**Data are from 1985
***Data are from 1984
(Source: The World Bank; The Economist Intelligence Unit; Central Intelligence Agency)

U.S. Exports to the Caribbean Basin

Since 1985, U.S. exports to the Caribbean Basin have grown at an average annual rate of 8.7 percent. In 1989, U.S. exports to the region were $9.4 billion, up 19 percent over the previous year. The U.S. balance of trade with the region went from a deficit of $2.5 billion in 1984 to a surplus of $2.4 billion in 1989. As shown in Figure 20:

Figure 20. U.S. Exports to the Caribbean Basin, 1989, ($ Millions)
(Source: U.S. Department of Commerce)

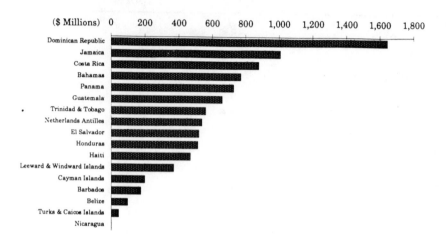

- The largest market for U.S. goods is the Dominican Republic, whose imports from the U.S. in 1989 totalled $1.6 billion.

- The Dominican Republic is followed by Jamaica ($1.0 billion), Costa Rica ($880 million), and the Bahamas ($773 million).

As indicated in Figure 21, principal U.S. exports to the Caribbean Basin are clothing (eight percent), oil and petroleum products (six percent), cereals and grains (five percent) and automobiles and parts (four percent). In the near future, the following areas offer the best export opportunities:

- Machinery for the booming apparel sector.

- A variety of goods and services for the expanding regional hotel market.

- Capital equipment for the manufacturing sector and the data entry industry.

- Capital equipment and agricultural inputs for the agribusiness sector.

Figure 21. Key U.S. Exports to the Caribbean Basin, 1989, (Total = $9.4 billion)
(Source: U.S. Department of Commerce)

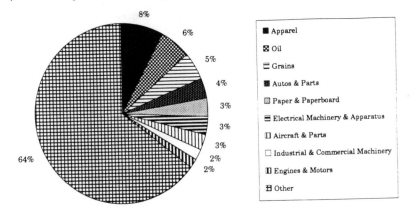

U.S. Investment in the Caribbean Basin

The CBI can benefit U.S. companies wishing to produce, manufacture, or refine in the region and export to the U.S. Not surprisingly, the industries that show the most promise for U. S. exports are also those where investment opportunities are abundant: tourism, data entry, agribusiness, and light manufacturing. Moreover, many countries in the region are also beneficiaries of similar trade preference programs with the European Community and Canada.

CBI Beneficiary Countries

Anguilla*   Antigua & Barbuda
Aruba   Bahamas
Barbados   Belize
British Virgin Islands   Cayman Islands*
Costa Rica   Dominica
Dominican Republic   El Salvador
Guatemala   Grenada
Guyana   Haiti
Honduras   Jamaica

CBI Beneficiary Countries (Continued)

Montserrat	Netherlands Antilles
Nicaragua*	Panama*
St. Christopher-Nevis	St. Lucia
St. Vincent and the Grenadines	Suriname*
Trinidad & Tobago	Turks and Caicos Islands*

---

*Eligible for CBI trade benefits, but, with the exception of Guyana, have not formally requested CBI designation.

COSTA RICA

Basic Data

Population (mid-1988):	2.7 million
Area (sq. kilometers):	51 thousand
Language:	Spanish

Key Economic Data

GDP (1988):	$4.7 billion
Real GDP Growth 1980-88:	2.4%
GDP/Capita (1988):	$1.740
Exchange Rate:	$1 = 91.33 Colón

Foreign Trade

Total Exports (1988):	$1.3 billion
Total Imports (1988):	$1.4 billion
Imports from U.S. (1989):	$880 million

Key Contacts

American Embassy
Avenida 3 y Calle 1
San Jose, Costa Rica
APO Miami 34020
Tel: 506-33-11-55

Costa Rican-American Chamber of
Commerce
Avda. 2, Calles 30-32, #3034
Apdo. 4946
San Jose 1000, Costa Rica
Tel: 506-33-21-33
Telex: 323-21286 POZUELO CR

Embassy of Costa Rica
1825 Connecticut Avenue, NW
Washington, DC 20009
Tel: (202) 234-2945
Telex: 3400

U.S. Exports to Costa Rica

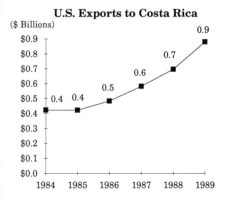

($ Billions)

Leading Imports from U.S. 1989

Paper and Paperboard
Miscellaneous Articles of Apparel
Men's and Boy's Coats
Est. of Shipments Valued Under $1,501
Women's and Girl's Coats
Ethylene Polymers
Wheat
Oil (not crude)
Woven Fabrics
Maize

DOMINICAN REPUBLIC

Basic Data

Population (mid-1988):	6.9 million
Area (sq. kilometers):	49 thousand
Language:	Spanish

Key Economic Data

GDP (1988):	$4.6 billion
Real GDP Growth 1980-88:	2.2%
GDP/Capita (1988):	$671
Exchange Rate:	$1 = 10.4125 Peso

Foreign Trade

Total Exports (1988):	$900 million
Total Imports (1988):	$1.6 billion
Imports from U.S. (1989):	$1.6 billion

Key Contacts

American Embassy Commercial Section
Calle Cesar Nicolas Penson con Calle
  Leopoldo Navarro
Santo Domingo, Dominican Republic
APO Miami 34041-2171
Telex: 3460013

American Chamber of Commerce
Av. Winston Churchill, P.O. Box 95-2
Santo Domingo, Dominican Republic
Tel: 809-544-2222
Telex: 346-0958 AMCHAM

Embassy of Dominican Republic
  Commercial Section
1715 22nd Street, NW
Washington, DC 20008
Tel: (202) 332-6280
Telex: 44-0031 DOR EMB

U.S. Exports to the Dominican Republic

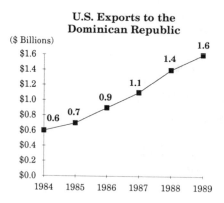

($ Billions)

Leading Imports from U.S. 1989

Men's and Boy's Coats
Electrical Switches
Women's and Girl's Coats
Tobacco
Articles of Apparel
Maize
Clothing Accessories
Leather
Oil (not crude)
Medical Instruments

THE MIDDLE EAST

To many Americans, the Middle East is a region of oil wealth, military conflict between nations, and terrorism against Westerners. Yet, looking behind these common perceptions, we see the region is of great political and economic importance to the United States. First, the region contains a large part of the world's oil resources, thus making it of strategic and economic importance. Second, the U.S. has strong political and economic ties with most countries in the region, including Israel, Egypt, Saudi Arabia, Oman and Kuwait.

The region can be divided into two groups:

- **Oil-Producing Countries.** This group consists of the countries of Iran, Saudi Arabia, Iraq, the United Arab Emirates, Kuwait, Oman, Qatar and Bahrain, all of which are members of the Organization of Petroleum Exporting Countries (OPEC). These countries' economies are dominated by the oil industry. They all enjoy high rates of GDP per capita.

- **Non-Oil-Producing Countries.** This group consists of the remaining countries in the Middle East, namely, Egypt, Israel, Syria, Jordan, Lebanon, North Yemen and South Yemen. These countries, with the exception of Israel, tend to have lower GDP per capita.

Recent trends in the region include:

- **The Changed Nature of the Oil Market.** The rapid rise in the price of oil during the 1970s led to an economic boom in the OPEC countries. During the 1980s, however, decreases in demand for oil in the rest of the world as well as an increase in oil production by non-OPEC countries, led to a steep decline in the price of crude oil and broke OPEC's monopoly power in the oil market.

- **Moderate Rates of Economic Growth.** Depressed oil prices from 1985–87 led to a sharp downturn in the economies of the Middle East. More recent rises in the price of oil have allowed oil-producing countries to achieve moderate rates of economic growth.

Table 11 outlines economic data for the region.

Table 11. Middle East Key Economic Data, 1988, ($ Billions)

Counry	GDP	Exports	Imports
Iran	184.4	9.8	11.8
Iraq	91.0	13.5	11.4
Saudi Arabia	69. 1	23.7	21.8
Egypt	45.6	2.6	9.4
Israel	41.9	9.4	12.3
United Arab Emirates	23.8	12.3	8.5
Kuwait	19.9	7.1	5.4
Syria	14.9	1.3	2.2
Oman	7.5	2.6	2.2
North Yemen	5.8	0.4	1.3
Qatar	5.2	1.7	1.2
Jordan	4.7	1.0	2.8
Bahrain	3.6	2.4	2.6
Lebanon*	1.8	1.0	1.5
South Yemen	1.3	.08	0.6
Middle East Total	**$520.5**	**$88.9**	**$95.0**

* GDP is from 1985; trade data is from 1987
(Source: The Economist Intelligence Unit; Central Intelligence Agency)

- **The Union of North and South Yemen.** The union of these two countries will more fully integrate South Yemen into the Gulf economy and improve its economic and political relationships with other cotmtries. The union is also expected to significantly reduce the Communist influence in the region.

U.S. Exports to the Middle East

U.S. exports to the region experienced periods of growth and decline during the 1980s. During the early part of the 1980s, U.S. exports grew steadily. From 1982–86, however, exports declined. In 1987, this trend was reversed when countries in the region began to achieve improved rates of economic growth. U.S. exports to the region in 1989 totalled $11.1 billion.

- As shown in Figure 22, the biggest importers of U.S. goods and services in the region are Saudi Arabia, Israel and Egypt.

- Major U.S. exports to the region are aircraft, spacecraft and parts; cereals and grains; industrial and commercial machinery; tobacco products; telecommunications equipment, and automobiles and parts. Figure 23 shows the relative importance of each of these categories of exports.

In the future, exports opportunities to the region are likely to be related to the following:

- The U.S.–Israel Free Trade Area (FTA) Agreement, which became effective in September 1985, provides for the elimination of all tar-

Figure 22. U.S. Exports to the Middle East, 1989, ($ Millions)
(Source: U.S. Department of Commerce)

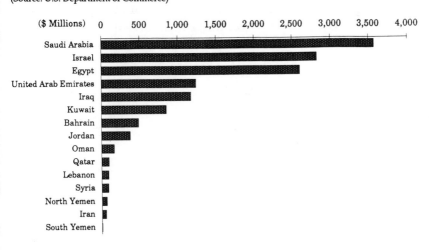

Figure 23. Key U.S. Exports to the Middle East, 1989, (Total = $11.1 billion)
(Source: U.S. Department of Commerce)

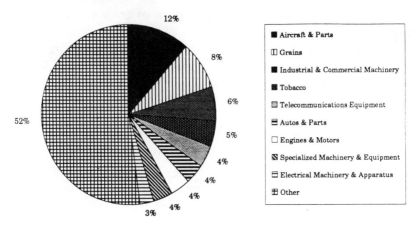

iffs and most non-tariff barriers between both countries by 1995. As of January 1989, more than 80 percent of U.S. exports to Israel were duty-free.

• Over 50 percent of U.S. foreign assistance goes to Israel and Egypt. Much of this aid, in turn, is used to finance the purchase of U.S. goods and services.

• As the oil-producing countries' economies start growing at high rates, opportunities will exist for the export of oil exploration and production equipment, telecommunications equipment, electrical equipment, computers, aircraft and parts, and agricultural goods.

EGYPT

Basic Data

Population (mid-1988):	50.2 million
Area (sq. kilometers):	1.0 million
Languages:	Arabic, English and French widely understood

Key Economic Data

GDP (1988):	$45.6 billion
Real GDP Growth 1980-88:	5.7%
GDP/Capita (1988):	$908
Exchange Rate:	$1 = 2.7034 Pound

Foreign Trade

Total Exports (1988):	$2.6 billion
Total Imports (1988):	$9.4 billion
Imports from U.S. (1989):	$2.6 billion

Key Contacts

American Embassy
5 Sharia Latin America
Cairo, Arab Republic of Egypt
FPO NY 09527
Tel: 20-2-355-7371
Telex: 93773 AMEMB

American Chamber of Commerce
Cairo Marriott Hotel, Suite 1537
P.O. Box 33, Zamalek
Cairo, Egypt
Tel: 20-2-340-8888
Telex: 20870 AMCHE UN

Embassy of Egypt
2310 Decatur Place, NW
Washington, DC 20008
Tel: (202) 232-5400
Telex: 89-2481 COMRAU WSH

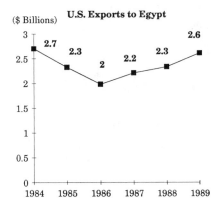

($ Billions) U.S. Exports to Egypt

Leading Imports from U.S. 1989

Wheat
Aircraft, Parts and Equipment
Arms and Ammunition
Maize
Meal and Flour
Telecommunications Equipment
Engineering Plant and Equipment
Cotton Textile Fibers
Engines and Motors
Vegetable Fats and Oils

IRAN

Basic Data

Population (mid-1988):	48.6 million
Area (sq. kilometers):	1.6 million
Languages:	Farsi, Turki, Kurdish, Arabic, English, French

Key Contacts

The United States has no official relations with Iran

Key Economic Data

GDP (1988):	$184.4 billion
Real GDP Growth 1980-88:	–2%%
GDP/Capita (1988):	$3,794
Exchange Rate:	$1 = 68.6838 Rial

Foreign Trade

Total Exports (1988):	$9.8 billion
Total Imports (1988):	$11.8 billion
Imports from U.S. (1989):	$60 million

U.S. Exports to Iran
($ Billions)

Leading Imports from U.S. 1989

Fertilizers
Additives for Mineral Oils
Internal Combustion Piston Engines
Engineering Plant and Equipment
Telecommunications Equipment
ADP and Office Machines
Crude animal materials
Industrial Machinery
Taps, Cocks and Valves
Valves

IRAQ

Basic Data

Population (mid-1988):	17.6 million
Area (sq. kilometers):	435 thousand
Languages:	Arabic, Kurdish, Assyrian, Armenian

Key Economic Data

GDP (1988):	$91 billion
Real GDP Growth 1980-88:	0%
GDP/Capita (1988):	$5,170
Exchange Rate:	$1 = .3217 Dinar

Key Contacts

American Embassy Commercial Section
P.O. Box 2447 Alwiyah
Baghdad, Iraq
Tel: 964-1-719-6138
Telex: 212287 USINTIK or 213966 USFCSIK

Embassy of Iraq Commercial Section
1801 P Street, NW
Washington, DC 20036
Tel: (202) 483-7500
Telex: 64437 IRAQI YA/64464 IRAQI YA

Foreign Trade

Total Exports (1988):	$13.5 billion
Total Imports (1988):	$11.4 billion
Imports from U.S. (1989):	$1.2 billion

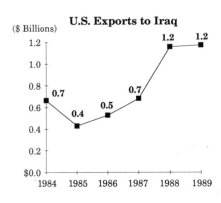

(\$ Billions) **U.S. Exports to Iraq**

Leading Imports from U.S. 1989

Wheat
Animal Feed
Rice
Maize
Wood and Railway Sleepers of Wood
Tobacco
Pulp and Waste Paper
Cotton Textile Fibers
Aircraft, Parts and Equipment
Sugars, Molasses and Honey

ISRAEL

Basic Data

Population (mid-1988):	4.4 million
Area (sq. kilometers):	21 thousand
Languages:	Hebrew, Arabic, English

Key Economic Data

GDP (1988):	$41.9 billion
Real GDP Growth 1980-88:	3.2%
GDP/Capita (1988):	$9,523
Exchange Rate:	$1 = 2.0383 Shekel

Foreign Trade

Total Exports (1988):	$9.4 billion
Total Imports (1988):	$12.3 billion
Imports from U.S. (1989):	$2.8 billion

Key Contacts

American Embassy
71 Hayarkon Street
Tel Aviv, Israel
APO NY 09672
Tel: 972-3-654338
Telex: 33376 or 371386 USFCSIL

American Chamber of Commerce
35 Shaul Hamelech Blvd.
P.O. Box 33174
64927 Tel Aviv, Israel
Tel: 972-3-252341/2
Telex: 23139 BETAM IL

Embassy of Israel
3514 International Drive, NW
Washington, DC 20008
Tel: (202) 364-5500
Fax: (202) 364-5647

($ Billions) U.S. Exports to Israel

Leading Imports from U.S. 1989

Aircraft, Parts and Equipment
Pearls and Gemstones
Telecommunications Equipment
Arms and Ammunition
ADP and Office Machines
Engines and Motors
Wheat
Measuring Instruments
Oilseed and Oleaginous Fruit
Valves

KUWAIT

Basic Data

Population (mid-1988):	2 million
Area (sq. kilometers):	18 thousand
Languages:	Arabic; English widely spoken

Key Economic Data

GDP (1988):	$19.9 billion
Real GDP Growth 1980-88:	–1.1%
GDP/Capita (1988):	$9,985
Exchange Rate:	$1 = .29070 Dinar

Key Contacts

American Embassy Commercial Section
P.O. Box 77 SAFAT
13001 SAFAT, Kuwait
Tel: 965-242-4151
Telex: 2039 HILTELS KT

Embassy of Kuwait
2940 Tilden Street, NW
Washington, DC 20008
Tel: (202) 966-0702
Telex: 64142 KUWAIT WSH

Foreign Trade

Total Exports (1988):	$7.1 billion
Total Imports (1988):	$5.4 billion
Imports from U.S. (1989):	$855 million

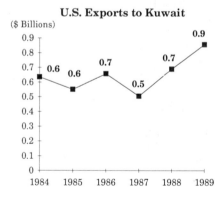

U.S. Exports to Kuwait
($ Billions)

Leading Imports from U.S. 1989

Automobiles and Other Vehicles
Commercial Vehicles
Aircraft, Parts and Equipment
Tobacco
Automobile Parts and Accessories
Heating and Cooling Equipment
Rotating Electric Plant and Parts
Telecommunications Equipment
Pumps, Gas Compressors and Fans
Internal Combustion Piston Engines

SAUDI ARABIA

Basic Data

Population (mid-1988):	14 million
Area (sq. kilometers):	2.2 million
Language:	Arabic

Key Economic Data

GDP (1988):	$69.1 billion
Real GDP Growth 1980-88:	-3.3%
GDP/Capita (1988):	$4,936
Exchange Rate:	$1 = 3.7495 Riyal

Foreign Trade

Total Exports (1988):	$23.7 billion
Total Imports (1988):	$21.8 billion
Imports from U.S. (1989):	$3.6 billion

Key Contacts

American Embassy
Collector Road M
Riyadh Diplomatic Quarter
P.O. Box 9041, Riyadh 11143, Saudi Arabia
APO NY 09038
Tel: 966-1-488-3800
Telex: 406866 AMEMB SJ

American Businessmen's Association,
    Eastern Province
c/o ARAMCO
P.O. Box 1329
Dhahran, Saudi Abrabia 31311
Tel: 966-3-875-2933
Telex: 801220

Embassy of Saudi Arabia
601 New Hampshire Avenue, NW
Washington, DC 20037
Tel: (202) 342-3800
Telex: 440132 NAJDI AH

U.S. Exports to Saudi Arabia
($ Billions)

Leading Imports from U.S. 1989

Automobiles and Other Vehicles
Aircraft, Parts and Equipment
Telecommunications Equipment
Tobacco
Heating and Cooling Equipment
Pumps, Gas Compressors and Fans
Rice
Nonelectrical Machinery
Automobile Parts and Accessories
Maize

OTHER COUNTRY DATA

INDIA

Basic Data

Population (mid-1988):	815.6 million
Area (sq. kilometers):	3.3 million
Languages:	Hindi, English, and 14 other official languages

Key Economic Data

GDP (1988):	$237.9 billion
Real GDP Growth 1980-88:	5.2%
GDP/Capita (1988):	$291
Exchange Rate:	$1 = 17.48 Rupee

Key Contacts

American Embassy Commercial Section
Shanti Path
Chanakyapuri 110021
New Delhi, India
Tel: 91-11-600651
Telex: 031-65269 USEMIN

Embassy of India Commercial Section
2107 Massachusetts Avenue, NW
Washington, DC 20008
Tel: (202) 939-7000
Fax: (202) 939-7027

Foreign Trade

Total Exports (1988):	$14.6 billion
Total Imports (1988):	$22.5 billion
Imports from U.S. (1989):	$2.5 billion

U.S. Exports to India
($ Billions)

Leading Imports from U.S. 1989

Fertilizers
Aircraft, Parts and Equipment
Ferrous Waste and Scrap
Measuring Instruments
Engineering Plant and Equipment
ADP and Office Machines
Pearls and Gemstones
Pulp and Waste Paper
Valves
Telecommunications Equipment

PAKISTAN

Basic Data

Population (mid-1988):	110.4 million
Area (sq. kilometers):	796 thousand
Languages:	Urdu, English, Punjabi, Sindhi, Pashtu, Baluchi

Key Economic Data

GDP (1988):	$34 billion
Real GDP Growth 1980-88:	6.5%
GDP/Capita (1988):	$320
Exchange Rate:	$1 = 21.72 Rupee

Foreign Trade

Total Exports (1988):	$4.4 billion
Total Imports (1988):	$7.5 billion
Imports from U.S. (1989):	$1.1 billion

Key Contacts

American Embassy Commercial Section
Diplomatic Enclave, Ramna 5
P.O. Box 1048
Islamabad, Pakistan
APO NY 09614
Tel: 92-51-8261-61
Telex: 952-5864

American Business Council of Pakistan
NIC Building, 6th Floor
Abbasi Shaheed Road Off Sharea Faisal
Karachi, Pakistan
Tel: 92-21-52-1635/5476
Telex: 25620 CHASE PK

Embassy of Pakistan Commercial Section
2315 Massachusetts Avenue, NW
Washington, DC 20008
Tel: (202) 939-6200
Telex: 89-2348 PARAP WSH

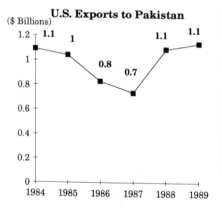

U.S. Exports to Pakistan
($ Billions)

Leading Imports from U.S. 1989

Wheat
Vegetable Fats and Oils
Aircraft, Parts and Equipment
Fertilizers
Arms and Ammunition
Measuring Instruments
Telecommunications Equipment
Rotating Electric Plant and Parts
Engineering Plant and Equipment
Animal Oils and Fats

SOURCES

Basic Data

Population

World Development Report 1990, Published
for the World Bank, Oxford University
Press, June 1990
The World Factbook 1989
Central Intelligence Agency, 1990

Area (sq. kilometers)

World Development Report 1990
The World Factbook 1989

Language

The World Factbook 1989

Key Economic Data

Gross Domestic Product (GDP)/
Gross National Product (GNP)

World Development Report 1990
The World Factbook 1989
The Economist, July, 1990, Survey, page 15

GDP Growth/GNP Growth

World Development Report 1990
The Economist Intelligence Unit
World Outlook 1990

GDP/capita-GNP/capita

World Development Report 1990
The World Factbook 1989

Exchange Rate

Journal of Commerce

Foreign Trade

Total Exports

World Development Report 1990
The World Factbook 1989

Total Imports

World Development Report 1990
The World Factbook 1989

Imports from U.S. (1989):

U.S. Foreign Trade Highlights 1989

Key Contacts

The *Arthur Young International Business Guide*
Key Officers of Foreign Service Posts, May
1990, U.S. Department of State
American Chambers of Commerce Abroad,
April 1990, U.S. Chamber of Commerce
The World is Your Market, (Ed. William A.
Delphos, Braddock Communications,
Washington, DC, 1990)

Charts

U.S. Exports to. . .
Leading Imports From U.S.

U.S. Foreign Trade Highlights 1989
U.S. Foreign Trade Highlights 1989

SECTION 3

GLOSSARY OF COMMON INTERNATIONAL BUSINESS TERMS

This glossary* defines terms which are common in international business ventures. These definitions are used by the U.S. Department of Commerce. Some of these terms have appeared in the preceding text; others have not. This glossary is not meant to be exhaustive or provide you with full definitions for all terms. Rather, it serves as a useful and quick reference guide.

Acceptance—This term has several related meanings:

1. A time draft (or bill of exchange) which the drawee has accepted and is unconditionally obligated to pay at maturity. The draft must be presented first for acceptance—the drawee becomes the "acceptor"—then for payment. The word "accepted" and the date and place of payment must be written on the face of the draft.

2. The drawee's act in receiving a draft and thus entering into the obligation to pay its value at maturity.

3. (Broadly speaking) Any agreement to purchase goods under specified terms. An agreement to purchase goods at a stated price and under stated terms.

Ad valorem—According to value. See **Duty**.

Advance against documents—A loan made on the security of the documents covering the shipment.

Advising bank—A bank, operating in the exporter's country, that handles letters of credit for a foreign bank by notifying the exporter that the credit has been opened in his or her favor. The advising bank fully informs the exporter of the conditions of the letter of credit without necessarily bearing responsibility for payment.

Advisory capacity—A term indicating that a shipper's agent or representative is not empowered to make definitive decisions or adjustments without approval of the group or individual represented. Compare **Without reserve.**

*Source: U.S. Department of Commerce.

145

Agent—See **Foreign sales agent.**

Air waybill—A bill of lading that covers both domestic and international flights transporting goods to a specified destination. This is a non-negotiable instrument of air transport that serves as a receipt for the shipper, indicating that the carrier has accepted the goods listed and obligates itself to carry the consignment to the airport of destination according to specified conditions. Compare **Inland bill of lading, Ocean bill of lading,** and **Through bill of lading.**

Alongside—A phrase referring to the side of a ship. Goods to be delivered "alongside" are to be placed on the dock or barge within reach of the transport ship's tackle so that they can be loaded aboard the ship.

Antidiversion clause—See **Destination control statement.**

Arbitrage—The process of buying **Foreign exchange,** stocks, bonds, and other commodities in one market and immediately selling them in another market at higher prices.

Asian dollars—U.S. dollars deposited in Asia and the Pacific Basin. Compare **Eurodollars.**

ATA Carnet—See **Carnet.**

Balance of trade—The difference between a country's total imports and exports; if exports exceed imports, a favorable balance of trade exists; if not, a trade deficit is said to exist.

Barter—Trade in which merchandise is exchanged directly for other merchandise without use of money. Barter is an important means of trade with countries using currency that is not readily convertible.

Beneficiary—The person in whose favor a **Letter of credit** is issued or a **Draft** is drawn.

Bill of exchange—See **Draft.**

Bill of lading—A document that establishes the terms of a contract between a shipper and a transportation company under which freight is to be moved between specified points for a specified charge. Usually prepared by the shipper on forms issued by the carrier, it serves as a document of title, a contract of carriage, and a receipt for goods. Also see **Air waybill, Inland bill of lading, Ocean bill of lading,** and **Through bill of lading.**

Bonded warehouse—A warehouse authorized by **Customs** authorities for storage of goods on which payment of **Duties** is deferred until the goods are removed.

Booking—An arrangement with a steamship company for the acceptance and carriage of freight.

Buying agent—See **Purchasing agent.**

Carnet—A customs document permitting the holder to carry or send merchandise temporarily into certain foreign countries (for display, demonstration, or similar purposes) without paying duties or posting bonds.

Cash against documents (C.A.D.)—Payment for goods in which a commission house or other intermediary transfers title documents to the buyer upon payment in cash.

Cash in advance (C.I.A.)—Payment for goods in which the price is paid in full before shipment is made. This method is usually used only for small purchases or when the goods are built to order.

Cash with order (C.W.O.)—Payment for goods in which the buyer pays when ordering and in which the transaction is binding on both parties.

Certificate of inspection—A document certifying that merchandise (such as perishable goods) was in good condition immediately prior to its shipment.

Certificate of manufacture—A statement (often notarized) in which a producer of goods certifies that manufacture has been completed and that the goods are now at the disposal of the buyer.

Certificate of origin—A document, required by certain foreign countries for tariff purposes, certifying the country of origin of specified goods.

C & F—"Cost and freight." A pricing term indicating that the cost of the goods and freight charges are included in the quoted price; the buyer arranges for and pays insurance.

Charter party—A written contract, usually on a special form, between the owner of a vessel and a "charterer" who rents use of the vessel or a part of its freight space. The contract generally includes the freight rates and the ports involved in the transportation.

C & I—"Cost and insurance." A pricing term indicating that the cost of the product and insurance are included in the quoted price. The buyer is responsible for freight to the named port of destination.

C.I.F.—"Cost, insurance, freight." A pricing term indicating that the cost of the goods, insurance, and freight are included in the quoted price.

Clean bill of lading—A receipt for goods issued by a carrier that indicates that the goods were received in "apparent good order and condition," without damages or other irregularities. Compare **Foul bill of lading.**

Clean draft—A **Draft** to which no documents have been attached.

Collection papers—All documents (**Commercial invoices, Bills of lading,** etc.) submitted to a buyer for the purpose of receiving payment for a shipment.

Commercial attache—The commerce expert on the diplomatic staff of his or her country's embassy or large consulate.

Commercial invoice—An itemized list of goods shipped, usually included among an exporter's **Collection papers.**

Commission agent—See **Purchasing agent.**

Common carrier—An individual, partnership, or corporation that transports persons or goods for compensation.

Confirmed letter of credit—A letter of credit, issued by a foreign bank, with validity confirmed by a U.S. bank. An exporter who requires a confirmed letter of credit from the buyer is assured of payment by the U.S. bank even if the foreign buyer or the foreign bank defaults. See **Letter of credit.**

Consignment—Delivery of merchandise from an exporter (the consignor) to an agent (the consignee) under agreement that the agent sell the merchandise for the account of the exporter. The consignor retains title to the goods until the consignee has sold them. The consignee sells the goods for commission and remits the net proceeds to the consignor.

Consular declaration—A formal statement, made to the consul of a foreign country, describing goods to be shipped.

Consular invoice—A document, required by some foreign countries, describing a shipment of goods and showing information such as the consignor, consignee, and value of the shipment. Certified by a consular official of the foreign country, it is used by the country's customs officials to verify the value, quantity, and nature of the shipment.

Convertible currency—A currency that can be bought and sold for other currencies at will.

Correspondent bank—A bank that, in its own country, handles the business of a foreign bank.

Countertrade—The sale of goods or services that are paid for in whole or in part by the transfer of goods or services from a foreign country. (See **Barter.**)

Credit risk insurance—Insurance designed to cover risks of nonpayment for delivered goods. Compare **Marine insurance.**

Customs—The authorities designated to collect duties levied by a country on imports and exports. The term also applies to the procedure involved in such collection.

Customhouse broker—An individual or firm licensed to enter and clear goods through Customs.

Date draft—A draft that matures in a specified number of days after the date it is issued, without regard to the date of **Acceptance** (Definition 2). See **Draft, Sight draft** and **Time draft.**

Deferred payment credit—Type of Letter of credit providing for payment some time after presentation of shipping documents by exporter.

Demand draft—See **Sight draft.**

Destination control statement—Any of various statements that the U.S. Government requires to be displayed on export shipments and that specify the destinations for which export of the shipment has been authorized.

Devaluation—The official lowering of the value of one country's currency in terms of one or more foreign currencies. (E.g., if the U.S. dollar is devalued in relation to the French franc, one dollar will "buy" fewer francs than before.)

Discrepancy—Letter of credit—When documents presented do not conform to the letter of credit, it is referred to as a "discrepancy."

Dispatch—An amount paid by a vessel's operator to a charterer if loading or unloading is completed in less time than stipulated in the charter party.

Distributor—A foreign agent who sells for a supplier directly and maintains an inventory of the supplier's products.

Dock receipt—A receipt issued by an ocean carrier to acknowledge receipt of a shipment at the carrier's dock or warehouse facilities. Also see **Warehouse receipt.**

Documentary draft—A Draft to which documents are attached.

Documents against acceptance (D/A)—Instructions given by a shipper to a bank indicating that documents transferring title to good should be delivered to the buyer (or drawee) only upon the buyer's acceptance of the attached draft.

Draft (or Bill of exchange)—An unconditional order in writing from one person (the drawer)

to another (the drawee), directing the Drawee to pay a specified amount to a named Drawer at a fixed or determinable future date. See Date draft, Sight draft, Time draft.

Drawback—Articles manufactured or produced in the United States with the use of imported components or raw materials and later exported are entitled to a refund of up to ninety-nine percent of the duty charged on the imported components. The refund of duty is known as a "drawback."

Drawee—The individual or firm on whom a draft is drawn and who owes the stated amount. Compare **Drawer.** Also see **Draft.**

Drawer—The individual or firm that issues or signs a draft and thus stands to receive payment of the stated amount from the drawee. Compare **Drawee.** Also see **Draft.**

Dumping—Exporting/importing merchandise into a country below the costs incurred in production and shipment.

Duty—A tax imposed on imports by the customs authority of a country. Duties are generally based on the value of the goods (ad valorem duties), some other factor such as weight or quantity (specific duties), or a combination of value and other factors (compound duties).

EMC—See **Export management company.**

ETC—See **Export trading company.**

Eurodollars—U.S. dollars placed on deposit in banks outside the United States; usually refers to deposits in Europe.

EX—"From." When used in pricing terms such as "Ex Factory" or "Ex Dock," it signifies that the price quoted applies only at the point of origin (in the two examples, at the seller's factory or a dock at the import point). In practice, this kind of quotation indicates that the seller agrees to place the goods at the disposal of the buyer at the specified place within a fixed period of time.

Exchange permit—A government permit

sometimes required by the importer's government to enable the importers to convert his or her own country's currency into foreign currency with which to pay a seller in another country.

Exchange rate—The price of one currency in terms of another, i.e., the number of units of one currency that may be exchanged for one unit of another currency.

Eximbank—The Export-Import Bank of the United States.

Export broker—An individual or firm that brings together buyers and sellers for a fee but does not take part in actual sales transactions.

Export commission house—An organization which, for a commission, acts as a purchasing agent for a foreign buyer.

Export declaration—See **Shipper's export declaration.**

Export license—A government document that permits the "Licensee" to engage in the export of designated goods to certain destinations. (See **General and Validated licenses.**)

Export management company—A private firm that serves as the export department for several manufacturers, soliciting and transacting export business on behalf of its clients in return for a commission, salary, or retainer plus commission.

Export trading company—A firm similar or identical to an export management company.

F.A.S.—"Free Alongside." A pricing term indicating that the quoted price includes the cost of delivering the goods alongside a designated vessel.

F.I.—"Free in." A pricing term indicating that the charterer of a vessel is responsible for the cost of loading and unloading goods from the vessel.

Floating policy—See **Open policy.**

F.O.—"Free out." A pricing term indicating that the charterer of a vessel is responsible for the cost of loading goods from the vessel.

F.O.B.—"Free on board." A pricing term indicating that the quoted price includes the cost of loading the goods into transport vessels at the specified place.

Force majeure—The title of a standard clause in marine contracts exempting the parties for nonfulfillment of their obligations as a result of conditions beyond their control, such as earthquakes, floods, or war.

Foreign exchange—The currency or credit instruments of a foreign country. Also, transactions involving purchase and/or sale of currencies.

Foreign freight forwarder—See **Freight forwarder.**

Foreign sales agent—An individual or firm that serves as the foreign representative of a domestic supplier and seeks sales abroad for the supplier.

Foreign sales corporation (FSC)—An organization formed by American manufacturers or export groups to obtain U.S. tax incentives for export sales. FSCs are a valuable tool for increasing export profits.

Foreign trade zone—See **Free trade zone.**

Foul bill of lading—A receipt for goods issued by a carrier with an indication that the goods were damaged when received. Compare **Clean bill of lading.**

Free port—An area such as a port city into which merchandise may legally be moved without payment of duties.

Free trade zone—A port designated by the government of a country for duty-free entry of any non-prohibited goods. Merchandise may be stored, displayed, used for manufacturing, etc., within the zone and reexported without duties being paid. Duties are imposed on the merchandise (or items manufactured from the merchandise) only when the goods pass from the zone into an area of the country subject to the Customs Authority.

Freight forwarder—An independent business which handles export shipments for compensation. (A freight forwarder is among the best sources of information and assistance on U.S. export regulations and documentation, shipping methods, and foreign import regulations.)

GATT—"General Agreement on Tariffs and Trade." A multilateral treaty intended to help reduce trade barriers between the signatory countries and to promote trade through tariff concessions.

General export license—Any of various export licenses covering export commodities for which **Validated export licenses** are not required. No formal application or written authorization is needed to ship exports under a General export license.

Gross weight—The full weight of a shipment, including goods and packaging. Compare **Tare weight.**

Import license—A document required and issued by some national governments authorizing the importation of goods into their individual countries.

Inland bill of lading—A bill of lading used in transporting goods overland to the exporter's international carrier. Although a **Through bill of lading** can sometimes be used, it is usually necessary to prepare both an inland bill of lading and an **Ocean bill of lading** for export shipments. Compare **Air waybill, Ocean bill of lading,** and **Through bill of lading.**

International freight forwarder—See **Freight forwarder.**

Irrevocable letter of credit—A letter of credit in which the specified payment is guaranteed by the bank if all terms and conditions are met by the drawee. Compare **Revocable letter of credit.**

Letter of credit (L/C)—A document, issued by a bank per instructions by a buyer of goods, authorizing the seller to draw a speci-

fied sum of money under specified terms, usually the receipt by the bank of certain documents within a given time.

Licensing—A business arrangement in which the manufacturer of a product (or a firm with proprietary rights over certain technology, trademarks, etc.) grants permission to some other group or individual to manufacture that product (or make use of that proprietary material) in return for specified royalties or other payment.

Manifest—See **Ship's manifest.**

Marine insurance—Insurance that compensates the owners of goods transported overseas in the event of loss that cannot be legally recovered from the carrier. Also covers air shipments. Compare **Credit risk insurance.**

Marking (or marks)—Letters, numbers, and other symbols placed on cargo packages to facilitate identification.

Ocean bill of lading—A Bill of lading (B/L) indicating that the exporter consigns a shipment to an international carrier for transportation to a specified foreign market. Unlike an **Inland B/L,** the **Ocean B/L** also serves as a collection document. If it is a "straight" **B/L,** the foreign buyer can obtain the shipment from the carrier by simply showing proof of identity. If a "negotiable" **B/L** is used, the buyer must first pay for the goods, post a bond, or meet other conditions agreeable to the seller. Compare **Air waybill, Inland bill of lading,** and **Through bill of lading.**

On board bill of lading (B/L)—A Bill of lading in which a carrier certifies that goods have been placed on board a certain vessel.

Open account—A trade arrangement in which goods are shipped to a foreign buyer without guarantee of payment. The obvious risk this method poses to the supplier makes it essential that the buyer's integrity be unquestionable.

Open insurance policy—A marine insurance policy that applies to all shipments made by an exporter over a period of time rather than to one shipment only.

"Order" fill of lading (B/L)—A negotiable **Bill of lading** made out to the order of the shipper.

Packing list—A list showing the number and kinds of items being shipped, as well as other information needed for transportation purposes.

Parcel post receipt—The postal authorities' signed acknowledgment of delivery to receiver of a shipment made by parcel post.

PEFCO (Private Export Funding Corporation)—lends to foreign buyers to finance exports from U.S.

Perils of the sea—A marine insurance term used to designate heavy weather, stranding, lightning, collision, and sea water damage.

Phytosanitary Inspection Certificate—A certificate, issued by the U.S. Department of Agriculture to satisfy import regulations for foreign countries, indicating that a U.S. shipment has been inspected and is free from harmful pests and plant diseases.

Political risk—In export financing the risk of loss due to such causes as currency inconvertibility, government action preventing entry of goods, expropriation or confiscation, war, etc.

Pro forma invoice—An invoice provided by a supplier prior to the shipment of merchandise, informing the buyer of the kinds and quantities of goods to be sent, their value, and important specifications (weight, size, etc.).

Purchasing agent—An agent who purchases goods in his or her own country on behalf of foreign importers such as government agencies and large private concerns.

Quota—The quantity of goods of a specific kind that a country permits to be imported without restriction or imposition of additional **Duties.**

Quotation—An offer to sell goods at a stated price and under specified conditions.

Remitting bank—Bank that sends the **Draft** to overseas bank for collection.

Representative—See **Foreign sales agent.**

Revocable letter of credit—A **Letter of credit** that can be cancelled or altered by the **Drawee** (buyer) after it has been issued by the drawee's bank. Compare **Irrevocable letter of credit.**

Schedule B—Refers to "Schedule B, Statistical Classification of Domestic and Foreign Commodities Exported from the United States." All commodities exported from the United States must be assigned a seven-digit Schedule B number.

Shipper's export declaration—A form required by the U.S. Treasury Department for all shipments and prepared by a shipper, indicating the value, weight, destination, and other basic information about an export shipment.

Ship's manifest—An instrument in writing, signed by the captain of a ship, that lists the individual shipments constituting the ship's cargo.

Sight draft (S/D)—A draft that is payable upon presentation to the drawee. Compare **Date draft, Time draft.**

Spot exchange—The purchase or sale of foreign exchange for immediate delivery.

Standard Industrial Classification (SIC)—A standard numerical code system used by the U.S. Government to classify products and services.

Standard International Trade Classification (SITC)—A standard numerical code system developed by the United Nations to classify commodities used in international trade.

Steamship conference—A group of steamship operators that operate under mutually agreed upon freight rates.

Straight bill of lading—A non-negotiable **Bill of lading** in which the goods are consigned directly to a named consignee.

Tare weight—The weight of a container and packing materials without the weight of the goods it contains. Compare **Gross weight.**

Tenor (or a Draft)—Designation of a payment as being due at sight, a given number of days after sight, or a given number of days after date.

Through bill of lading—A single **Bill of lading** converting both the domestic and international carriage of an export shipment. An **Air waybill,** for instance, is essentially a through bill of lading used for air shipments. Ocean shipments, on the other hand, usually require two separate documents—an **Inland bill of lading** for domestic carriage and an **Ocean bill of lading** for international carriage. **Through bills of lading** are insufficient for ocean shipments. Compare **Air waybill, Inland bill of lading, Ocean bill of lading.**

Time draft—A draft that matures either a certain number of days after acceptance or a certain number of days after the date of the draft. Compare **Date draft, Sight draft.**

Tramp steamer—A ship not operating on regular routes or schedules.

Transaction statement—A document that delineates the terms and conditions agreed upon between the importer and exporter.

Trust receipt—Release of merchandise by a bank to a buyer in which the bank retains title to the merchandise. The buyer, who obtains the goods for manufacturing or sales purposes, is obligated to maintain the goods (or the proceeds from their sale) distinct from the remainder of his or her assets and to hold them ready for repossession by the bank.

Validated export license—A required document issued by the U.S. Government authorizing the export of specific commodities. This license is for a specific transaction or time period in which the exporting is to take place. Compare **General export license.**

Warehouse receipt—A receipt issued by a warehouse listing goods received for storage.

Wharfage—A charge assessed by a pier or dock owner for handling incoming or outgoing cargo.

Without reserve—A term indicating that a shipper's agent or representative is empowered to make definitive decisions and adjustments abroad without approval of the group or individual represented. Compare **Advisory capacity.**

SECTION 4

DIRECTORY OF FEDERAL ASSISTANCE *

Here we provide a directory of federal agencies which offer international services to private individuals, companies, and associations. Services offered include technical assistance, grants, low-interest loans, and project financing. It's a good idea to get to know individuals in these agencies as they can be helpful in providing you with specific information about industries and markets, contact names, and so forth. Most of these agencies are set up to answer even the most general or basic questions relating to international business—don't be afraid to use these resources!

This directory covers the federal agencies most directly connected to international business. If these agencies cannot help you, they frequently are able to refer you to other agencies and/or organizations that can.

1. U.S. Department of Commerce
2. Small Business Administration
3. Export-Import Bank
4. U.S. Department of Agriculture
5. Overseas Private Investment Corporation (OPIC)
6. Department of the Treasury/U.S. Customs Service
7. Agency for International Development
8. U.S. Trade Representative

1. U.S. Department of Commerce

The U.S. Department of Commerce can provide a wealth of information to exporters. The first step an exporter should take is to contact the nearest US&FCS District Office. For more specific information on who to contact in Washington, D.C., the Export Counseling Center (below) can help guide the exporter to the right person or office.

* Source: U.S. Department of Commerce.

153

To send inquiries to or to communicate with the following offices, the address should include the office name, the office room number, followed by: U.S. Department of Commerce, Washington, DC 20230 (exceptions noted).

Area Code: 202

U.S. and Foreign Commercial Service

Office of Domestic Operations
* Export Counseling Center: Room 1066 (Export counseling and marketing assistance) 377-3181

Export Promotion Services
* Office of Information Product Development and Distribution: P.O. Box 14207, Washington, DC 20044 (Information on foreign markets, customers, and trade leads) 377-2432
* Office of Marketing Programs: (Trade show and trade mission information) Room 2116 377-4231
* Information on *Commercial News USA* and other Commerce export-related publications 377-5367

Office of Foreign Operations

Regional Coordinators for:
* Africa, Near East and South Asia: Room 3104 377-2736
* East Asia and Pacific: Room 3104 377-2736
* Europe: Room 3122 377-1599
* Western Hemisphere: Room 3122 377-1599

Trade Development

Product/Service Specialists:
* Aerospace: Room 6877 377-8228
* Automotive Affairs and Consumer Goods: Room 4324 377-0823
* Basic Industries: Room 4045 377-0614
* Capital Goods & International Construction: Rm 2001B . . . 377-5023
* Export Trading Company Affairs: Room 1223 377-5131

* International Major Projects: Room 2015B 377-5225
* Services: Room 1128 377-5261
* Telecommunications: Room 1001A 377-4466
* Textiles and Apparel: Room 3100 377-3737
* Trade Information and Analysis: Room 3814B 377-1316

Trade Administration

Office of Export Administration
* Exporter's Service Staff: (Export licensing, controls, etc.) Room 1099 377-4811

Office of Antiboycott Compliance: Room 6098 377-2381

Minority Business Development Agency

Minority Export Development Consulting Program Office: Room 5096 377-3237

International Economic Policy

Country Desk Officers can provide specific country information relating to international trade. The following is a list of country desk officers.

Listing of ITA desk officers

Country	Phone	Room
Afghanistan	377-2954	2029-B
Albania	377-2645	3419
Algeria	377-4652	2033
Angola	377-5148	3317
Argentina	377-5427	3021
ASEAN	377-3875	2032
Australia	377-3647	2310
Austria	377-2920	3411
Bahamas	377-2527	3029-A
Bahrain	377-5545	2039
Bangladesh	377-2954	2029-B
Barbados	377-2527	3029-A
Belgium	377-5401	3415
Belize	377-2527	3029-A

Listing of ITA desk officers (continued)

Country	Phone	Room
Benin	377-4564	3317
Bermuda	377-2527	3029-A
Bhutan	377-2954	2029-B
Bolivia	377-4302	3314
Botswana	377-5148	3317
Brazil	377-3871	3017
Brunei	377-3875	2310
Bulgaria	377-2645	3419
Burkina Faso	377-4564	3317
Burma	377-5334	3820
Burundi	377-0357	3318
Cambodia	377-4681	2323
Cameroon	377-0357	3317
Canada	377-3101	3314
Cape Verde	377-4564	3317
Caymans	377-2527	3029-A
Central African Rep.	377-0357	3317
Chad	377-4564	3317
Chile	377-1495	3027
Columbia	377-1659	3027
Comoros	377-4564	3317
Congo	377-0357	3317
Costa Rica	377-2527	3029-A
Cuba	377-2527	3029-A
Cyprus	377-3945	3044
Czechoslovakia	377-2645	3419
Denmark	377-3254	3413
D'Jibouti	377-4564	3320
Dominican Rep.	377-2527	3016
East Caribbean	377-2527	3022
Ecuador	377-4302	3027
Egypt	377-4652	2033
El Salvador	377-2527	3029-A
Equatorial Guinea	377-0357	3318
Ethiopia	377-4564	3320
European Community	377-5276	3034
Finland	377-3254	3413
France	377-8008	3042
French Guyana	377-2523	3029-A
Gabon	377-0357	3317
Gambia	377-4564	3317
German Democratic Rep.	377-2645	3419
Germany (West)	377-2434	3411
Ghana	377-4388	3317
Greece	377-3945	3044

Country	Phone	Room
Grenada	377-2527	3029-A
Guatemala	377-2527	3022
Guadeloupe	377-2527	3029-A
Guinea	377-4564	3317
Guinea-Bissau	377-4564	3317
Guyana	377-2527	3029-A
Haiti	377-2527	3029-A
Honduras	377-2527	3029-A
Hong Kong	377-2462	2323
Hungary	377-2645	3421
Iceland	377-3254	3413
India	377-2954	2029-B
Indonesia	377-3875	2032
Iran	377-5767	2039
Iraq	377-4781	2039
Ireland	377-4104	3415
Israel	377-4652	2039
Italy	377-2177	3045
Ivory Coast	377-4388	3317
Jamaica	377-2527	3029-A
Japan	377-2425	2318
Jordan	377-5767	2038
Kampuchea	377-4681	2323
Kenya	377-4564	3317
Korea	377-4957	2034
Kuwait	377-4441	2039
Laos	377-3583	2325
Lebanon	377-5767	2039
Lesotho	377-5148	3317
Liberia	377-4564	3317
Libya	377-5737	2039
Luxembourg	377-5401	3415
Macao	377-3853	2325
Madagascar	377-0357	3317
Malaysia	377-3875	2310
Malawi	377-5148	2310
Maldives	377-2954	2029-B
Mali	377-4564	3320
Malta	377-5401	3415
Martinique	377-2527	3029-A
Mauritania	377-4564	3317
Mauritius	377-0357	3317
Mexico	377-4464	3028
Mongolia	377-3932	3217
Morocco	377-5737	2039
Mozambique	377-5148	3317
Namibia	377-5148	3319
Nepal	377-2954	2029-B
Netherlands	377-5401	3415

Listing of ITA desk officers (continued)

Country	Phone	Room
Netherlands		
Antilles	377-2527	3029-A
New Zealand	377-3647	2310
Nicaragua	377-2527	3029-A
Niger	377-4564	3317
Nigeria	377-4388	3321
Norway	377-4414	3413
Oman	377-5545	2039
Pacific Islands	377-3647	2310
Pakistan	377-2954	1029-B
Panama	377-2527	3029-A
Paraguay	377-5427	3021
People's Republic		
of China	377-3583	2317
Peru	377-4302	3027
Philippines	377-3875	2310
Poland	377-2645	3419
Portugal	377-3945	3042
Puerto Rico	377-2527	3029-A
Qatar	377-5545	2039
Romania	377-2645	3419
Rwanda	377-0357	3317
Sao Tome &		
Principe	377-0357	3317
Saudi Arabia	377-4652	2039
Senegal	377-4564	3317
Seychelles	377-4564	3320
Sierra Leone	377-4564	3317
Singapore	377-3875	2310
Somalia	377-4564	3317
South Africa	377-4564	3317
Spain	377-4508	3042
Sri Lanka	377-2954	2029-B
St. Barthelemy	377-2527	3029-A
St. Martin	377-2527	3029-A
Sudan	377-4564	3317
Suriname	377-2527	3029-A
Swaziland	377-2920	3317
Sweden	377-4414	3413
Switzerland	377-2897	3044
Syria	377-5767	2039
Taiwan	377-4957	2034
Tanzania	377-4564	3317
Thailand	377-3875	2032
Togo	377-4564	3317
Trinidad &		
Tobago	377-2527	3029-A
Tunisia	377-4652	2039

Country	Phone	Room
Turks & Caicos		
Islands	377-2527	3029-A
Turkey	377-3945	3042
Uganda	377-4564	3317
U.S.S.R.	377-4655	3414
United Arab		
Emirates	377-5545	2039
United Kingdom	377-3748	4212
Uruguay	377-5427	3021
Venezuela	377-4303	3027
Vietnam	377-4681	2323
Virgin Islands (U.K.)	377-2527	3029-A
Virgin Islands (U.S.)	377-2912	3016
Yemen	377-4652	2039
Yugoslavia	377-5373	3046
Zaire	377-0357	3317
Zambia	377-5148	3317
Zimbabwe	377-5148	3317

2. Small Business Administration (SBA)

All export programs administered through SBA are available through SBA Field Offices. More information about the programs can be obtained through:

Small Business Administration (SBA)(202) 653-6365
Office of International Trade(800) 368-5855
1441 L Street, NW.
Washington, DC 20416

3. Export Import Bank

Export Import Bank
811 Vermont Ave., NW.
Washington, D.C. 20571

Area Code: 202
Main phone number 566-2117
Assistance 566-8944
Engineering Division 566-8802
Small Business Assistance
Hotline . . . . (800) 424-5201

4. U.S. Department of Agriculture

U.S. Department of Agriculture
14th Street and Independence Avenue, SW.
Washington, D.C. 20250Area Code: 202

Foreign Agriculture Service

Commodity and Marketing Programs:

Dairy, Livestock and Poultry . .	447-8031
Grain and Feed Division . . .	447-6219
Horticulture and Tropical Plants	447-6590
Oilseed and Oilseed Products	447-7037
Tobacco, Cotton and Seed . .	382-9516
Forest Products	382-8138

Export Programs
   Division—Processed Foods . 447-3031

Minority and Small Business
   Coordinator 382-9458
Agricultural Information & Marketing Service
   (AIMS) 447-7103

5. Overseas Private Investment Corporation (OPIC)

Overseas Private Investment Corporation
   (OPIC) . . . . (202) 457-7010
1615 M St., NW., Suite 400
Washington D.C. 20527

6. U.S. Department of Treasury

U.S. Department of Treasury
15th Street and Pennsylvania Ave., NW.
Washington, D.C. 20220
U.S. Customs Strategic Investigation
   Division . . . . (202) 566-2140

7. Agency for International Development (AID)

Agency for International Development (AID)
Department of State Building
320 21st Street, NW.
Washington, D.C. 20523
Office of Business
   Relations . . . . (202) 647-1850

8. Office of the United States Trade Representative

Winder Building
600 17th Street, NW.
Washington, D.C. 20506 . Area Code: 202

General Counsel	395-3150
Private Sector Liaison	395-6120
Agricultural Affairs &	
Commodity Policy	395-6127
The Americas Trade Policy . . .	395-6135
East-West & Non-Market	
Economies	395-4543
Europe & Mediterranean	395-4620
General Agreement on Tariff	
& Trade (GATT)	395-6843
Services and Investment	395-7320
Pacific, and Asia Trade Policy . .	395-3430
Japan	395-3900

SECTION 5

U.S. DEPARTMENT OF COMMERCE DISTRICT OFFICES

District offices of the U.S. Department of Commerce are set up specifically to help local companies in their business dealings overseas. Should you or your company wish to "go international," should you need information about U.S. customs or trade regulations, or should you simply have questions about new markets or industries, your local Commerce office is a good first stop for information. If they are unable to help you, district Commerce offices will refer you to other bureaus and/or organizations which can.

ALABAMA, Birmingham—2015 2nd Ave. N., 3rd Flr. Berry Bldg., 35203. Tel: (205) 731-1331.

ALASKA, Anchorage—222 West 7th Ave., P.O. Box 32, 99513. Tel: (907) 271-5041.

ARIZONA, Phoenix—Fed. Bldg. & U.S. Courthouse, 230 N. 1st Ave., Rm. 3412, 85025. Tel: (602) 261-3285.

ARKANSAS, Little Rock—Ste. 811, 320 W. Capitol Ave., 72201. Tel: (501) 378-5794.

CALIFORNIA, Los Angeles—Rm. 800, 11777 San Vicente Blvd., 90049. Tel: (213) 209-6705.

San Diego—6363 Greenwich Dr., 92122. Tel: (619) 557-5395.

San Francisco—Fed. Bldg. Box 6013, 450 Golden Gate Ave., 94102. Tel: (415) 556-5860.

COLORADO, Denver—Suite 600, 1625 Broadway, 80202. Tel: (303) 844-3246.

CONNECTICUT, Hartford—Rm. 610-B, Fed. Bldg., 450 Main St., 06103. Tel: (203) 240-3530.

DELAWARE, Serviced by Philadelphia D.O.

DISTRICT OF COLUMBIA, Serviced by Baltimore D.O.

159

FLORIDA, Miami—224 Fed. Bldg., 51 SW. 1st Ave., 33130. Tel: (305) 536-5267.

Clearwater—128 N. Osceola Ave., 34615. Tel: (813) 461-0011.

Jacksonville—3100 University Blvd., 5, Independence Square, 32202. Tel: (904) 791-2796.

Orlando—111 N. Orange Ave., 32802. Tel: (407) 648-1608.

Tallahassee—107 W. Gaines St., Rm. 401, 32304. Tel: (904) 488-6469.

GEORGIA, Atlanta—Suite 504, 1365 Peachtree St., NE., 30309. Tel: (404) 347-7000.

Savannah—Fed. Bldg., Rm. A-107, 120 Barnard St., 31401. Tel: (912) 944-4202.

HAWAII, Honolulu—4106 Fed. Bldg., P.O. Box 50026, 300 Ala Moana Blvd., 96850. Tel: (808) 541-1782

IDAHO, Boise—2nd Floor, 700 W. State St., 83720. Tel: (208) 334-3857.

ILLINOIS, Chicago—1406 Mid Continental Plaza Bldg., 55 East Monroe St., 60603. Tel: (312) 353-4450.

Palatine—Harper College, Algonquin & Roselle Rd., 60067. Tel: (312) 397-3000.

Rockford—515 N. Court St., P.O. Box 1747, 61110-0247. Tel: (815) 987-8123

INDIANA, Indianapolis—One N. Capital, Ste. 520, 46204. Tel: (317) 226-6214.

IOWA, Des Moines—817 Fed. Bldg., 210 Walnut St., 50309. Tel: (515) 284-4222.

KANSAS, Wichita (Kansas City, MO, District)—River Park Pl., Ste. 580, 727 N. Waco, 67203. Tel: (316) 269-6160.

KENTUCKY, Louisville—Rm 636B, 601 W. Broadway, 40202. Tel: (502) 582-5066.

LOUISIANA, New Orleans—432 World Trade Ctr. No. 2 Canal St. 70130. Tel: (504) 589-6546.

MAINE, Augusta (Boston, MA, Districts)—77 Sewell St. 04330. Tel: (207) 622-8249.

MARYLAND, Baltimore—415 U.S. Customhouse, Gay & Lombard Sts., 21202. Tel: (301) 962-3560.

MASSACHUSETTS, Boston—World Trade Center Boston, Commonwealth Pier, Ste. 307, 02210. Tel: (617) 565-8563.

MICHIGAN, Detroit—1140 McNamara Bldg., 477 Michigan Ave., 48226. Tel: (313) 226-3650.

Grand Rapids—300 Monroe N.W., Rm. 409, 49503. Tel: (616) 456-2411.

MINNESOTA, Minneapolis—108 Fed. Bldg., 110 S. 4th St., 55401. Tel: (612) 348-1638.

MISSISSIPPI, Jackson—300 Woodrow Wilson Blvd., Ste. 328, 39213. Tel: (601) 965-4388.

MISSOURI, St. Louis—7911 Forsyth Blvd., Ste. 610, 63105. Tel: (314) 425-3302.

Kansas City—Rm. 635, 601 E. 12th St., 64106. Tel: (816) 374-3141.

MONTANA, Serviced by Denver D.O.

NEBRASKA, Omaha—1133 "O" St., 68137. Tel: (402) 221-3664.

NEVADA, Reno—1755 E. Plumb Ln., #152, 89502. Tel: (702) 784-5203.

NEW HAMPSHIRE, Serviced by Boston D.O.

NEW JERSEY, Trenton—3131 Princeton Pike, Bldg. 6, Ste. 100, 08648. Tel: (609) 989-2100.

NEW MEXICO, Albuquerque—5000 Marble NE, Ste. 320, 87110. Tel: (505) 262-6024.

NEW YORK, Buffalo—1312 Fed. Bldg., 111 W. Huron St., 14202. Tel: (716) 846-4191.

Rochester—121 E. Ave., 14604. Tel: (716) 263-6480.

New York—Fed. Bldg., 26 Fed. Plaza, Foley Sq., 10278. Tel: (212) 264-0634.

NORTH CAROLINA, Greensboro—203 Fed. Bldg., 324 W. Market St., P.O. Box 1950, 27402. Tel: (919) 333-5345.

NORTH DAKOTA, Serviced by Omaha D.O.

OHIO, Cincinnati—9504 Fed. Bldg., 550 Main St., 45202. Tel: (513) 684-2944.

Cleveland—Rm. 668, 666 Euclid Ave., 44114. Tel: (216) 522-4750.

OKLAHOMA, Oklahoma City—6601 Broadway Ext., Ste. 200, 73116. Tel: (405) 231-5302.

Tulsa—440 S. Houston St., 74127. Tel: (918) 581-7650.

OREGON, Portland—Rm. 618, 1220 SW. 3rd Ave., 97204. Tel: (503) 221-3001.

PENNSYLVANIA, Philadelphia—475 Allendale Rd., Ste. 202, King of Prussia, 19406. Tel: (215) 962-4980.

Pittsburgh—2002 Fed. Bldg., 1000 Liberty Ave., 15222. Tel: (412) 644-2850.

PUERTO RICO, San Juan (Hato Rey)—Rm. G-55 Fed. Bldg., 00918. Tel: (809) 766-5555.

RHODE ISLAND, Providence (Boston, MA, District)—7 Jackson Walkway, 02903. Tel: (401) 528-5104.

SOUTH CAROLINA, Columbia—Fed. Bldg., Suite 172, 1835 Assembly St. 29201. Tel: (803) 765-5345.

Charleston—Rm. 128, 9 Liberty St., 29424. Tel: (803) 724-4361.

SOUTH DAKOTA, Serviced by Omaha D.O.

TENNESSEE, Nashville—Ste. 1114 Parkway Towers, 404 Jas. Robertson Pkwy., 37219-1505. Tel: (615) 736-5161.

Memphis—22 N. Front St., Ste. 200, 38101. Tel: (901) 521-4137.

TEXAS, Dallas—Rm. 7A5, 1100 Commerce St., 75242. Tel: (214) 767-0542.

Austin—400 1st City Ctr., 816 Congress Ave., 78711. Tel: (512) 482-5939.

Houston—2625 Fed. Courthouse, 515 Rusk St., 77002. Tel: (713) 229-2578.

UTAH, Salt Lake City—Rm. 340 U.S. Courthouse, 350 S. Main St., 84101. Tel: (801) 524-5116.

VERMONT, Serviced by Boston D.O.

VIRGINIA, Richmond—8010 Fed. Bldg., 400 N. 8th St., 23240. Tel: (804) 771-2246.

WASHINGTON, Seattle—3131 Elliott Ave., Ste. 290, 98121. Tel: (206) 442-5616.

Spokane—W. 808 Spokane Falls Blvd., Rm. 623, 99210. Tel: (509) 439-4557.

WEST VIRGINIA, Charleston—3000 New 42 Fed. Bldg., 500 Quarrier St., 25301. Tel: (304) 347-5123.

WISCONSIN, Milwaukee—Fed. Bldg., U.S. Courthouse, 517 E. Wisc. Ave., 53202. Tel: (414) 291-3473.

WYOMING, Serviced by Denver D.O.

SECTION 6

SOURCES OF STATE ASSISTANCE

Most states offer assistance to companies that wish to enter, or are already players in, the global market. State assistance can take a variety of forms, such as seminars and conferences, counseling and technical assistance, market research, trade show sponsorship and coordination, trade missions, and financing assistance. State assistance can be provided by state offices of federal government agencies and organizations, or by state government agencies. Information and incentives are highly decentralized across the country and forms of assistance differ from state to state. State officials are in the best position to ensure that you take advantage of any and all opportunities for state aid and resources.

SOURCES OF STATE ASSISTANCE*

	ALABAMA	ALASKA	ARIZONA	ARKANSAS	CALIFORNIA	COLORADO	CONNECTICUT	DELAWARE	FLORIDA	GEORGIA	HAWAII	IDAHO	ILLINOIS	INDIANA	IOWA	KANSAS	KENTUCKY	LOUISIANA (d)	MAINE	MARYLAND	MASSACHUSETTS	MICHIGAN	MINNESOTA
Seminars/ conferences	●		●	●	●	●	●	●	●	●	●	●	●	●	●	●	●	●		●	●	●	●
One-on-one counseling	●		●	●	●	●	●		●	●	●		●	●	●	●	●	●		●	●	●	●
Market studies prepared			●	●		●	●		●	●			●			●					●	●	
Language bank			●	●											●	●							
Referrals to local export services	●			●			●	●	●		●	●		●			●	●			●		●
Newsletter			●	●	●(a)		●										●			●		●	●
How-to handbook	●				●(b)										●	●	●					●	
Sales leads disseminated	●		●	●	●	●	●	●	●	●	●	●	●	●	●	●	●	●		●	●	●	●
Trade shows	●	●	●	●	●	●	●	●	●	●	●	●	●	●	●	●	●	●			●	●	●
Trade missions	●	●	●	●	●	●	●		●	●	●	●	●	●	●	●	●	●		●	●	●	●
Foreign offices reps.	●	●		●				●		●	●(c)		●	●	●		●			●		●	●
Operational financing program					●									●	●								●

*Source: National Association of State Development Agencies, State Export Program Database, January 1985.

MISSISSIPPI	MISSOURI	MONTANA	NEBRASKA	NEVADA	NEW HAMPSHIRE	NEW JERSEY	NEW MEXICO	NEW YORK	NORTH CAROLINA	NORTH DAKOTA	OHIO	OKLAHOMA	OREGON	PENNSYLVANIA	RHODE ISLAND	SOUTH CAROLINA	SOUTH DAKOTA	TENNESSEE	TEXAS	UTAH	VERMONT	VIRGINIA	WASHINGTON	WEST VIRGINIA	WISCONSIN	WYOMING
●	●	●	●	●	●	●	●	●	●	●	●	●	●	●	●	●	●	●	●	●	●	●	●	●	●	●
●	●	●	●		●	●	●	●	●	●	●	●	●	●	●	●	●	●	●	●	●	●				●
●	●	●						●			●		●	●		●	●	●	●	●			●	●		
			●	●				●			●	●				●					●					
●	●	●	●		●	●	●	●	●		●	●		●	●	●						●		●		
●	●			●		●	●	●		●	●	●	●	●	●						●			●		●
●	●	●	●		●		●	●				●	●					●	●	●		●	●			
●	●	●	●		●	●	●	●	●	●	●	●	●	●	●	●	●	●	●	●	●		●		●	●
●	●	●	●			●	●	●	●	●	●	●	●	●	●	●	●		●	●	●			●		●
●	●	●		●		●	●		●	●		●	●		●	●		●		●		●	●	●	●	●
	●					●	●	●		●			●			●	●	●		●	●	●	●		●	
●										●																

Notes: See next page for notes and explanation of programs.

State trade development services explanation and footnotes

- **Seminars/conferences**—State sponsors seminars for exporters, either basic, specific function, or specific market.
- **One-on-one counseling**—State staff provides actual export counseling to individual businesses in addition to making appropriate referrals.
- **Market studies prepared**—State staff prepares specific market studies for individual companies.
- **Language bank**—State program to match foreign-speaking visitors with bilingual local residents who provide volunteer translation services.
- **Referrals to local export services**—Matching exporters with exporter services, e.g. matchmaker fair, export service directory, individual referrals, etc.
- **Newsletter**—State publishes an international trade newsletter.
- **How-to handbook**—State publishes a basic how-to-export handbook.
- **Sales leads disseminated**—State collects and distributes sales leads to in-state businesses.
- **Trade shows**—State assists with and accompanies or represents businesses on trade shows.
- **Trade missions**—State assists with and accompanies businesses on trade missions.
- **Foreign offices/reps**—State office or contractual representative located abroad.
- **Operational financing program**—State export financing assistance program that is currently operational.

Footnotes:

(a) California issues a bimonthly column to local chambers and trade groups for publication in their newsletters.

(b) California produces a "road map" to low cost and free trade services.

(c) Georgia's foreign offices are only active in attracting reverse investment.

(d) Louisiana has recently established a new Office of International Trade, Finance and Development within the Department of Commerce and Industry. The office is expected to offer a full range of trade promotion services.

State & local sources of assistance

Alabama

U.S. Department of Commerce

US&FCS District Office
3rd Floor, Berry Building
2015 2nd Avenue North
Birmingham, Alabama 35203
(205) 254-1331

U.S. Small Business Administration
2121 8th Avenue North
Suite 3200, 35203-2398
(205) 731-1344

Office of International Trade
Department of Economic and
  Community Affairs
P.O. Box 2939
Montgomery, Alabama 36105-0939
(205) 284-8721

Alaska

U.S. Department of Commerce

US&FCS District Office
701 C Street
P.O. Box 32
Anchorage, Alaska 99513
(907) 271-5041

U.S. Small Business Administration
222 West 8th Avenue, #67
Anchorage, Alaska 99513-7559
(907) 271-4022

U.S. Small Business Administration
101 12th Avenue, Box 14
Fairbanks, Alaska 99701
(907) 452-0211

Alaska State Chamber of Commerce
217 Second Street, Suite 201
Juneau, Alaska 99801
(907) 586-2323

Anchorage Chamber of Commerce
437 East Street, Suite 300
Anchorage, Alaska 99501
(907) 272-2401

Department of Commerce
and Economic Development
P.O. Box D
Juneau, Alaska 99811
(907) 465-2500

Fairbanks Chamber of Commerce
First National Center
P.O. Box 74446
Fairbanks, Alaska 99707
(907) 452-1105

Arizona

U.S. Department of Commerce

US&FCS District Office
Fed. Building & U.S. Courthouse
230 North 1st Avenue, Room 3412
Phoenix, Arizona 85025
(602) 254-3285

U.S. Small Business Administration
2005 North Central Avenue, 5th Floor
Phoenix, Arizona 85004
(602) 261-3732

U.S. Small Business Administration
301 West Congress Street, Box FB 33
Tucson, Arizona 85701
(602) 629-6715

Arizona World Trade Association
34 West Monroe, Suite 900
Phoenix, Arizona 85003
(602) 254-5521

Director of International Trade
Office of Economic Planning
and Development
1700 West Washington Street,
Room 505
Phoenix, Arizona 85007
(602) 542-5371

Foreign Trade Zone No. 48
Papago Agency
P.O. Box 578
Sells, Arizona 85634
(602) 383-2611

Foreign Trade Zone No. 60
Border Industrial Development, Inc.
P.O. Box 578
Nogales, Arizona 85621
(602) 281-2029

Arkansas

U.S. Department of Commerce

US&FCS District Office
320 West Capitol Avenue,
Room 635
Little Rock, Arkansas 72201
(501) 378-5794

U.S. Small Business Administration
320 West Capitol Avenue, Room 601
Little Rock, Arkansas 72201
(501) 378-5871

International Marketing
Department of Economic Development
1 Capitol Mall
Little Rock, Arkansas 72201
(501) 682-7678

California

U.S. Department of Commerce

US&FCS District Office
11777 San Vicente Boulevard
Room 800
Los Angeles, California 90049
(213) 209-6707

U.S. Department of Commerce
US&FCS District Office
Federal Building, Room 15205
450 Golden Gate Avenue
Box 36013
San Francisco, California 94102
(415) 556-5860

U.S. Small Business Administration
2719 North Air Fresno Drive
Fresno, California 93727
(209) 487-5605

U.S. Small Business Administration
350 South Figueroa Street, 6th Floor

Los Angeles, California 90071
(213) 894-3016

U.S. Small Business Administration
660 J Street, Room 215
Sacramento, California 95814
(916) 440-4461

U.S. Small Business Administration
880 Front Street, Room 4-S-29
San Diego, California 85701
(619) 557-5440

U.S. Small Business Administration
450 Golden Gate Avenue, Room 15307
San Francisco, California 94102

U.S. Small Business Administration
211 Main Street, 4th Floor
San Francisco, California 94105
(415) 974-0649

U.S. Small Business Administration
901 West Civic Center Drive, Suite 160
Santa Ana, California 92703
(714) 836-2494

California State World Trade Commission
1121 L Street, Suite 310
Sacramento, California 95814
(916) 324-5511

California Chamber of Commerce
International Trade Department
1027 10th Street, 4th Floor
P.O. Box 1736
Sacramento, California 95814
(916) 444-6670

Century City Chamber of Commerce
International Business Council
2020 Avenue of the Stars, Plaza Level
Century City, California 90067
(213) 553-4062

Custom Brokers & Freight Forwarders
Association
303 World Trade Center
San Francisco, California 94111
(415) 982-7788

Export Managers Association of California
14549 Victory Boulevard
Suite 5
Van Nuys, California 91411
(818) 782-3350

Foreign Trade Association of Southern
California
900 Wilshire Boulevard
Los Angeles, California 90017
(213) 627-0634

Inland International Trade Association, Inc.
Bob Watson
World Trade Center
West Sacramento, California 95691
(916) 371-8000

International Marketing Association of
 Orange County
Cal State Fullerton
Marketing Department
Fullerton, California 92634
(714) 773-2223

Long Beach Area Chamber of Commerce
International Business Association
1 World Trade Center
Long Beach, California 90831
(213) 436-1251

Los Angeles Area Chamber of Commerce
International Commerce Division
404 South Bixel Street
Los Angeles, California 90017
(213) 629-0722

Los Angeles International Trade
 Development Corporation
555 South Flower Street, #2014
Los Angeles, California 90071
(213) 622-4832

Oakland World Trade Association
1939 Harrison Street
Oakland, California 94612
(415) 388-8829

San Diego Chamber of Commerce
110 West "C" Street, Suite 1600
San Diego, California 92101
(619) 232-0124

San Francisco Chamber of Commerce
San Francisco World Trade Association
465 California Street, 9th Floor
San Francisco, California 94104
(415) 392-4511

Santa Clara Valley World Trade Association
180 South Market Street

San Jose, California 95113
(408) 998-7000

Valley International Trade Association
(San Fernando Valley)
1323 Carmelina Avenue, Suite 214
Los Angeles, California 90025
(213) 207-1802

World Trade Association of Orange County
Hutton, 200 East Sandpointe #480
Santa Ana, California 92707
(714) 549-8151

World Trade Association of San Diego
P.O. Box 81404
San Diego, California 92138
(619) 453-4605

World Trade Council of San Mateo County
4 West Fourth Avenue, Suite 501
San Mateo, California 94402
(415) 345-8300

Colorado

U.S. Department of Commerce

US&FCS District Office
U.S. Customhouse, Room 119
721 19th Street
Denver, Colorado 80202
(303) 837-3246

U.S. Small Business Administration
U.S. Customhouse Room 407
721 19th Street
Denver, Colorado 80202
(303) 844-2607

Colorado Association of Commerce and
  Industry
1860 Lincoln Street, Suite 550
Denver, Colorado 80295
(303) 831-7411

Denver Chamber of Commerce
1600 Sherman Street
Denver, Colorado 80203
(303) 894-8500

Foreign Trade Office
Department of Commerce & Development
625 Broadway, Suite 680
Denver, Colorado 80202
(303) 892-3850

Connecticut

U.S. Department of Commerce

US&FCS District Office
Federal Building Room 610-B
450 Main Street
Hartford, Connecticut 06103
(203) 722-3530

U.S. Small Business Administration
330 Main Street
Hartford, Connecticut 06106
(203) 240-4700

International Division
Department of Economic Development
865 Brook Street
Rocky Hill, Connecticut 06067
(203) 258-4200

Delaware

U.S. Department of Commerce

US&FCS District Office
See listing for Philadelphia, Pennsylvania

U.S. Small Business Administration
844 King Street, Room 5207
Wilmington, Delaware 19801
(302) 573-6294

Delaware State Chamber of Commerce
One Commerce Center, Suite 200
Wilmington, Delaware 19801
(302) 655-7221

Delaware-Eastern Pennsylvania Export
  Council
9448 Federal Building
600 Arch Street
Philadelphia, Pennsylvania 19106
(215) 597-2850

Division of Economic Development
Box 1401
99 Kings Highway
Dover, Delaware 11903
(302) 736-4271

Florida

U.S. Department of Commerce

US&FCS District Office
Federal Building, Suite 224
51 Southwest First Avenue

Miami, Florida 33130
(305) 350-5267

U.S. Small Business Administration
400 West Bay Street, Room 261
Jacksonville, Florida 32202
(904) 791-3782

U.S. Small Business Administration
2222 Ponce de Leon Boulevard, 5th Floor
Miami, Florida 33134
(305) 536-5521

U.S. Small Business Administration
700 Twiggs Street, Room 607
Tampa, Florida 33602
(813) 228-2594

U.S. Small Business Administration
5601 Corporate Way
West Palm Beach, Florida 33407
(407) 689-2223

Bureau of International Trade and
   Development
Department of Commerce
331 Collins Building
Tallahassee, Florida 32399
(904) 488-6124

Georgia

U.S. Department of Commerce

US&FCS District Office
1365 Peachtree Street, Northeast, Suite 504
Atlanta, Georgia 30309
(404) 881-7000

U.S. Department of Commerce

US&FCS District Office
Federal Building, Room A-107
120 Barnard Street
Savannah, Georgia 31401
(912) 944-4202

U.S. Small Business Administration
1720 Peachtree Road, Northwest,
Suite 600
Atlanta, Georgia 30309
(404) 347-2441

U.S. Small Business Administration
52 North Main Street, Room 225
Statesboro, Georgia 30458
(912) 489-8719

Department of Industry and Trade
285 Peachtree Center Avenue
Atlanta, Georgia 30303
(404) 656-3746

International Trade Division
Division of Marketing
Department of Agriculture
330 Agriculture Building
Capitol Square
Atlanta, Georgia 30334
(404) 656-3600

Hawaii

U.S. Department of Commerce

US&FCS District Office
4106 Federal Building
300 Ala Moana Boulevard
P.O. Box 50026
Honolulu, Hawaii 96850
(808) 546-8694

U.S. Small Business Administration
P.O. Box 50207
Honolulu, Hawaii 96850
(808) 541-2987

Chamber of Commerce of Hawaii
World Trade Association
735 Bishop Street, Suite 220
Honolulu, Hawaii 96813
(808) 522-8800

Economic Development Corporation of
   Honolulu
1001 Bishop Street
Suite 855, Pacific Tower
Honolulu, Hawaii 96813
(808) 545-4533

International Services Agency
   Department of Planning & Economic
   Development
P.O. Box 2359
Honolulu, Hawaii 96804
(808) 548-3048

Idaho

U.S. Department of Commerce

US&FCS District Office
—See listing for Salt Lake City, Utah

U.S. Small Business Administration
1020 Main Street, Suite 290
Boise, Idaho 83702
(208) 334-1696

Idaho Department of Commerce
700 West State
Boise, Idaho 83720
(208) 334-2470

Department of Agriculture
International Trade Division
P.O. Box 790
Boise, Idaho 83701
(208) 334-3240

District Export Council
Statehouse, Room 225
Boise, Idaho 83720
(208) 334-2200

World Trade Committee
Greater Boise Chamber of Commerce
P.O. Box 2368
Boise, Idaho 83701
(208) 344-5515

Illinois

U.S. Department of Commerce

US&FCS District Office
Mid-Continental Plaza Building, Room 1406
55 East Monroe Street
Chicago, Illinois 60603
(312) 353-4450

U.S. Small Business Administration
219 South Dearborn Street
Room 437
Chicago, Illinois 60604
(312) 353-4528

U.S. Small Business Administration
511 West Capitol, Suite 302
Springfield, Illinois 62704
(217) 492-4416

American Association of Exporters and
  Importers
5901 North Cicero Avenue
Suite 309
Chicago, Illinois 60643
(312) 283-7555

Chamber of Commerce of Upper Rock
  Island County
622 19th Street
Moline, Illinois 61265
(309) 762-3661

Chicago Association of Commerce and
  Industry
World Trade Division
200 North La Salle Street
Chicago, Illinois 60601
(312) 580-6990

Chicago Economic Development
  Commission
International Business Division
Merchandise Mart
Suite 1503
Chicago, Illinois 60654
(312) 744-9550

Department of Commerce & Community
  Affairs
International Business Division
100 West Randolph Street
Chicago, Illinois 60601
(312) 917-7179

Foreign Credit Insurance Association
20 North Clark Street, Suite 910
Chicago, Illinois 60602
(312) 641-1915

Illinois Department of Agriculture
1010 Jorie Boulevard
Oak Brook, Illinois 60521
(312) 990-8256

Illinois Manufacturers' Association
175 West Jackson Boulevard
Suite 1321
Chicago, Illinois 60566
(312) 922-6575

Illinois State Chamber of Commerce
International Trade Division
20 North Wacker Drive, Suite 1960
Chicago, Illinois 60606
(312) 372-7373

Peoria Area Chamber of Commerce
124 Southwest Adams Street
Peoria, Illinois 61602
(309) 676-0755

World Trade Center of Northern Illinois

515 North Court
Rockford, Illinois 61101
(815) 987-8100

Indiana

U.S. Department of Commerce

US&FCS District Office
One North Capitol
Indianapolis, Indiana 46204-2248
(317) 232-8846
U.S. Department of Commerce

US&FCS District Office

357 U.S. Courthouse & Federal Office
  Building
46 East Ohio Street
Indianapolis, Indiana 46204
(317) 269-6214

U.S. Small Business Administration
575 North Pennsylvania Street
Room 578
Indianapolis, Indiana 46204
(317) 226-7272

Fort Wayne Chamber of Commerce
International Development Group
826 Ewing Street
Fort Wayne, Indiana 46802
(219) 424-1435

Greater Lafayette
Tippecanoe World Trade Council
Chamber of Commerce
P.O. Box 348
Lafayette, Indiana 47902

Indiana Manufacturers Association
54 Monument Circle
Suite 700
Indianapolis, Indiana 46204
(317) 632-2474

Indiana State Chamber of Commerce
1 North Capitol, No. 200
Indianapolis, Indiana 46204
(317) 634-6407

Indianapolis Chamber of Commerce
Development and World Trade
320 North Meridian, Suite 928
Indianapolis, Indiana 46204
(317) 267-2900

Indianapolis Economic Development
  Corporation
320 North Meridian Street
Indianapolis, Indiana 46204
(317) 236-6262

Michiana World Trade Club
230 West Jefferson Boulevard
P.O. Box 1677
South Bend, Indiana 46634
(219) 289-7323

TransNational Business Club
College of Business
Ball State University
Muncie, Indiana 47306
(317) 285-5207

Tri State World Trade Council
100 Northwest 2nd Street
Suite 202
Evansville, Indiana 47708
(812) 425-8147

World Trade Club of Indiana, Inc.
P.O. Box 986
Indianapolis, Indiana 46206
(317) 261-1169

Iowa

U.S. Department of Commerce

US&FCS District Office
817 Federal Building
210 Walnut Street
Des Moines, Iowa 50309
(515) 284-4222

U.S. Small Business Administration
373 Collins Road, Northeast
Cedar Rapids, Iowa 52402
(310) 399-2571

U.S. Small Business Administration
749 Federal Building
210 Walnut Street
Des Moines, Iowa 50309
(515) 284-4422

International Trade
Iowa Development Commission
600 East Court Avenue, Suite A
Des Moines, Iowa 50309
(515) 281-3581

Iowa Office of Economic Development
200 East Grand Avenue
Des Moines, Iowa 50309

Iowa-Illinois International Trade
Association
112 East Third Street
Davenport, Iowa 52801
(319) 322-1706

Siouxland International Trade Association
Legislative & Agriculture Affairs
101 Pierce Street
Sioux City, Iowa 51101
(712) 255-7903

Kansas

U.S. Department of Commerce

US&FCS District Office
—See listing for Kansas City, Missouri

U.S. Small Business Administration
110 East Waterman Street
Wichita, Kansas 67202
(316) 269-6571

Department of Economic Development
International Trade Development Division
400 West 8th Street
Topeka, Kansas 66603-3957
(913) 296-3483

International Trade Institute
1627 Anderson Avenue
Manhattan, Kansas 66502
(913) 532-6799

Kansas District Export Council
c/o Sunflower Manufacturing Company
1 Sunflower Drive
P.O. Box 566
Beloit, Kansas 67420
(913) 738-2261

Kentucky

U.S. Department of Commerce

US&FCS District Office
U.S. Post Office & Courthouse Building,
Room 636-B
Louisville, Kentucky 40202
(502) 582-5066

U.S. Small Business Administration
600 Dr. Martin Luther King, Jr. Place,
Room 188
Louisville, Kentucky 40202
(502) 582-5971

Kentuckiana World Commerce Council
P.O. Box 58456
Louisville, Kentucky 40258
(502) 583-5551

Kentucky District Export Council
601 West Broadway, Room 636-B
Louisville, Kentucky 40202
(502) 582-5066

Louisville Economic Development Cabinet
515 West Market Street
Suite 650
Louisville, Kentucky 40202
(502) 625-3051

Office of International Marketing
Kentucky Commerce Cabinet
Capitol Plaza Tower, 24th Floor
Frankfort, Kentucky 40601
(502) 564-2170

Kentucky World Trade Center, Lexington
410 West Vine Street
Suite 290
Lexington, Kentucky 40507
(606) 258-3139

Louisiana

U.S. Department of Commerce

US&FCS District Office
432 International Trade Mart
2 Canal Street
New Orleans, Louisiana 70130
(504) 589-6546

U.S. Small Business Administration
1661 Canal Street, Suite 2000
New Orleans, Louisiana 70112
(504) 589-6685

U.S. Small Business Administration
500 Fannin Street
Room 8A-08
Shreveport, Louisiana 71101
(318) 226-5196

Chamber of Commerce/New Orleans and
the River Region
301 Camp Street
New Orleans, Louisiana 70130
(504) 527-6900

Office of International Trade Finance and
Development
Louisiana Department of Congress
P.O. Box 94185
Baton Rouge, Louisiana 70804-9185
(504) 342-5361

World Trade Club of Greater New Orleans
1132 International Trade Mart
2 Canal Street
New Orleans, Louisiana 70130
(504) 525-7201

Maine

U.S. Department of Commerce

US&FCS District Office
—See listing for Boston, Massachusetts

U.S. Small Business Administration
The Federal Building
40 Western Avenue, Room 512
Augusta, Maine 04330
(207) 622-8378

State Development Office
State House, Station 59
Augusta, Maine 04333
(207) 289-5700

Maryland

U.S. Department of Commerce

US&FCS District Office
415 U.S. Customhouse
Gay and Lombard Streets
Baltimore, Maryland 21202
(301) 962-3560

U.S. Small Business Administration
Equitable Building
3rd Floor
10 North Calvert Street
Baltimore, Maryland 21202
(301) 962-4392

Baltimore Economic Development Crop.
36 South Charles Street, Suite 1600
Baltimore, Maryland 21201
(301) 837-9305

Division of Economic Development
Arundel Center
P.O. Box 1831
Annapolis, Maryland 21404
(301) 280-1122

Massachusetts

U.S. Department of Commerce

US&FCS District Office
441 Stuart Street, 10th Floor
Boston, Massachusetts 02116
(617) 233-2312

U.S. Small Business Administration
10 Causeway Street, Room 265
Boston, Massachusetts 02222-1093
(617) 565-5590

U.S. Small Business Administration
1550 Main Street, Suite 212
Springfield, Massachusetts 01103
(413) 785-0268

Associated Industries of Massachusetts
441 Stuart Street
Boston, Massachusetts 02116
(617) 262-1180

Brockton Regional Chamber of Commerce
One Centre Street
Brockton, Massachusetts 02401
(508) 586-0500

Central Berkshire Chamber of Commerce
66 West Street
Pittsfield, Massachusetts 01201
(413) 499-4000

Chamber of Commerce of the Attleboro
Area
42 Union Street
Attleboro, Massachusetts 02703
(508) 222-0801

Fall River Area Chamber of Commerce
P.O. Box 1871
200 Pocasset Street
Fall River, Massachusetts 02722
(508) 676-8226

Greater Boston Chamber of Commerce
125 High Street
Boston, Massachusetts 02110
(617) 227-4500

Greater Fitchburg Chamber of Commerce
344 Main Street
Fitchburg, Massachusetts 01420
(508) 343-6487

Greater Gardner Chamber of Commerce
301 Central Street
Gardner, Massachusetts 01440

Greater Lawrence Chamber of Commerce
264 Essex Street
Lawrence, Massachusetts 01840
(508) 686-0900

Greater Springfield Chamber of Commerce
1350 Main Street, 3rd Floor
Springfield, Massachusetts 01103
(413) 787-1555

Massachusetts Department of Commerce &
    Development
100 Cambridge Street, 13th Floor
Boston, Massachusetts 02202
(617) 727-3218

Massachusetts Department of Food &
    Agriculture
100 Cambridge Street, 21st Floor
Boston, Massachusetts 02202
(617) 727-3018

New Bedford Area Chamber of Commerce
P.O. Box G-827
838 Purchase Street
New Bedford, Massachusetts 02742
(508) 999-5231

North Suburban Chamber of Commerce
7 Alfred Street, Suite 100
Woburn Massachusetts 01801
(617) 933-3499

Office of Economic Affairs
100 Cambridge Street
Suite 902
Boston, Massachusetts 02202
(617) 367-1830

South Middlesex Area
Chamber of Commerce
600 Worcester Road

Framingham, Massachusetts 01701
(508) 879-5600

South Shore Chamber of Commerce
36 Miller Stile Road
Quincy, Massachusetts 02169
(617) 479-1111

Waltham/West Suburban Chamber of
    Commerce
663 Main Street
Waltham, Massachusetts 02154
(617) 894-4700

Watertown Chamber of Commerce
P.O. Box 45
75 Main Street
Watertown, Massachusetts 02172
(617) 926-1017

Worcester Chamber of Commerce
33 Waldo Street
Worcester, Massachusetts 01608
(508) 753-2924

Michigan

U.S. Department of Commerce

US&FCS District Office
445 Federal Building
231 West Lafayette
Detroit, Michigan 48226
(313) 226-3650

U.S. Small Business Administration
515 Patrick V. McNamara Building
477 Michigan Avenue, Room 515
Detroit, Michigan 48226
(313) 226-6075

U.S. Small Business Administration
220 West Washington Street, Room 310
Marquette, Michigan 49885
(906) 225-1108

Ann Arbor Chamber of Commerce
211 East Huron
Ann Arbor, Michigan 48104
(313) 665-4433
City of Detroit

Community & Economic Development
    Department
50 Michigan Avenue, 7th Floor
Detroit, Michigan 48226
(313) 224-6533

Downriver Community Conference
15100 Northline
Southgate, Michigan 48195
(313) 283-8933

Flint Area Chamber of Commerce
708 Root
Flint, Michigan 49503
(313) 232-7101

(Greater) Detroit Chamber of Commerce
600 West Lafayette Boulevard
Detroit, Michigan 48226
(313) 964-4000

(Greater) Grand Rapids Chamber of
Commerce
17 Fountain Street, Northwest
Grand Rapids, Michigan 49503
(616) 771-0300

(Greater) Port Huron-Marysville Chamber of
Commerce
920 Pine Grove Avenue
Port Huron, Michigan 48060
(313) 985-7101

(Greater) Saginaw Chamber of Commerce
901 South Washington
Saginaw, Michigan 48601
(517) 752-7161

Kalamazoo Chamber of Commerce
128 North Kalamazoo Mall
Kalamazoo, Michigan 49007
(616) 381-4000

Macomb County Chamber of Commerce
58 North Avenue
P.O. Box 855
Mt. Clemens, Michigan 48043
(313) 463-1528

Michigan Department of Agriculture
Office of International Trade
North Ottawa Building, 4th Floor
611 West Ottawa
Lansing, Michigan 48909
(517) 373-1054

Michigan Manufacturers Association
124 East Kalamazoo
Lansing, Michigan 48933
(517) 372-5900

Michigan State Chamber of Commerce
Small Business Programs

600 South Walnut
Lansing, Michigan 48933
(517) 371-2100

Muskegon Area Chamber of Commerce
1065 Fourth Street
Muskegon, Michigan 48909
(616) 722-3751

Office of International Development
Michigan Department of Commerce
Law Building, 5th Floor
Lansing, Michigan 48909
(517) 373-6390

Twin Cities Area Chamber of Commerce
777 Riverview Drive, Building V
Benton Harbor, Michigan 49022
(616) 925-0044

West Michigan World Trade Club
445 Sixth Street, Northwest
Grand Rapids, Michigan 49504
(616) 451-7651

World Trade Club of Detroit
150 Michigan Avenue
Detroit, Michigan 48226
(313) 964-4000

Minnesota

U.S. Department of Commerce

US&FCS District Office
108 Federal Building
110 South 4th Street
Minneapolis, Minnesota 55401
612) 349-3338

U.S. Small Business Administration
100 North 6th Street
610 C Butler Square
Minneapolis, Minnesota 55403
(612) 370-2324

Minnesota Export Finance Authority
1000 World Trade Center
300 East 7th Street
St. Paul, Minnesota 55101
(612) 297-4659

Minnesota World Trade Association
33 East Wentworth Avenue, 101
West St. Paul, Minnesota 55118
(612) 431-1289

Mississippi

U.S. Department of Commerce

US&FCS District Office
300 Woodrow Wilson Boulevard, Suite 328
Jackson, Mississippi 39213
(601) 960-4388

U.S. Small Business Administration
100 West Capitol Street, Suite 322
Jackson, Mississippi 39269
(601) 965-4378
Marketing Division

Mississippi Department of Economic
   Development
P.O. Box 849
Jackson, Mississippi 39205
(601) 359-3444

Missouri

U.S. Department of Commerce

US&FCS District Office
120 South Central, Suite 400
St. Louis, Missouri 53105
(314) 425-3301
U.S. Department of Commerce

US&FCS District Office
601 East 12th Street, Room 635
Kansas City, Missouri 64106
(816) 374-3142

U.S. Small Business Administration
1103 Grande Avenue
Kansas City, Missouri 64106-2445
(816) 374-6757

U.S. Small Business Administration 620
   South Glenstone, Suite 110
Springfield, Missouri 65802
(417) 864-7670
International Business Development

Department of Commerce & Economic
   Development
P.O. Box 118
Jefferson City, Missouri 65102
(314) 751-4855

International Trade Club of Greater Kansas
   City
920 Main Street, Suite 600

Kansas City, Missouri 64105
(816) 221-1462

Missouri Department of Agriculture
International Marketing Division
P.O. Box 630
Jefferson City, Missouri 65102
(314) 751-5611

Missouri District Export Council
120 South Central, Suite 400
St. Louis, Missouri 63105
(314) 425-3302

World Trade Club of St. Louis, Inc.
111 North Taylor Avenue
Kirkwood, Missouri 63122
(314) 965-9940

Montana

U.S. Department of Commerce

US&FCS District Office
—See listing for Denver, Colorado

U.S. Small Business Administration
301 South Park, Room 528, Drawer 10054
Helena, Montana 59626
(406) 449-5381

U.S. Small Business Administration
   Post-of-Duty
2601 First Avenue North, Room 216
Billings, Montana 59101
(406) 657-6047

Governor's Office of Commerce & Small
   Business Development
1424 Ninth Avenue
Helena, Montana 59620
(406) 444-3923

Nebraska

U.S. Department of Commerce

US&FCS District Office
Empire State Building, 1st Floor
300 South 19th Street
Omaha, Nebraska 68102
(402) 221-3664

U.S. Small Business Administration
Empire State Building

1145 Mill Valley Road
Omaha, Nebraska 68154
(402) 221-4691
International Division

Nebraska Department of Economic
  Development
P.O. Box 94666
301 Centennial Mall South
Lincoln, Nebraska 68509
(402) 471-1311

Midwest International Trade Association
c/o NBC, 1248 O Street
Lincoln, Nebraska 68508
(402) 472-4321

Omaha Chamber of Commerce
International Affairs
1301 Harney Street
Omaha, Nebraska 68102
(402) 346-5000

Nevada

U.S. Department of Commerce

US&FCS District Office
1755 East Plumb Lane, Room 152
Reno, Nevada 89502
(702) 784-5203

U.S. Small Business Administration
301 East Steward Street
Las Vegas, Nevada 89125
(702) 385-6611

U.S. Small Business Administration
50 South Virginia Street, Room 238
Box 3216
Reno, Nevada 89505
(702) 784-5268

Commission on Economic Development
Capital Complex
600 East Williams, Suite 203
Carson City, Nevada 89710
(702) 885-4325

Economic Development Authority of
  Western Nevada
5190 Neil Road, Suite 111
Reno, Nevada 89502
(702) 322-4004

Latin Chamber of Commerce
P.O. Box 7534
Las Vegas, Nevada 89125-2534
(702) 385-7367

Nevada Development Authority
P.O. Box 11128
Las Vegas, Nevada 89111

New Hampshire

U.S. Department of Commerce

US&FCS District Office
—See listing for Boston, Massachusetts

U..S. Small Business Administration
55 Pleasant Street, Room 211
P.O. Box 1257
Concord, New Hampshire 03301
(603) 225-1400
Foreign Trade & Commercial Development

Department of Resources & Economic
  Development
105 Loudon Road, Building 2
P.O. Box 856
Concord, New Hampshire 03301
(603) 271-2591

New Jersey

U.S. Department of Commerce

US&FCS District Office
3131 Princeton Pike, 4-D, Suite 211
Trenton, New Jersey 08648
(609) 989-2100

U.S. Small Business Administration
60 Park Place, 4th Floor
Newark, New Jersey 07102
(201) 645-2434

U.S. Small Business Administration
2600 Mount Ephraim Road
Camden, New Jersey 08104
(609) 757-5183

Department of Commerce & Economic
  Development

Division of International Trade
Gateway 4, 10th Floor
100 Mulberry Street
Newark, New Jersey 07102-4006
(201) 648-3518

World Trade Association of New Jersey
5 Commerce Street
Newark, New Jersey 07102
(201) 623-7070

New Mexico

U.S. Department of Commerce

US&FCS District Office
517 Gold, Southwest, Suite 4303
Albuquerque, New Mexico 87102
(505) 766-2386

Department of Development
International Trade Division
Joseph Montoya Building
1100 Street Francis Drive
Santa Fe, New Mexico 87503
(505) 827-6208

New Mexico Department of Agriculture
Department 30005
P.O. Box 5600
Las Cruces, New Mexico 88003
(505) 646-4929

New Mexico Industry Development
    Corporation
5301 Central Avenue, Northeast, Suite 705
Albuquerque, New Mexico 87110
(505) 262-2247

New York

U.S. Department of Commerce

US&FCS District Office
1312 Federal Building
111 West Huron Street
Buffalo, New York 14202
(716) 846-4191

U.S. Department of Commerce

US&FCS District Office
Federal Office Building, Room 3718
26 Federal Plaza, Foley Square
New York, New York 10278
(212) 264-0634

U.S. Small Business Administration
26 Federal Plaza, Room 3100
New York, New York 10278
(212) 264-4355

U.S. Small Business Administration
35 Pinelawn Road, Room 102E
Melville, New York 11747
(516) 454-0750

U.S. Small Business Administration
Federal Building
100 S. Clinton Street, Room 1071
Syracuse, New York 13260
(315) 423-5383

U.S. Small Business Administration
111 West Huron Street, Room 1311
Buffalo, New York 14203
(716) 846-4301

U.S. Small Business Administration
333 East Water Street
Elmira, New York 14901
(607) 733-4686

U.S. Small Business Administration
445 Broadway, Room 222
Albany, New York 12207
(518) 472-6300

U.S. Small Business Administration
100 State Street, Room 601
Rochester, New York 14614
(716) 263-6700

Albany-Colonie Regional Chamber of
    Commerce
518 Broadway
Albany, New York 12207
(518) 434-1214

American Association of Exporters and
    Importers
11 West 42nd Street, 30th Floor
New York, New York 10036
(212) 944-2230

Buffalo Area Chamber of Commerce
Economic Development
107 Delaware Avenue
Buffalo, New York 14202
(716) 852-7100

Buffalo World Trade Association
146 Canterbury Square
Williamsville, New York 14221
(716) 634-8439

Foreign Credit Insurance Association
40 Rector Street, 11th Floor

New York, New York 10006
(212) 306-5000

International Business Council of the
  Rochester Area Chamber of Commerce
International Trade & Transportation
55 St. Paul Street
Rochester, New York 14604
(716) 454-2220

Long Island Association, Inc.
80 Hauppage Road
Commack, New York 11725
(516) 499-4400

Long Island Association, Inc.
World Trade Club
Legislative & Economic Affairs
80 Hauppage Road
Commack, New York 11725
(516) 499-4400

Mohawk Valley World Trace Council
P.O. Box 4126
Utica, New York 13540
(315) 797-9530 ext. 319

New York Chamber of Commerce &
Industry
200 Madison Avenue
New York, New York 10016
(212) 561-2028

New York State Department of Commerce
International Division
1515 Broadway, 51st Floor
New York, New York 10036
(212) 827-6100

Rochester Area Chamber of Commerce
World Trade Department
International Trade & Transportation
55 St. Paul Street
Rochester, New York 14604
(716) 454-2220

Rockland International Development
  Corporation
Tappan Zee International Trade Association
1 Blue Hill Plaza
Pearl River, New York 10965
(914) 735-7040

U.S. Council of the International Chamber
  of Commerce
1212 Avenue of the Americas

New York, New York 10036-1689
(212) 354-4480

Westchester County Association, Inc.
World Trade Club of Westchester
235 Mamaroneck Avenue
White Plains, New York 10605
(914) 948-6444

World Commerce Association of Central
  New York
100 East Onondaga
Syracuse, New York 13202
(315) 470-1343

World Trade Club of New York, Inc.
200 Madison Avenue
New York, New York 10016
(212) 561-2028

World Trade Institute
1 World Trade Center, 55 West
New York, New York 10048
(212) 466-4044

North Carolina

U.S. Department of Commerce

US&FCS District Office
203 Federal Building
324 West Market Street
P.O. Box 1950
Greensboro, North Carolina 27402
(919) 378-5345

U.S. Small Business Administration
222 South Church Street, Suite 300
Charlotte, North Carolina 28202
(704) 371-6563

U.S. Small Business Administration
Greenville, North Carolina 27834
(919) 752-1000

Department of Commerce
International Division
430 North Salisbury Street
Raleigh, North Carolina 27611
(919) 733-7193

North Carolina Department of Agriculture
1 West Edenton Street
P.O. Box 27647
Raleigh, North Carolina 27611
(919) 733-7912

North Dakota

U.S. Department of Commerce

US&FCS District Office
—See listing for Omaha, Nebraska

U.S. Small Business Administration
P.O. Box 3086
Fargo, North Dakota 58103
(701) 239-5131

North Dakota Economic Development
   Commission

International Trade Division
604 East Boulevard Avenue
Bismarck, North Dakota 58505
(701) 224-2810

Fargo Chamber of Commerce
321 North 4th Street
Fargo, North Dakota 58102
(701) 237-5678

Ohio

U.S. Department of Commerce

US&FCS District Office
9504 Federal Building
550 Main Street
Cincinnati, Ohio 45202
(513) 684-2944

U.S. Department of Commerce

US&FCS District Office
668 Euclid Avenue, Room 600
Cleveland, Ohio 44114
(216) 522-4750

U.S. Small Business Administration
Federal Building
1240 East 9th Street, Room 317
Cleveland, Ohio 44199
(216) 522-4180

Small Business Administration
85 Marconi Boulevard
Columbus, Ohio 43215
(614) 469-6860

U.S. Small Business Administration
550 Main Street, Room 5028
Cincinnati, Ohio 45202
(513) 684-2814

Cleveland World Trade Association
690 Huntington Building
Cleveland, Ohio 44115
(216) 621-3300

Columbus Area Chamber of Commerce
Economic Development
37 North High Street
Columbus, Ohio 43215
(614) 221-1321

Columbus Council on World Affairs
P.O. Box 10044
Columbus, Ohio 43216
(614) 249-8450

Commerce & Industry Association of
   Greater Elyria
360 Second Street
P.O. Box 179
Elyria, Ohio 44036
(216) 322-5438

Dayton Council on World Affairs
P.O. Box 9190
Wright Brother's Branch
Dayton, Ohio 45409

Dayton Development Council
1880 Kettering Tower
Dayton, Ohio 45423
(513) 226-8222

Department of Development
International Trade Division
30 East Broad Street
P.O. Box 1001
Columbus, Ohio 43266-0101
(614) 466-5017

(Greater) Cincinnati Chamber of
Commerce
Export Development
300 Carew Tower
441 Vine Street
Cincinnati, Ohio 45202
(513) 579-3122

International Business & Trade Association
   of Akron
Regional Development Board
1 Cascade Plaza, 8th Floor
Akron, Ohio 44308
(216) 376-5550

North Central Ohio Trade Club

Chamber of Commerce
55 North Mulberry Street
Mansfield, Ohio 44902
(419) 522-3211

Ohio Department of Agriculture
Ohio Department Building, Room 607
65 South Front Street
Columbus, Ohio 43215
(614) 466-8789

Toledo Area International Trade Association
Toledo, Ohio 43604
(419) 243-8191

Oklahoma

U.S. Department of Commerce

US&FCS District Office
4024 Lincoln Boulevard
Oklahoma City, Oklahoma 73105
(405) 231-5302

U.S. Small Business Administration
200 Northwest 5th Street, Suite 670
Oklahoma City, Oklahoma 73102
(405) 231-4301

Department of Economic Development
International Trade Division
4024 North Lincoln Boulevard
P.O. Box 53424
Oklahoma City, Oklahoma 73152

(Metropolitan) Tulsa Chamber of Commerce
Economic Development Division
616 South Boston Avenue
Tulsa, Oklahoma 74119
(918) 585-1201

Oklahoma City Chamber of Commerce
Economic and Community Development
One Santa Fe Plaza
Oklahoma City, Oklahoma 73102
(405) 278-8900

Oklahoma City International Trade
   Association
c/o Ditch Witch International
P.O. Box 66
Perry, Oklahoma 73077
(405) 336-4402

Oklahoma District Export Council
4024 Lincoln Boulevard

Oklahoma City, Oklahoma 73105
(405) 231-5302

Oklahoma State Chamber of Commerce
4020 Lincoln Boulevard
Oklahoma City, Oklahoma 73105
(405) 424-4003

Tulsa World Trade Association
1821 North 106th East Avenue
Tulsa, Oklahoma 74116
(918) 836-0338

Oregon

U.S. Department of Commerce

US&FCS District Office
1220 Southwest 3rd Avenue, Room 618
Portland, Oregon 97204
(503) 221-3001

U.S. Small Business Administration
222 Southwest Columbia, Suite 500
Portland, Oregon 97201-6605
(503) 326-2682

Department of Economic Development
International Trade Division
121 West Salmon, Suite 300
Portland, Oregon 97204
(503) 229-5625 or (800) 452-7813

Eugene Area Chamber of Commerce
1401 Willamette
P.O. Box 1107
Eugene, Oregon 97440
(503) 484-1314

Institute for International Trade and
   Commerce
One World Trade Center
121 Southwest Salmon, Suite 230
Portland, Oregon 97204
(503) 229-3246

Oregon District Export Council
1220 Southwest 3rd Avenue, Room 618
Portland, Oregon 97209
(503) 292-9219

Western Wood Products Association
Yeon Building, 522 Southwest 5th Avenue
Portland, Oregon 97204
(503) 224-3930

Pennsylvania

U.S. Department of Commerce

US&FCS District Office
9448 Federal Building
600 Arch Street
Philadelphia, Pennsylvania 19106
(215) 597-2866

U.S. Department of Commerce

US&FCS District Office
2002 Federal Building
1000 Liberty Avenue
Pittsburgh, Pennsylvania 15222
(412) 644-2850

U.S. Small Business Administration
475 Allendale
King of Prussia, Pennsylvania 19406
(215) 962-3700

U.S. Small Business Administration
Branch Office
100 Chestnut Street, Suite 309
Harrisburg, Pennsylvania 17101
(717) 782-3840

U.S. Small Business Administration
Branch Office
20 North Pennsylvania Avenue
Wilkes-Barre, Pennsylvania 18701
(717) 826-6497

U.S. Small Business Administration
District Office
960 Pennsylvania Avenue,
Convention Tower, 5th Floor
Pittsburgh, Pennsylvania 15222
(412) 644-2780

(City of) Philadelphia
Commerce Department
International Division
Room 1660
Philadelphia, Pennsylvania 19102-684
(215) 686-3647

Economic Development Council of
Northwestern Pennsylvania
1151 Oak Street
Pittston, Pennsylvania 18640
(717) 655-5581

Erie Manufacturers Association
P.O. Box 1779

Erie, Pennsylvania 16507
(814) 453-4454

(Greater) Pittsburgh Chamber of
Commerce
3 Gateway Center
Pittsburgh, Pennsylvania 15222
(412) 392-4500

Pennsylvania Department of Agriculture
Bureau of Agricultural Development
2301 North Cameron Street
Harrisburg, Pennsylvania 17110
(717) 783-8460

Philadelphia Export Network
3508 Market Street,
Suite 100
Philadelphia, Pennsylvania 19104
(215) 898-4189

Reading Foreign Trade Association
601 Penn Street
Reading, Pennsylvania 19601
(215) 320-2976

Smaller Manufacturers Council
1900 South Braddock Avenue
Pittsburgh, Pennsylvania 15218
(412) 371-1500

Southwestern Pennsylvania Economic
Development District
355 Fifth Avenue,
Room 1411
Pittsburgh, Pennsylvania 15222
(412) 391-1240

Western Pennsylvania District Export
Council

1000 Liberty Avenue, Room 2002
Pittsburg, Pennsylvania 15222
(412) 644-2850

Women's International Trade Association
P.O. Box 40004
Continental Station
Philadelphia, Pennsylvania 19106
(215) 925-5780

World Trade Association of
Philadelphia, Inc.
1317 Spruce Street
Philadelphia, Pennsylvania 19107
(215) 735-0711

Rhode Island

U.S. Department of Commerce

US&FCS District Office
—See listing for Boston, Massachusetts

U.S. Small Business Administration
380 Westminster Mall
Providence, Rhode Island 02903
(401) 528-4562

Department of Economic Development
7 Jackson Walkway
Providence, Rhode Island 02903
(401) 277-2601

South Carolina

U.S. Department of Commerce

US&FCS District Office
Strom Thurmond Federal Building
Suite 172
1835 Assembly Street
Columbia, South Carolina 29201
(803) 765-5345

U.S. Small Business
Strom Thurmond Federal Building
P.O. Box 2786
1835 Assembly, 3rd Floor
Columbia, South Carolina 29202-2786
(803) 765-5376

South Carolina District Export Council
Strom Thurmond Federal Building
Suite 172
1835 Assembly Street
Columbia, South Carolina 29201
(803) 765-5345

South Carolina International Trade Club
Strom Thurmond Federal Building
Suite 172
1835 Assembly Street
Columbia, South Carolina 29201
(803) 765-5345

South Carolina State Development Board
International Division
P.O. Box 927
Columbia, South Carolina 29202
(803) 737-0400

South Dakota

U.S. Department of Commerce

US&FCS District Office
—See listing for Omaha, Nebraska

U.S. Small Business Administration
101 South Main Avenue, Suite 101
Sioux Falls, South Dakota 57102
(605) 330-4231

Rapid City Area Chamber of Commerce
P.O. Box 747
Rapid City, South Dakota 57709
(605) 343-1744

Sioux Falls Chamber of Commerce
315 South Phillips
Sioux Falls, South Dakota 57101
(605) 336-1620

South Dakota Bureau of Industrial and
   Agricultural Development
711 Wells Street
Pierre, South Dakota 57501
(605) 773-5032

Tennessee

U.S. Department of Commerce

US&FCS District Office
Suite 1114, Parkway Tower
404 James Robertson Parkway
Nashville, Tennessee 37219-1505
(615) 736-5161

U.S. Small Business Administration
404 James Robertson Parkway
Suite 1012, Parkway Towers
Nashville, Tennessee 37219
(615) 736-5881

Department of Economic & Community
   Development

Export Promotion Office
Rachel Jackson Building
326 Avenue North, 7th Floor
Nashville, Tennessee 37219-5308
(615) 741-5870

Mid-South Exporters' Roundtable
P.O. Box 3521
Memphis, Tennessee 38103
(901) 761-3490

Tennessee Department of Agriculture
Ellington Agricultural Center
P.O. Box 40627, Melrose Station
Nashville, Tennessee 37204
(615) 360-0103

Tennessee District Export Council
c/o Aladdin Industries
P.O. Box 100255
Nashville, Tennessee 37210
(615) 748-3575

Texas

U.S. Department of Commerce

US&FCS District Office
1100 Commerce Street, Room 7A5
Dallas, Texas 75242
(214) 767-0542

U.S. Department of Commerce

US&FCS District Office
2625 Federal Building
515 Rusk Street
Houston, Texas 77002
(713) 229-2578

U.S. Small Business Administration
300 East 8th Street, Room 520
Austin, Texas 78701
(512) 482-5288

U.S. Small Business Administration
400 Mann Street, Suite 403
Corpus Christi, Texas 78408
(512) 888-3331

U.S. Small Business Administration
1100 Commerce Street, Room 3C36
Dallas, Texas 75242
(214) 767-0605

U.S. Small Business Administration
10737 Gateway West, Suite 320
El Paso, Texas 79935
(915) 541-7586

U.S. Small Business Administration
819 Taylor Street
Ft. Worth, Texas 76102
(817) 334-3777

U.S. Small Business Administration
222 East Van Buren Street, Room 500

Harlingen, Texas 78550
(512) 429-8533

U.S. Small Business Administration
2525 Murworth, Room 112
Houston, Texas 77054
(713) 660-4401

U.S. Small Business Administration
1611 Tenth Street, Suite 200
Lubbock, Texas 79401
(806) 743-7462

U.S. Small Business Administration
505 East Travis, Room 103
Marshall, Texas 75670
(214) 935-5257

U.S. Small Business Administration
7400 Blanco Road, Room 200
San Antonio, Texas 78216-4300
(512) 229-4535

Amarillo Chamber of Commerce
Amarillo Building
1301 South Polk
Amarillo, Texas 79101
(806) 373-7800

Dallas Chamber of Commerce
1201 Elm Street, Suite 2000
Dallas, Texas 75270
(214) 746-6600

Dallas Council on World Affairs
World Trade Center
P.O. Box 58232
Dallas, Texas 75258
(214) 748-5663

El Paso Chamber of Commerce
10 Civic Center Plaza
P.O. Box 9738
El Paso, Texas 79987
(915) 534-0500

Foreign Credit Insurance Association
600 Travis
Suite 2860
Houston, Texas 77002
(713) 227-0987

Fort Worth Chamber of Commerce
777 Taylor Street
Suite 900
Fort Worth, Texas 76102
(817) 336-2491

Greater San Antonio Chamber of
Commerce
P.O. Box 1628
San Antonio, Texas 78296
(512) 229-2100

Houston Chamber of Commerce
1100 Milam Building, 25th Floor
Houston, Texas 77002
(713) 651-1313

Houston World Trade Association
1100 Milam Building, 24th Floor
Houston, Texas 77002
(713) 658-2401

Lubbock Chamber of Commerce
14th Street & Avenue K
P.O. Box 561
Lubbock, Texas 79408
(806) 763-4666

Odessa Chamber of Commerce
P.O. Box 3626
400 West 4th
Odessa, Texas 79760
(915) 332-9111

Texas Department of Agriculture
Export Services Division
P.O. Box 12847, Capitol Station
Austin, Texas 78711
(512) 475-2760

Texas Economic Development Commission
International Trade Department
P.O. Box 12728
Austin, Texas 78711
(512) 472-5059

Texas Industrial Development Council, Inc.
P.O. Box 1002
College Station, Texas 77841
(409) 845-2911

U.S. Chamber of Commerce
4835 LBJ Freeway, Suite 750
Dallas, Texas 75244
(214) 387-0404

Utah

U.S. Department of Commerce

US&FCS District Office
U.S. Post Office Building
Room 340

350 South Main Street
Salt Lake City, Utah 84101
(801) 524-5116

U.S. Small Business Administration
125 South State Street
Room 2237
Salt Lake City, Utah 84138
(801) 524-5800

Salt Lake Area Chamber of Commerce
Export Development Committee
175 East 400 South
Suite 600
Salt Lake City, Utah 84111
(801) 364-3631

Utah Economic & Industrial Development
Division
6150 State Office Building
Salt Lake City, Utah 84114
(801) 538-3037

World Trade Association of Utah
10 Exchange Place
Suite 301-302
Salt Lake City, Utah 84111
(801) 531-1515

Vermont

U.S. Department of Commerce

US&FCS District Office
—See listing for Boston, Massachusetts

U.S. Small Business Administration
87 State Street, Room 204
P.O. Box 605
Montpelier, Vermont 05602
(802) 828-3221

Department of Economic Development
Pavilion Office Building
Montpelier, Vermont 05602
(802) 828-3221

Virginia

U.S. Department of Commerce

US&FCS District Office
8010 Federal Building
400 North 8th Street
Richmond, Virginia 23240
(804) 771-2246

U.S. Small Business Administration
3015 Federal Building
400 North 8th Street
Richmond, Virginia 23240
(804) 771-2617

International Trade Association of Northern
Virginia
P.O. Box 2982
Reston, Virginia 22090

International Trade Development
Division of Industrial Development
1010 Washington Building
Richmond, Virginia 23219
(804) 786-3791

Newport News Export Trading System
Department of Development
Peninsula Export Program
2400 Washington Avenue
Newport News, Virginia 32607
(804) 247-8751

Vextrac/Export Trading Company of the
Virginia Port Authority
600 World Trade Center
Norfolk, Virginia 23510
(804) 683-8000

(Virginia) Chamber of Commerce
9 South Fifth Street
Richmond, Virginia 23219
(804) 644-1607

Virginia Department of Agriculture &
Consumer Services
P.O. Box 1163
Richmond, Virginia 23209
(804) 786-3501

Virginia District Export Council
P.O. Box 10190
Richmond, Virginia 23240
(804) 771-2246

Washington

U.S. Department of Commerce
706 Lake Union Building
1700 Westlake Avenue North
Seattle, Washington 98109
(206) 442-5616

U.S. Small Business Administration
915 Second Avenue

Room 1792
Seattle, Washington 98174
(206) 442-5534

U.S. Small Business Administration
Farm Credit Building
10th Floor East
West 601 First Avenue
Spokane, Washington 99214
(509) 353-2800

Department of Trade & Economic
Development
International Trade & Investment Division
312 1st Avenue North
Seattle, Washington 98109
(206) 464-6282

Economic Development Council of Puget
Sound
219 First Avenue, South
Suite 305
Seattle, Washington 98104
(206) 623-2744

Inland Empire World Trade Club
P.O. Box 3727
Spokane, Washington 99220
(509) 922-8609

Seattle Chamber of Commerce
Trade & Transportation Division
600 University Street
Suite 1200
Seattle, Washington 98101
(206) 461-7200

Washington Council on International Trade
2615 4th Avenue
Suite 350
Seattle, Washington 98121
(206) 443-3825

Washington State Department of Agriculture
406 General Administration Building
Mail Stop: AX41
Olympia, Washington 98504
(206) 753-5046

World Affairs Council
Stouffer–Madison Hotel
Suite 501
515 Madison Street
Seattle, Washington 98104
(206) 682-6986

World Trade Club of Bellevue
10500 Northeast Eighth Street
Suite 750
Bellevue, Washington 98004
(206) 454-2464

World Trade Club of Seattle
1402 Third Avenue, Suite 414
Seattle, Washington 98101
(206) 621-0344

West Virginia
U.S. Department of Commerce
US&FCS District Office
3000 New Federal Office Building
500 Quarrier Street
Charleston, West Virginia 25301
(304) 347-5123

U.S. Small Business Administration
P.O. Box 1608
Clarksburg, West Virginia 26302-1608
(304) 623-5631

U.S. Small Business Administration
550 Eagan Street, Room 309
Charleston, West Virginia 25301
(304) 347-5220

Governor's Office of Economic &
   Community Development
State Capitol, Room B-517
Charleston, West Virginia 25305
(304) 348-2234

West Virginia Chamber of Commerce
P.O. Box 2789
Charleston, West Virginia 25330
(304) 342-1115

West Virginia Manufacturers Association
405 Capitol Street
Suite 505
Charleston, West Virginia 25301
(304) 342-2123

Wisconsin

U.S. Department of Commerce

US&FCS District Office
605 Federal Building
517 East Wisconsin Avenue

Milwaukee, Wisconsin 53202
(414) 291-3473

U.S. Small Business Administration
212 East Washington Avenue
Room 213
Madison, Wisconsin 53703
(608) 264-5261

U.S. Small Business Administration
500 South Barstow Street
Room 17
Eau Claire, Wisconsin 54701
(715) 834-9012

U.S. Small Business Administration
310 West Wisconsin Avenue, Room 400
Milwaukee, Wisconsin 53203
(414) 291-3941

Milwaukee Association of Commerce
756 North Milwaukee Street
Milwaukee, Wisconsin 53202
(414) 273-3000

Small Business Development Center
602 State Street
Madison, Wisconsin 53703
(608) 263-7766

Wisconsin Department of Development
123 West Washington Avenue
Madison, Wisconsin 53702
(608) 266-1767

Wyoming

U.S. Department of Commerce

US&FCS District Office
—See listing for Denver, Colorado

U.S. Small Business Administration
100 East "B" Street, Room 4001
Casper, Wyoming 82602
(307) 261-5761

Department of Economic Planning
Industrial Development Division
Barrett Building, 3rd Floor
Cheyenne, Wyoming 82002
(307) 777-7285

SECTION 7

ORGANIZATIONS OF INTEREST

There are many associations and organizations set up nationally and locally to facilitate U.S.–overseas trade and investment. We have listed some of the most relevant ones here. Some are industry associations which provide information and services to member companies and the interested public. These associations also frequently play a lobbying role to protect the interests of the industry against unfavorable laws and regulations. One example of such an industry association is the American Association of Exporters and Importers. Other types of organizations of interest to potential international business persons include councils designed to promote U.S. trade with, and investment in, specific regions of the world, such as the ASEAN–U.S. Business Council. There are also organizations that play the role of advocate for, and advisor to, U.S. business, such as the International Insurance Advisory Council. Still another category includes multilateral organizations that facilitate international business transactions, such as the International Bank for Reconstruction and Development (the World Bank). Finally, some organizations are more along the lines of a "think tank" or policy center, such as the Council on Foreign Relations.

ASEAN-U.S. Business Council
1400 L Street NW, Suite 650
Washington, D.C. 20062
Tel: (202) 289-1911

Academy of International Business
World Trade Education Center
Cleveland State University
Cleveland, Ohio 44115
Tel: (216) 687-3733

Advisory Council on Japan-U.S. Economic
   Relations
1020 19th Street, NW, Suite 130
Washington, D.C. 20036
Tel: (202) 728-0068

Affiliated Advertising Agencies International
World Headquarters
2280 Xanadu Way, Suite 300
Aurora, Colorado 80014
Tel: (303) 671-8551

American Arbitration Association
140 West 51st Street
New York, New York 10020
Tel: (212) 484-4000

American Association of Exporters and
   Importers
30th Floor, 11 West 42nd Street
New York, New York 10036
Tel: (212) 944-2230

American Enterprise Institute for Public
   Policy Research
1150 17th Street, NW, Suite 1200
Washington, D.C. 20036
Tel: (202) 862-5800

American Institute of Marine Underwriters
14 Wall Street, 21st Floor
New York, New York 10005
Tel: (212) 233-0550

American Management Association
440 1st Street, NW
Washington, D.C. 20001
Tel: (202) 347-3092

American National Metric Council
1010 Vermont Avenue, NW, Suite 1010
Washington, D.C. 20005
Tel: (202) 628-5757

American Society of International
Executives

Dublin Hall, 1777 Walton, Suite 419
Blue Bell, Pennsylvania 19422
Tel: (215) 643-3040

American Society of International Law
2223 Massachusetts Avenue, NW
Washington, D.C. 20008
Tel: (202) 265-4313

Bankers Association for Foreign Trade
1600 M Street, NW, 7th Floor
Washington, D.C. 20036
Tel: (202) 452-0952

Brazil-U.S. Business Council
Chamber of Commerce of the United States
International Division
1615 H Street, NW
Washington, D.C. 20062
Tel: (202) 463-5485

Brookings Institution
1775 Massachusetts Avenue, NW
Washington, D.C. 20036
Tel: (202) 797-6000

Bulgarian-U.S. Economic Council
25 East Algonquin
Des Plains, Illinois 60017-5017
Tel: (708) 391-2000

Caribbean Central American Action
1333 New Hampshire Avenue, NW
Washington, D.C. 20036
Tel: (202) 466-7464

Chamber of Commerce of the United States
1615 H Street, NW
Washington, D.C. 20062
Tel: (202) 659-6000

Coalition for Employment Through Exports,
   Inc.
1801 K Street, NW, 8th Floor
Washington, D.C. 20006
Tel: (202) 296-6107

Committee for Economic Development
1700 K Street, NW
Washington, D.C. 20006
Tel: (202) 296-5860

Committee for Production Sharing
1629 K Street, NW
Washington, D.C. 20006
Tel: (202) 296-3232

Committee for Small Business Exports
P.O. Box 6
Aspen, Colorado 81612
Tel: (303) 925-7567

Committee on Canada–U.S. Relations
Chamber of Commerce of the United States
International Division
1615 H Street, NW
Washington, D.C. 22062
Tel: (202) 463-5478

Conference Board
845 Third Avenue
New York, New York 10022
Tel: (212) 759-0900

Council for Export Trading Companies
1225 Connecticut Avenue, NW,
Suite 415
Washington, D.C. 20036
Tel: (202) 861-4705

Council of the Americas
680 Park Avenue
New York, New York 10021
Tel: (212) 628-3200

Council on Foreign Relations, Inc.
58 East 68th Street
New York, New York 10021
Tel: (212) 734-0400

Customs and International Bar Association
475 Park Avenue
New York, New York 10016
Tel: (212) 725-0200

Czechoslovak-U.S. Economic Council
Chamber of Commerce of the United States
International Division
1615 H Street, NW
Washington, D.C. 20062
Tel: (202) 463-5482

Egypt-U.S. Business Council
Chamber of Commerce of the United States
International Division
1615 H Street, NW
Washington, D.C. 20062
Tel: (202) 463-5487

Emergency Committee for American Trade
1211 Connecticut Avenue,
Suite 801

Washington, D.C. 20036
Tel: (202) 659-5147

Foreign Credit Interchange Bureau
National Association of Credit Management
520 8th Avenue
New York, New York 10018
Tel: (212) 947-5070

Fund for Multinational Management
   Education
680 Park Avenue
New York, New York 10021
Tel: (212) 535-9386

Hungarian-U.S. Economic Council
Chamber of Commerce of the United States
International Division
1615 H Street, NW
Washington, D.C. 20062
Tel: (202) 463-5482

Ibero American Chamber of Commerce
2100 M Street, NW,
Suite 607
Washington, D.C. 20037
Tel: (202) 737-2676

India–U.S. Business Council
Chamber of Commerce of the United States
International Division
1615 H Street, NW
Washington, D.C. 20062
Tel: (202) 463-5492

International Advertising Association
342 Madison Avenue, 20th Floor,
Suite 2000
New York, New York 10077
Tel: (212) 557-1133

International Airforwarders and Agents
   Association
310 Swann Avenue
Alexandira, Virginia 22301
Tel: (703) 463-4800

International Bank for Reconstruction and
   Development
1818 H Street, NW
Washington, D.C. 20006
Tel: (202) 477-1234

International Business Council MidAmerica
401 N. Wabash Avenue,
Suite 538

Chicago, Illinois 60611
Tel: (312) 222-1424

International Cargo Gear Bureau
17 Battery Place
New York, New York 10004
Tel: (212) 425-2750

International Economic Policy Association
1625 Eye Street, NW
Washington, D.C. 20006
Tel: (202) 331-1974

International Finance Corporation
1818 H Street, NW
Washington, D.C. 20433
Tel: (202) 477-1234

International Insurance Advisory Council
Chamber of Commerce of the United States
International Division
1615 H Street, NW
Washington, D.C. 20062
Tel: (202) 463-5480

International Trade Council
750 13th Street, SE
Washington, D.C. 20003
Tel: (202) 233-4880

Israel–U.S. Business Council
Chamber of Commerce of the United States
International Division
1615 H Street, NW
Washington, D.C. 20062
Tel: (202) 463-5478

National Association of Export Companies
17 Battery Place
Suite 1425
New York, New York 10004
Tel: (212) 809-8023

National Association of Manufacturers
1331 Pennsylvania Avenue, NW
Washington, D.C. 20006
Tel: (202) 637-3000

National Association of State Development
  Agencies
Hall of State,
Suite 345
444 North Capitol, NW
Washington, D.C. 20001
Tel: (202) 624-5411

National Council for U.S.–China Trade

1818 Street, NW
Washington, D.C. 20036
Tel: (202) 429-0340

National Custom Brokers and Forwarders
  Association of America
Five World Trade Center,
Suite 9273
New York, New York 10048
Tel: (212) 432-0050

National Export Traffic League
234 Fifth Avenue
New York, New York 10001
Tel: (212) 697-5895

National Foreign Trade Council
100 E. 42nd Street
New York, New York 10017
Tel: (212) 867-5630

Nigeria–U.S. Economic Council
Chamber of Commerce of the United States
International Division
1615 H Street, NW
Washington, D.C. 20062
Tel: (202) 463-5734

Organization of American States
19th & Constitution Avenue, NW
Washington, D.C. 20006
Tel: (202) 789-3000

Overseas Development Council
1717 Massachusetts Avenue, NW
Washington, D.C. 20036
Tel: (202) 234-8701

Overseas Sales and Marketing Association
  of America
P.O. Box 37
Lake Bluff, Illinois 60044
Tel: (312) 234-1760

Pacific Agricultural Cooperative for Export
21 Tamal Vista Boulevard,
Suite 106
Corte Madera, California 94925
Tel: (415) 924-2442

Pan American Development Foundation
1889 F Street, NW
Washington, D.C. 20006
Tel: (202) 789-3969

Partners of the Americas
1424 K Street, NW

Washington, D.C. 20005
Tel: (202) 628-3300

Partnership for Productivity International
2001 S Street, NW
 Suite 610
Washington, D.C. 20009
Tel: (202) 234-0340

Polish–U.S. Economic Council
Chamber of Commerce of the United States
International Division
1615 H Street, NW
Washington, D.C. 20062
Tel: (202) 463-5482

Romanian–U.S. Economic Council
Chamber of Commerce of the United States
International Division
1615 H Street, NW
Washington, D.C. 20062
Tel: (202) 463-5482

Sell Overseas America, The Association of
 American Export
2500 Artesia Boulevard
Redondo Beach, California 90278
Tel: (213) 318-2678

Sudan–U.S. Business Council
Chamber of Commerce of the United States
International Division
1615 H Street, NW
Washington, D.C. 20062
Tel: (202) 463-5487

Trade Relations Council of the
 United States, Inc.
1001 Connecticut Avenue, NW,
Room 901
Washington, D.C. 20036
Tel: (202) 785-4194

U.S.–Republic of China Economic Council
200 Main Street
Crystal Lake, Illinois 60014
Tel: (815) 459-5875

U.S.–U.S.S.R. Trade and Economic Council
805 3rd Avenue,
14th Floor
New York, New York 10022
Tel: (212) 644-4550

The U.S.–Yugoslav Economic Council, Inc.
1511 K Street, NW,
Suite 431
Washington, D.C. 20005
Tel: (202) 737-9652

Western International Trade Group
P.O. Box 20551
Phoenix, Arizona 85038
Tel: (602) 271-6361

World Trade Institute
One World Trade Center, 55 West
New York, New York 10048
(212) 466-4044

SECTION 8

FURTHER READING/BIBLIOGRAPHY*

This bibliography contains more information on specific aspects of the global market. Once again, this bibliography is by no means exhaustive, but it does provide references for those who need more in-depth information on specific industries, countries and regions of the world, project financing, exporting and importing, market research, etc. Many of the books and publications listed also provide bibliographies, this opening the way even more for the hungry reader.

1. Market identification and assessment

Addresses to AID Missions Overseas, Office of Small and Disadvantaged Business Utilization/Minority Business Center, Agency for International Development, Washington, D.C. 20523. Free.

AID Commodity Eligibility Listing, Office of Small and Disadvantaged Business Utilization/Minority Resource Center, Agency for International Development, Washington, D.C. 20523, 1984 revised. This document lists groups of commodities, presents the agency for International Development (AID) commodity eligibility list, gives eligibility re-

quirements for certain commodities and describes commodities that are not eligible for financing by the agency. Free.

AID Regulation 1, Office of Small and Disadvantaged Business Utilization/Minority Resource Center, Agency for International Development, Washington, D.C. 20523. This tells what transactions are eligible for financing by the Agency for International Development (AID), and the responsibilities of importers, as well as the bid procedures. Free.

AID Financed Export Opportunities, Office of Small and Disadvantaged Business Utilizations/Minority Resource Center, Agency for International Development, Washington,

*Source: U.S. Department of Commerce, Ernst & Young.

D.C. 10523. These are fact sheets also referred to as "Small Business Circulars." They present procurement data about proposed foreign purchases. Free.

American Bulletin of International Technology Transfer, International Advancement, P.O. Box 75537, Los Angeles, CA 90057. Bimonthly. This is a comprehensive listing of product and service opportunities offered and wanted for licensing and joint ventures agreements in the United States and overseas. $72 per year.

Annual Worldwide Industry Reviews (AWIR), Export Promotion Services, U.S. Department of Commerce, P.O. Box 14207, Washington, D.C. 20044; Tel: (202) 377-2432. These reports provide a combination of country by country market assessments, export trends, and a 5-year statistical table of U.S. exports for a single industry integrated into one report. They quickly show an industry's performance for the most recent year in most countries. Each report covers 8 to 18 countries. A single report is $200; two reports within the same industry are $350; and three reports within the same industry are $500.

Big Business Blunders: Mistakes in Multinational Marketing, 1982, David A. Ricks, Dow Jones-Irwin, Homewood, IL 60430. 200 pp. $13.95.

Business America, International Trade Administration, U.S. Department of Commerce. This magazine is the principal Commerce Department publication for presenting domestic and international business news and news of the application of technology to business and industrial problems. Available through the Superintendent of Documents, Government Printing Office, Washington, D.C. 20402. Annual subscription, $57.

Business Guide to EC Initiatives, 1989, American Chamber of Commerce in Belgium, EC Affairs Office, Avenues des Arts 50, bte 5, 1040 Brussels, Belgium; Tel: 513.6892. 88 pp., $35.

Catalogo de Publicaciones de la OPS, Pan American Health Organization/World Health Organization, 525 23rd Street, NW., Washington, D.C. 20037. A free guide of publications, many of which are in English. This catalog is published in Spanish.

The China Venture: America's Corporate Encounter with the People's Republic of China, Christopher Engholm, 1989, Scott, Foresman, and Company, Glenview, IL. 377 pp., $24.95.

Commodity Trade Statistics, Series D, United Nations, annual. Imports and exports of member countries by SITC product classifications.

Country Market Surveys (CMS), Export Promotions Services, U.S. Department of Commerce, P.O. Box 14207, Washington, D.C. 20044; Tel: (202) 377-2432. This report series offers short summaries of International Market Research (IMR) geared to the needs of the busy executive. They highlight market size, trends and prospects in an easy-to-read format. $10 per copy or $9 per copy for six or more.

Country Trade Statistics (CTS), Export Promotion Services, U.S. Department of Commerce, P.O. Box 14207, Washington, D.C. 20044; Tel: (202) 377-2432. This is a set of four key tables that indicate which U.S. products are in the greatest demand, in a specific country over the most recent five-year period. They indicate which U.S. industries look best for export to a particular country and the export performance of single industries. Tables highlight the top U.S. exports, those with the largest market share, the fastest growing, and those which are the primary U.S. market. The CTS is $25 for the first country, and $10 for each additional country up to 25.

Cracking the Global Market: How to Do Business Around the Corner and Around the World, Jack Nadel, 1987, American Management Association, 246 pp., $17.95.

Creative Countertrade: A Guide to Doing Business Worldwide, Kenton W. Elderkin and Warren E. Norquist, 1987, Ballinger Publishing Company, 236 pp., $32.

Current Economic Indicators, United Nations, quarterly. Lists about 500 economic indicators for the world's countries.

Custom Statistical Service, Export Promotion Services, U.S. Department of Commerce, P.O. Box 14207, Washington, D.C. 20044; Tel: (202) 377-2432. Individually tailored tables of U.S. exports or imports. The custom service provides data for specific products or countries of interest, or for ones which may not appear in the standard ESP country and product rankings for a chosen industry. With Custom Statistics one can also obtain data in other formats such as quantity, unit quantity, unit value and percentages. Custom orders are priced by the number of products, countries, or other data desired, and range from $50 to $500.

Developments in International Trade Policy, International Monetary Fund, Publications Unit, 700 19th Street, NW., Washington, D.C. 20431. This paper focuses on the main current issues in trade policies of the major trading nations. $5.

Direction of Trade Statistics, International Monetary Fund, Publications Unit, 700 19th Street, NW., Washington, D.C. 20431. This monthly publication provides data on the country and area distribution of countries' exports and imports as reported by themselves or their partners. A yearbook is published annually which gives seven years of data for 157 countries and two sets of world and area summaries. $36 for 12 monthly issues, including the yearbook. Single monthly issue is $14, the yearbook is $10.

Directory of Leading U.S. Export Management Companies, 1984, Bergamo Book Co., 15 Ketchum Street, Westport, CT 06881. $37.50.

Economic and Social Survey for Asia and the Pacific, UNIPUB, P.O. Box 1222, Ann Arbor, MI 48106; Tel: (800) 521-8110. This publication analyzes recent economic and social developments in the region in the context of current trends. It examines agriculture, food, industry, transport, public finance, wages and prices, and external trade sectors. $19.

Element of Export Marketing, John Stapleton, 1984, Woodhead-Faulkner, Dover, NH, $11.25.

Entry Strategies for Foreign Markets—From Domestic to International Business, Franklin R. Root, American Management Association, 1977, 51 pp. $10.

EC Information Handbook, 1989, EC Committee of the American Chamber of Commerce in Belgium, Avenue des Arts 50, bte 5, 1040 Brussels, Belgium; Tel: 513.6892, 124 pp.

EC 1992: A Commerce Department Analysis of European Community Directives, 1989, Debra L. Miller, ed., Office of Industrial Trade, Department of Commerce, U.S. Government Printing Office, Washington, D.C. 20402; Tel: (202) 783-3238. This report assesses the impact of the European Community's 1992 program on U.S. industry, analyzing 66 key EC 1992 directives on manufactured products and services. The first in a series of three volumes, 161 pp., $10.

EXIM Bank Information Kit, Public Affairs Office, Export-Import Bank of the United States, 811 Vermont Avenue, NW., Washington, D.C. 20571. This includes the bank's annual report, which provides information on interest rates and the Foreign Credit Insurance Association.

Export Development Strategies: U.S. Promotion Policy, Michael R. Czinkota and George Tasar, Praeger, New York, NY, 1982, $27.95.

Export Directory, Foreign Agricultural Services, Department of Agriculture, 14th & Independence Avenues, SW., Room 5918-S, Washington, D.C. 20230. The directory describes the principal functions of the Foreign Agricultural Service and lists agricultural attaches. Free.

Export Directory: Buying Guide, biennial, Journal of Commerce. 110 Wall Street, New York, NY 10005. $225.

Export-Import Bank: Financing for American Exports—Support for American Jobs, Export-Import Bank of the United States, 1980. Free.

Export/Import Operations: A Manager's "How to" and "Why" Guide, Robert M. Franko, 1979, Professional Business Services, Inc. $35.

Export Sales and Marketing Manual, John R. Jagoe, 1989, Export USA Publications, P.O. Box 35422, Minneapolis, MN 55435; Tel: (800) 876-0624. 320 pp., $298.50

Export Statistics Profiles (ESP), Export Promotion Services, U.S. Department of Commerce, P.O. Box 14207, Washington, D.C. 20044; Tel: (202) 377-2432. These tables of U.S. exports for a specific industry help identify the best export markets and analyze the industry's exports product-by-product, country-by-country over each of the last five years to date. Data is rank-ordered by dollar value. The price is $70.00 for each ESP.

Export Strategies: Markets and Competition, Nigel Percy, 1982, Allen & Unwin, Winchester, MA 01890, $30 (cloth), $13.95 (paper).

Exporters Directory/U.S. Buying Guide, The Journal of Commerce, latest edition, Phillipsburg, NJ. Includes a nationwide directory of 40,000 U.S. exporters, and an SITC product index listing 1,300 products together with their U.S. exporters.

Exporter's Guide to Federal Resources for Small Business, U.S. Small Business Administration, 1988, U.S. Government Printing Office. Available through the Superintendent of Documents, U.S. Government Printing Office, Washington, DC 20402-9325; Tel: (202) 783-3238. 111 pp., $4.50.

Exporter's Encyclopedia, annual with semi-monthly updates, Dun & Bradstreet International, One Exchange Plaza, Suite 715, Jersey City, NJ 07302. This provides a comprehensive, country-by-county coverage of 220 world markets. It contains an examination of each country's communications and transporta-

tion facilities, customs and trade regulations, documentation, key contacts, and unusual conditions that may affect operations. Financing and credit abroad are also examined. $365 per year.

Exporting: A Practical Manual for Developing Export Markets and Dealing with Foreign Customs, 2nd edition, Earnst Y. Maitland, 1982, 150 pp., Self-Counsel Press, $12.50.

Exporting from the U.S.A.: How to Develop Export Markets and Cope with Foreign Customs, A.B. Marring, 1981, 114 pp., Self-Counsel Press, $12.95.

Exporting to Japan, American Chamber of Commerce in Japan, 1982, A.M. Newman. $10.

FAS Commodity Reports, U.S. Department of Agriculture, Foreign Agriculture Service, Room 5918, Washington, D.C. 20250; Tel: (202) 477-7937. These reports provide information on foreign agricultural production in 22 commodity areas. Reports are based on information submitted by Foreign Agricultural Service (FAS) personnel overseas. The publication frequency varies with the commodity. The price is $1-$460 depending on commodity and whether the report is mailed or picked up at the USDA office.

FATUS: Foreign Agricultural Trade of the United States, U.S. Department of Agriculture, Foreign Agriculture Service, Room 5918, Washington, D.C. 20250; Tel: (202) 477-7937. This report of trends in U.S. agricultural trade by commodity and country and of events affecting this trade is published six times a year with two supplements. The price is $19 per year.

Findex: The Directory of Market Research Reports, Studies and Surveys, FIND/SVP, The Information Clearinghouse, 500 Fifth Avenue, New York, NY 10036; Tel: (212) 354-2424. Over 10,000 listings. $245.

Foreign Agriculture, U.S. Department of Agriculture, Foreign Agriculture Service, Room 5918, Washington, D.C. 20250; Tel: (202)

477-7937. A monthly publication containing information on overseas markets and buying trends, new competitors and products, trade policy developments and overseas promotional activities. The price is $16 per year.

Foreign Agriculture Circulars, U.S. Department of Agriculture, Foreign Agriculture Service, Room 5918, Washington, D.C. 20250; Tel: (202) 477-7937. These individual circulars report on the supply and demand for commodities around the world. Products covered include: dairy, livestock, poultry, grains, coffee, and wood products. The frequency of publication varies with the commodity. The price is $3 to $66 depending on commodity.

Foreign Commerce Handbook, Chamber of Commerce of the United States, 1615 H Street, NW., Washington, D.C. 20062. A publication containing organizations of assistance to U.S. exporters, as well as up-to-date published information on all important phases of international trade and investment. $10.

Foreign Economic Trends (FET), Superintendent of Documents, U.S. Government Printing Office, Washington, D.C. 20402. Prepared by the U.S. and Foreign Commercial Service. This presents current business and economic developments and the latest economic indications in more than 100 countries. Annual subscription, $70; single copies are available for $1 from ITA Publications Distribution, Rm. 1617D, U.S. Department of Commerce, Washington, D.C. 20230.

Foreign Market Entry Strategies, Franklin R. Root, 1982, AMACOM, New York, NY 10020, 304 pp. $24.95.

Foreign Trade Bulletins, Series C, OECD, semiannual. For 21 OECD countries, this publication gives in two volumes (imports and exports) the quantity and value of international trade for 272 commodity categories.

General Economic Problems, OECD Publications and information Center, Suite 1207, 1750 Pennsylvania Avenue, NW., Washington, D.C. 20006-4582; Tel: (202) 724-1859.

This contains the latest monographs on: economic policies and forecasts; growth; inflation; national accounts; international trade and payments; capital markets; interest rates; taxation; and energy, industrial and agricultural policies. $144.25.

Global Risk Assessments: Issues, Concepts, and Applications, Book 3, 1988, Jerry Rodgers, ed., Global Risk Assessments, Inc., 239 pp., $32.50.

Glossary of International Terms, International Trade Institute, Inc., 5055 N. Main Street, Dayton, OH 45415; Tel: (800) 543-2453. 68 pp. $17.50.

A Guide to Export Marketing, International Trade Institute, Inc., 5055 North Main Street, Suite 270, Dayton, OH 45415; Tel: (800) 453-2453. $50.

Guide to Foreign Trade Statistics, U.S. Department of Commerce, latest edition. Identifies and describes the coverage of all foreign trade reports and tabulations prepared by Census.

Handbook of International Business, Second Edition, 1988, Ingo Walter and Tracy Murray, eds., John Wiley & Sons, Inc.

Handbook of International Statistics, UNIPUB, P.O. Box 1222, Ann Arbor, MI 48106; Tel: (800) 521-8110. The handbook examines structural trends in 70 developing and developed countries, including: changes in the pattern of consumption for specific commodities; long-term patterns of growth; and the export performance of key industries, $22.

Highlights of U.S. Import and Export Trade, Superintendent of Documents, U.S. Government Printing Office, Washington, D.C. 20402. Statistical book of U.S. imports and exports. Compiled monthly by the Bureau of the Census. $41 per year; single copies, $4.50.

How to Build an Export Business: An International Marketing Guide for Minority-Owned Businesses, Superintendent of Documents, U.S. Government Printing Office, Washington, D.C. 20402, $10.

Import/Export Can Make You Rich, L.B. Lanze, 1988, Prentice-Hall, Inc., Englewood Cliffs, NJ 07632, 307 pp., $19.95.

Import/Export: A Guide to Growth, Profits, and Market Share, Howard R. Goldsmith, 1989, Prentice-Hall, Inc., Englewood Cliffs, NJ 07632, 484 pp., $19.95.

Index to Foreign Market Reports, U.S. Department of Commerce, monthly. Monthly. Lists all the Foreign Market Reports prepared by Department of Commerce by country and SIC product code.

Inside Washington: The International Business Executive's Guide to Government Resources, 1988, William A. Delphos, ed., Madison Books, Lanham, MD. This reference makes Government services more accessible to American investors, exporters, contractors, and service firms by organizing the information by product or service rather than by government agency. Available through Venture Marketing Corporation, 600 Watergate NW, Suite 850, Washington, D.C. 20037; Tel: (202) 377-6300. 295 pp., $19.95.

International Development, OECD Publications and Information Center, Suite 1207, 1750 Pennsylvania Avenue, NW., Washington, D.C. 20006-4582; Tel: (202) 724-1857. This contains the latest monographs on: financial resources and aid policies, general problems of development, industrialization, transfer of technology, rural development, employment, human resources, immigration, and demography. $173.

International Financial Statistics, International Monetary Fund, Publications Unit, 700 19th Street, NW., Washington, D.C. 20431. This monthly publication is a standard source of international statistics on all aspects of international and domestic finance. It reports, for most countries of the world, current data needed in the analysis of problems of international payments and of inflation and deflation, i.e., data on exchange rates, international liquidity, money and banking,

international transactions, prices, production, government finance, interest rates, and other items. $10 per issue, or $100 per year, including a yearbook and two supplement series.

International Market Research (IMR) Reports, Export Promotion Services, U.S. Department of Commerce, P.O. Box 14207, Washington, D.C. 20044; Tel: (202) 377-2432.. This is an in-depth industry sector analysis for those who want the complete data for one industry in one country. A report includes information such as behavior characteristics, trade barriers, market share figures, end user analysis, and trade contact. $50 to $250.

International Market Information (IMI), Export Promotion Services, U.S. Department of Commerce, P.O. Box 14207, Washington, D.C. 20044; Tel: (202) 377-2432. These are special "bulletins" that point out unique market situations and new opportunities to U.S. exporters in specific markets. $15.00 to $100.

International Marketing, 5th edition, 1983, Phillip R. Cateora, Irwin, Homewood, IL 60430. $29.95.

International Marketing, Michael R. Czinkota and Ilkka A. Ronkainen, 1988, The Dryden Press, 649, pp., $42.

International Marketing, Raul Kahler, 1983, Southwestern Publishing Co., Cincinnati, OH 45227. 426 pp.

International Marketing, 3rd edition, Vern Terpstra, 1983, Dryden Press, Hinsdale, IL 60521. 624 pp., $32.95.

International Marketing, Revised edition, Hans Thorelli & Helmut Becker, eds., 1980, Pergamon Press, Elmsford, NY 10523. 400 pp., $14.25.

International Marketing, 2nd edition, 1981, L.S. Walsh, International Ideas, Philadelphia, PA 19103. $15.95.

International Marketing: An Annotated Bibliography, 1983, S.T. Cavusgil & John R.

Nevin, eds., American Marketing Association. 139 pp., $8.

International Marketing Handbook, 1985, 3 vols., Frank S. Bair, eds., Gale Research Co., Detroit, MI 48226. 3,637 pp. $200.

International Marketing Research, 1983, Susan P. Douglas & C. Samuel Craig, Prentice-Hall, Englewood Cliffs, NJ 07632. 384 pp., $27.95.

International Monetary Fund: Publications Catalog, International Monetary Fund, Publications Unit, 700 19th Street, NW., Washington, D.C. 20431. Free.

International Trade Names Dictionary, First Edition, 1988-89, Donna Wood, ed., Gale Research, Inc., Book Tower, Detroit, MI 48226-9948. This publication provides current information about brand-named products in foreign countries. 366 pp., $240.

International Trade Operations...A Managerial Approach, R. Duane Hall, Unz & Co., 190 Baldwin Ave., Jersey City, NJ 07303. $42.50.

Local Chambers of Commerce Which Maintain Foreign Trade Services, 1983. International Division, Chamber of Commerce of the United States, 1615 H Street, NW., Washington, D.C. 20062. This is a list of chambers of commerce that have programs to aid exporters. Free.

Main Economic Indicators, OECD, monthly. Indicators include national accounts, industrial production, deliveries, stocks and orders, construction, retail sales, and other data for the 21 OECD countries.

Market Share Reports for U.S. Exports, U.S. Department of Commerce, latest issue. Compares exports of 14 major supplying countries (including the United States) to 92 foreign markets. Data are usually at the four or five-digit level of product classification.

Marketing Aspects of International Business, 1983, Gerald M. Hampton & Aart Van Gent, Klewer-Nijhoff Publishing. Bingham, MA., $39.50.

Marketing High-Technology, William L. Shanklin & John K. Ryans, Jr., DC Heath & Co., 125 Spring Street, Lexington, MA 02173. $24.

Marketing in Europe, Economic Intelligence Unit, Ltd., 10 Rockefeller Plaza, New York, NY 10020, monthly. This journal provides detailed analysis of the European market for consumer goods. The issues are published in three subject groups: food, drink, and tobacco; clothing, furniture, and consumer goods; and chemists' goods such as pharmaceuticals and toiletries. $380 for three groups per year.

Marketing in the Third World, Erdener Kaynak, Praeger, New York, NY 10175. 302 pp. $29.95.

Metric Laws and Practices in International Trade—Handbook for U.S. Exporters, U.S. Government Printing Office, Washington, D.C. 20402. 1982, 113 pp., $4.75.

Monthly Bulletin of Statistics, United Nations. Monthly supplement to Statistical Yearbook.

Monthly Trade Reports, FT 410, U.S. Department of Commerce, monthly. U.S. exports by product and country of destination. Uses five-digit Schedule B classification for products.

Monthly World Crop Production, U.S. Department of Agriculture, Foreign Agriculture Service, Room 5918, Washington, D.C. 20250; Tel: (477-7937. This report provides estimates on the projection of wheat, rice, coarse grains, oilseeds, and cotton in selected regions and countries around the world.

The Multinational Marketing and Employment Directory, 8th edition, World Trade Academy Press, Inc., 50 East 42nd Street, New York, NY 10017, 1982, two volumes. This directory lists more than 7,500 American corporations operating in the United States and overseas. The directory is recognized as an outstanding marketing source for products, skills and services in the United States and abroad. It is of particular value to manufacturers, distributors, international traders, investors, bankers, advertising agencies and libraries. It is also helpful for placement bureaus, executive recruiters, direct mail marketers, and technical and management consultants. The specialized arrangement of the information expedites sales in domestic and foreign markets. $90.

Multinational Marketing Management, 3rd edition, 1984, Warren J. Keegan, Prentice-Hall, Englewood Cliffs, NJ 07632. 720 pp., $31.95.

The 1988-89 Caribbean American Directory, 1988, North American Communications, 1377 K Street NW, Washington, D.C. 20005; Tel: (202) 544-3238. This directory, now in its fourth edition, lists each firm with current business interests in the Caribbean, Central America, Puerto Rico, and the U.S. Virgin Islands, and purpose and activity, key personnel, and products and services of those firms. 650 pp., $100.

1992: The European Community's Internal Market Program—Opportunities and Challenges for U.S. Firms, 1989, Manufacturers' Alliance for Productivity and Innovation, 1200 18th Street NW, Washington, D.C. 20036; Tel: (202) 331-8430. 98 pp., $30.

OECD Publications, OECD Publications and Information Center, Suite 1207, 1750 Pennsylvania Avenue, NW., Washington, D.C. 20006-4582; Tel: (202) 724-4582. Free.

Outlook for U.S. Agriculture Exports, U.S. Department of Agriculture, Foreign Agriculture Service, Room 5918, Washington, D.C. 20250; Tel: (202) 477-7937. This report analyzes current developments and forecasts U.S. farm exports in coming months by commodity and region. Country and regional highlights discuss the reasons why sales of major commodities are likely to rise or fall in those areas. The price is $7 per year.

Overseas Business Reports (OBR), Superintendent of Documents, U.S. Government Printing Office, Washington, D.C. 20402. These reports are prepared by the country

specialists in the International Trade Administration (ITA). The include current marketing information, trade forecasts, statistics, regulations, and marketing profiles. Annual subscription, $26. Single copies are available from ITA Publications, Rm. 1617D, U.S. Department of Commerce, Washington, D.C. 20230.

Practical Guide for Marketing to the Pacific Rim, Export Today, 1988, SIRCo International, P.O. Box 28189, Washington, D.C. 20038. $425 per year, subscription includes monthly *Special Update Report.*

Product/Country Market Profiles, Export Promotion Services, U.S. Department of Commerce, P.O. Box 14702, Washington, D.C. 20044; Tel: (202) 377-2432. These products are tailor-made, single product/multicountry; or single country/multiproduct reports. They include trade contacts, specific opportunities, and statistical analyses. $300 to $500.

Profitable Export Marketing: A Strategy for U.S. Business, Maria Ortiz-Buonafina, Prentice-Hall, Englewood Cliffs, NJ 07632. $9.95.

Reference Book for World Traders, Annual, Croner Publications, Inc., 211 Jamaica Avenue, Queens Village, NY 11428. A loose-leaf reference book for traders. Gives information about export documentation, steamship lines and airlines, free trade zones, credit and similar matters. Supplemented monthly.

Profitable Exporting: A Complete Guide to Marketing Your Products Abroad, John S. Gordon and Jack R. Arnold, 1988, John Wiley & Sons, 605 Third Avenue., New York, NY 10158. 353 pp., $42.50.

Setting Up a Company in the European Community: A Country by Country Guide, 1989, Brebner & Co., London; Oryx Press, 2214 North Central at Encanto, Phoenix, AZ 85004-1483; Tel: (800) 457-ORYX. 264 pp., $49.50.

Source Book... The "How to" Guide for Exporters and Importing, Unz & Co., 190 Baldwin Avenue, Jersey City, NJ 07036.

Statistical Classification of Domestic and Foreign Commodities Exported from the United States (Schedule B Manual), U.S. Department of Commerce, latest edition. Describes Schedule B product classifications used in all official U.S. export statistics.

Statistical Yearbook, United Nations. Data for more than 150 countries on broad range of economic and social subjects, including population, manpower, mining, agriculture, construction, manufacturing, trade, and national accounts.

Statistics of Foreign Trade, Series A, OECD, monthly. Shows trade statistics for each OECD country, including the composition of trade by SITC categories.

Trade and Development Report, UNIPUB, P.O. Box 1222, Ann Arbor, MI 48106; Tel: (800) 521-8110. This report reviews current economic issues and longer run development in international trade. $15.00.

Trade Directories in the World, Annual, Croner Publications, Inc., 211 Jamaica Avenue, Queens Village, NY 11428. $59.95 plus supplements.

Trends in World Production and Trade, UNIPUB, P.O. Box 1222, Ann Arbor, MI 48106; Tel: (800) 521-8110. This report discusses the structural change in world output, industrial growth patterns since 1960, changes in the pattern of agricultural output, and changes in patterns of trade in goods and services. Product groups and commodity groups are defined according to SITC criteria. $6.

United Nations Publications, United Nations and Information Center, 1889 F Street, NW, Washington, D.C. 20006. Free.

U.S. Export Sales. U.S. Department of Agriculture, Foreign Agriculture Service, Room 5918, Washington, D.C. 20250; Tel: (202) 477-7937. A weekly report of agricultural export sales based on reports provided by private exporters. There is no cost for this publication.

U.S. Export Weekly—International Trade Reporter, Bureau of National Affairs, Inc. $352 per year.

U.S. Farmers Export Arm, U.S. Department of Agriculture, Foreign Agricultural Service, Room 5918, Washington, D.C. 20250, 1980. Free.

U.S. Foreign Trade Highlights, 1988, Government Printing Office, 1990. The publication presents data on U.S. merchandise trade with major trading partners and regions. It also contains an overview that summarizes major trends in U.S. trade, with particular focus on 1989 developments. Available through the Superintendent of Documents, Government Printing Office, Washington, D.C. 20402-9325; Tel: (202) 783-3238. 492 pp., $25.

Weekly Roundup of World Production and Trade, U.S. Department of Agriculture, Foreign Agriculture Service, Room 5918, Washington, D.C.. 20250; Tel: (202) 477-7937. This publication provides a summary of the week's important events in agricultural foreign trade and world production. Free.

World Agriculture, U.S. Department of Agriculture, Foreign Agriculture Service, Room 5918, Washington, D.C. 20250; Tel: (202) 477-7937. Provides production information, data and analyses by commodity and country, along with a review of recent economic conditions and changes in food and trade policies. Price: $9 per year.

World Agriculture Regional Supplements, U.S. Department of Agriculture, Foreign Agriculture Service, Room 5918, Washington, D.C. 20250; Tel: (202) 477-7937. Provides a look by region at agricultural developments during the previous year and the outlook for the year ahead. Reports are published on North America/Oceania, Latin America, Eastern Europe, Western Europe, U.S.S.R., Middle East and North Africa, Subsaharan Africa, East Asia, China, South Asia, and Southeast Asia. Price: $18 per year.

The World Bank Catalog of Publications, World Bank Publications, P.O. Box 37525, Washington, D.C. 20013. Free.

World Economic Outlook: A Survey by the Staff of the International Monetary Fund, International Monetary Fund, Publications Unit, 700 19th Street, NW., Washington, D.C. 20431. This report provides a comprehensive picture of the international situation and prospects. It highlights the imbalances that persist in the world economy and their effects on inflation, unemployment, real rates of interest and exchange rates. Published yearly. $8.

World Economic Survey, UNIPUB, P.O. Box 1222, Ann Arbor, MI 48106; Tel: (800) 521-8110. This publications assesses the world economy. It provides an overview of developments in global economics for the past year and provides an outlook for the future. $12.

The World Factbook, 1990, Central Intelligence Agency, National Technical Information Service, Springfield, VA 22161; Tel: (703) 487-4650. 375 pp., $33.50.

Yearbook of International Trade Statistics, UNIPUB, P.O. Box 1222, Ann Arbor, MI 48106; Tel: (800) 521-8110. This yearbook offers international coverage of foreign trade statistics. Tables are provided for overall trade by regions and countries. Vol. I: Trade by Commodity. Vol II: Commodity Matrix Tables. Both volumes $80.

Yearbook of National Account Statistics, United Nations. Per-capita gross domestic product, national growth, disposable income, expenditure on gross domestic product, annual growth rates, and other aspects of national accounts.

2. Selling & sales contacts

American Export Register, Thomas Publishing Co., 1 Penn Plaza, 250 34th Street, New York, NY 10010, 1984. A listing of more than 25,000 firms, this book is designed for per-

sons searching for U.S. suppliers, for foreign manufacturers seeking U.S. buyers or representatives for their products. It contains product lists in four languages, an advertiser's index, information about and a list of U.S. Chambers of Commerce abroad, and a list of banks with international services and shipping, financing, and insurance information. $112.

Background Notes, Superintendent of Documents, U.S. Government Printing Office, Washington, DC 20402. These are four to twelve page summaries on the economy, people, history, culture, and government of about 160 countries. $42 per set; binders, $3.75.

A Business Guide to the Near East and North Africa, 1981. Superintendent of Documents, U.S. Government Printing Office, Washington, D.C. 20402, 28 pp. This guide is designed to provide U.S. business with information on the nature of these markets, how to do business in these areas, and how the Department of Commerce can help in penetrating these markets. $4.75.

Commercial News USA (CN), Monthly export promotion magazine circulated only overseas, listing specific products and services of U.S. firms. Applications for participation in the magazine are available from the District Office of the U.S. and Foreign Commercial Service, U.S. Department of Commerce.

Directory of American Firms Operating in Foreign Countries, 10th edition, 1984, World Trade Academy Press, 50 E. 42nd Street, New York, NY 10017, 1600 pp. This directory contains the most recent data on more than 4,200 American corporations controlling and operating more than 16,500 foreign business enterprises. It lists every American firm under the country in which it has subsidiaries or branches, together with their home office branch in the United States. It also gives the names and addresses of their subsidiaries or branches, products manufactured or distributed. $150.

Export Mailing List Services (EMLS), Export Promotion Services, U.S. Department of Commerce, P.O. Box 14207, Washington, D.C. 20044; Tel: (202) 377-2432. These are targeted mailing lists of prospective overseas customers from the Commerce Department's automated worldwide file of foreign firms. EMLs identify manufacturers, agents, retailers, service firms, government agencies and other one-to-one contacts. Information includes name and address, cable and telephone numbers, name and title of a key official, product/service interests, and additional data. $35 and up.

How to Get the Most from Overseas Exhibitions, International Trade Administration, Publications Distribution, Room 1617D, U.S. Department of Commerce, Washington, D.C. 20230. This eight-page booklet outlines the steps an exporter should take to participate in an overseas exhibition sponsored by the Department of Commerce. Free.

Japan: Business Obstacles and Opportunities, 1983, McKinney & Co., John Wiley, NY. $24.95.

Management of International Advertising: A Marketing Approach, 1984, Dean M. Peeples & John K. Ryans. Allyn & Bacon, Boston, MA 02159. 600 pp., $48.

The NEFEA Directory of Export Trade Intermediaries, 1989, National Federation of Export Associations, 4905 Del Ray Avenue, Suite 302, Bethesda, MD 20814; Tel: (301) 907-8647. This directory serves as a matchmaking resource between manufacturers and distributors and export management and trading companies that are seeking new products to market abroad. $15.

Service Industries and Economic Development: Case Studies in Technology Transfer, Praeger Publishers, New York, NY 10175, 1984. 190 pp., $24.95.

Top Bulletin, Export Promotion Services, U.S. Department of Commerce, P.O. Box 14207, Washington, D.C. 20044; Tel: (202) 377-2432. A weekly publication of trade opportunities received each week from overseas embassies and consulates. $175 per year. Also available on computer tape.

Trade Lists, Export Promotion Services, U.S. Department of Commerce, P.O. Box 14207, Washington, D.C. 20044; Tel: (202) 377-2432. Preprinted trade lists are comprehensive directories listing all the companies in a country across all product sectors, or all the companies in a single industry across all countries. Trade lists are priced from $12 to $40, depending on the age of the publication.

World Traders Data Reports (WTDRs), Export Promotion Services, U.S. Department of Commerce, P.O. Box 14207, Washington, D.C. 20044; Tel: (203) 377-2432. This service provides background reports on individual foreign firms. WTDRs are designed to help U.S. firms evaluate potential foreign customers before making a business commitment. $75 per report.

3. Financing exports

Chase World Guide for Exporters, Export Credit Reports, Chase World Information Corporation, One World Trade Center, Suite 4533, New York, NY 10048. The Guide, covering 180 countries, contains current export financing methods, collection experiences and charges, foreign import and exchange regulations and related subjects. Supplementary bulletins keep the guide up to date throughout the year. The Reports, issued quarterly, specify credit terms granted for shipment to all the principal world markets. The reports show the credit terms offered by the industry groups as a whole, thereby enabling the reader to determine whether his or her terms are more liberal or conservative than the average for specific commodity groups. Annual subscription for both the Guide and Reports, $345.

Commercial Export Financing: An Assist to Farm Products Sales, U.S. Department of Agriculture, Foreign Agricultural Service, Room 5918, Washington, D.C. 20250, 1980, brochure. Free.

Export-Import Financing—A Practical Guide, Gerhart W. Schneider, Ronald Press, 1974. This book presents details of foreign trade financing and services available for making international payments. $59.95.

Exporting From Start to Finance, L. Fargo Wells and Karin B. Dulat, 1989, Liberty House, 443 pp., $39.95.

FCIB International Bulletin, FCIB-NACM Corp., 475 Park Avenue South, New York, NY 10016, twice monthly. The bulletin presents export information and review of conditions and regulations in overseas markets. $175 per year.

Financing and Insuring Exports: A User's Guide to Eximbank and FCIA Programs, Export-Import Bank of the United States, User's Guide, 811 Vermont Avenue, NW., Washington, D.C. 20571. A 350-page guide which covers Eximbank's working capital guarantees, credit risk protection (guarantees and insurance), medium-term and long-term lending programs. Includes free updates during calendar year in which the guide is purchased. $50 (plus $5 postage and handling).

Financial Institutions and Markets in the Far east, Morgan Guarantee Trust Company of New York, 23 Wall Street, New York, NY 10015. The book discusses export letters of credit, drafts, and other methods of payment and regulations of exports and imports.

A Guide to Checking International Credit, International Trade Institute, Inc., 5055 North Main Street, Suite 270, Dayton, OH 45415.

A Guide to Financing Exports, U.S. and Foreign Commercial Service, International Trade Administration Publications Distribution, Room 1617D, U.S. Department of Commerce, Washington, D.C. 20230, 1985. Brochure, 40 pp. Free.

A Guide to Understanding Drafts, International Trade Institute, Inc., 5055 N. Main Street, Dayton, OH 45415; Tel: (800) 543-2455, 64 pp. $17.50.

A Guide to Understanding Letters of Credit, International Trade Institute, Inc., 5055 N. Main Street, Dayton, OH 45415, 138 pp. $34.50.

A Handbook on Financing U.S. Exports–5th Edition, Paul Pratt, 1988, MAPI, 1200 18th Street NW, Washington, D.C. 20036. 190 pp., $30.

Official U.S. and International Financing Institutions: A Guide for Exporters and Investors, International Trade Administration, U.S. Department of Commerce. Available from the Superintendent of Documents, U.S. Government Printing Office, Washington, D.C. 20402. $2.75.

A Practical Guide to Export Financing and Risk Management, Louis G. Guadagnoli, 1989, Government Information Services, 1611 North Kent St., Suite 508, Arlington, VA 22209; Tel: (703) 528-1000. 208 pp., $79.95.

Special Report on Financing Exports, Export Today, 1988, SIRCo International, P.O. Box 28189, Washington, D.C. 20038, $49.95.

Specifics on Commercial Letters of Credit and Bankers Acceptances, James A. Harrington, 1979, UNZ & Co., Division of Scott Printing Corp., 190 Baldwin Avenue, Jersey City, NJ 07036, 1979.

4. Laws and regulations

Customs Regulations of the United States, Superintendent of Documents, Government Printing Office, Washington, D.C. 20402, 1971. Reprint includes amended text in revised pages nos. 1 through 130 (includes subscription to revised pages). This contains regulations for carrying out customs, navigation and other laws administered by the Bureau of Customs.

Distribution License, 1985 Office of Export Administration, Room 1620, U.S. Department of Commerce, Washington, D.C. 20230. Free.

Export Administration Regulations, Superintendent of Documents, Government Printing Office, Washington, D.C. 20402. Covers U.S. export control regulations and policies, with instructions, interpretations and explanatory material. Last revised Oct. 1, 1984, $65 plus supplements.

Export Marketing of Capital Goods to the Socialist Countries of Eastern Europe, 1978, M.R. Hill, Gower Publishing Company, 200 pp. $50.75.

Guide to The New Trade Law: What's in it for U.S. Exporters? Export Today, 1988, SIRCo International, P.O. Box 28189, Washington, D.C. 20038, $34.50.

Manual for the Handling of Applications for Patents, Designs and Trademarks Throughout the World, Ocrooibureau Los En Stigter B.V., Amsterdam, the Netherlands.

Summary of U.S. Export Regulations, 1985, Office of Export Administration, Room 1620, Department of Commerce, Washington, D.C. 20230.

Technology and East-West Trade, 1983, Summarizes the major provisions of the Export Administration Act of 1979 and its implications in East-West trade, Office of Technology Assessment, U.S. Department of Commerce, Washington, D.C.. 20230. $4.75.

5. Shipping and logistics

Export Documentation Handbook, 1984 edition, Dun & Bradstreet International, 49 Old Bloomfield Avenue, Mt. Lakes, NJ 07046. Compiled by Ruth E. Hurd, Dun's Marketing Services, 200 pp., $60.

Export-Import Traffic Management and Forwarding, 6th edition, 1979. Alfred Murr, Cornell Maritime Press, Box 456, Centerville, MD 21617, 667 pp., $22.50. This publication presents the diverse functions and varied services concerned with the entire range of ocean traffic management.

Export Shipping Manual, Indexed, looseleaf reference binder. Detailed current information on shipping and import regulations for all areas of the world. Bureau of National Affairs, 1231 25th Street, NW., Washington, D.C. 20037. $186 per year.

Guide to Canadian Documentation, International Trade Institute, Inc., 5055 N. Main Street, Dayton, OH 45415, 68 pp. $24.50.

Guide to Documentary Credit Operations, ICC Publishing Corporation, New York, NY 1985, 52 pp. $10.95.

Guide to Export Documentation, International Trade Institute, Inc., 5055 N. Main Street, Dayton, OH 45415, 168 pp. $44.50.

Guide to International Air Freight Shipping, International Trade Institute, 5055 N. Main Street, Dayton, OH 45415. $17.50.

Guide to International Ocean Freight Shipping, International Trade Institute, 5055 N. Main Street, Dayton, OH 45415. $34.50.

Guide to Selecting the Freight Forwarder, International Trade Institute, Inc. 5055 N. Main Street, Suite 270, Dayton, OH 45415.

Journal of Commerce Export Bulletin, 110 Wall Street, New York, NY 10005, $200 per year. This is a weekly newspaper that reports port and shipping developments. It lists products shipped from New York and ships and cargoes departing from 25 other U.S. ports. A "trade prospects" column lists merchandise offered and merchandise wanted.

Shipping Digest, Geyer-McAllister Publications, Inc., 51 Madison Avenue, New York, NY 10010. $26 per year. This is a weekly, which contains cargo sailing schedules from every U.S. port to every foreign port, as well as international air and sea commerce news.

6. Licensing

Foreign Business Practices...Material on Practical Aspects of Exporting, International

Licensing and Investment, 1981, International Trade Administration, U.S. Department of Commerce. Available from the Superintendent of Documents, U.S. Government Printing Office, Washington, D.C. 20402, 124 pp. $5.50

American Bulletin of International Technology Transfer, International Advancement, P.O. Box 75537, Los Angeles, CA 90057, $72 per year, bimonthly. This is a comprehensive listing of product and service opportunities offered and sought for licensing and joint ventures agreements in the United States and overseas.

Forms and Agreements on Intellectual Property and International Licensing, 3rd edition, 1979, Leslie W. Melville, Clark Boardman Co., Ltd., New York, NY 10014, 800 pp., looseleaf. $210.

International Technology Licensing: Competition, Costs, and Negotiation, 1981, J. Farok Contractor, Lexington Books, Lexington, MA 02173. $23.95.

The International Transfer of Technology: Theory, Issues, and Practice, Richard D. Robinson, 1988, Ballinger Publishing, 2350 Virginia Ave., Hagerstown, MD 21740; Tel: (800) 638-0300. 225 pp., $27.95.

Investing, Licensing, and Trading Conditions Abroad, Business International Corporation, base volume with monthly updates. $964.

Licensing Guide for Developing Countries, 1978, UNIPUB, 345 Park Avenue South, New York, NY 10010. $25. This book by the World Intelligence Property Organization covers the legal aspects of industrial property licensing and technology transfer agreements. It includes discussion of the negotiation process, the scope of licensing agreements, technical services and assistance, production, trademarks, management, compensation, default, and the expiration of agreements.

Technology, Licensing and Multinational Enterprises, 1979, Piero Telesio, Praeger Publishers, New York, NY 10175, 132 pp. $29.95.

INDEX

D

E

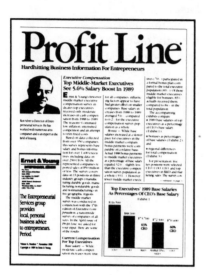

Profit Line is the newsletter of the Entrepreneurial Services Group of Ernst & Young. Distributed nationally on a bi-monthly basis to approximately 150,000 companies, the newsletter contains articles on topics ranging from financing assistance and business management to employee benefit programs and tax-related topics. Topics of international interest are covered on a regular basis.

To receive your *free* year of *Profit Line* (6 issues), complete the coupon by printing your name and complete address. Mail your coupon to:

John Wiley & Sons, Inc.
605 Third Avenue
New York, NY 10158-0012
Attn: Jeff Brown, *Profit Line*

Print Name_____Date_____

Address _____

City_____ State _____ Zip _____

This coupon must accompany your request. Offer expires January 1, 1992.